Be Your Dog's Best Friend

"Dogs in Our World" Series

*Be Your Dog's Best Friend: The Benefits of Mutual Bonding
and Relationship Building* (Katya Lidsky, 2025)

Canine Agility and the Meaning of Excellence (Beth A. Dixon, 2025)

Canine Crania: Your Dog's Head and Why It Looks That Way
(Bryan D. Cummins with Kaelyn Racine, 2025)

*The Dog as Guide, Guard and Healer: A Journey with People
Since Ancient Times* (Cinde L. Bauer, 2025)

*Dogs of the Railways: Canine Guardians, Companions
and Mascots Since the 19th Century* (Jill Lenk Schilp, 2024)

*The Force-Free Dilemma: Truth and Myths
in Modern Dog Training* (Nicola Ferguson, 2024)

*I Know Your Dog Is a Good Dog: A Trainer's Insights on Reactive,
Aggressive or Anxious Behavior* (Linda Scroggins, 2024)

My Broken Dog: Living with a Handicapped Pet (Sandy Kubillus, 2024)

*The Peace Puppy: A Memoir of Caregiving
and Canine Solace* (Susan Hartzler, 2024)

Police Dogs of Trinidad and Tobago: A 70-Year History (Debbie Jacob, 2024)

We Saved Each Other (Christopher Dale, 2024)

Horror Dogs: Man's Best Friend as Movie Monster (Brian Patrick Duggan, 2023)

*The Most Painful Choice: A Dog Owner's Story
of Behavioral Euthanasia* (Beth Miller, 2023)

Your Service Dog and You: A Practical Guide (Nicola Ferguson, 2023)

*Dog of the Decade: Breed Trends and What They Mean
in America* (Deborah Thompson, 2022)

Laboratory Dogs Rescued: From Test Subjects to Beloved Companions
(Ellie Hansen, 2022)

Beware of Dog: How Media Portrays the Aggressive Canine (Melissa Crawley, 2021)

I'm Not Single, I Have a Dog: Dating Tales from the Bark Side (Susan Hartzler, 2021)

Dogs in Health Care: Pioneering Animal-Human Partnerships
(Jill Lenk Schilp, 2019)

*General Custer, Libbie Custer and Their Dogs: A Passion for Hounds,
from the Civil War to Little Bighorn* (Brian Patrick Duggan, 2019)

*Dog's Best Friend: Will Judy, Founder of National Dog Week and
Dog World Publisher* (Lisa Begin-Kruysman, 2014)

*Man Writes Dog: Canine Themes in Literature,
Law and Folklore* (William Farina, 2014)

*Saluki: The Desert Hound and the English Travelers
Who Brought It to the West* (Brian Patrick Duggan, 2009)

Be Your Dog's Best Friend
The Benefits of Mutual Bonding and Relationship Building

Katya Lidsky

Dogs in Our World
Series Editor Brian Patrick Duggan

McFarland & Company, Inc., Publishers
Jefferson, North Carolina

ISBN (print) 978-1-4766-9661-4
ISBN (ebook) 978-1-4766-5610-6

Library of Congress cataloging data are available

Library of Congress Control Number 2025026991

© 2025 Katya Lidsky. All rights reserved

No part of this book may be reproduced or transmitted in any form or by any means, electronic or mechanical, including photocopying or recording, or by any information storage and retrieval system, without permission in writing from the publisher.

Front cover image: © Alina Kruk/Shutterstock, layout design by Ashley Prine, Tandem Books.

Printed in the United States of America

*McFarland & Company, Inc., Publishers
Box 611, Jefferson, North Carolina 28640
www.mcfarlandpub.com*

For E, E, & S
And for Ophelia, always Ophelia

Acknowledgments

I feel like I thanked a lot of animals already in this book, so I'm going to stick to humans for the most part in this section. Not the humans in the boxes across the chapters—those got their special placement—but the humans who are part of all the boxes, my whole life, not just when it comes to dogs, but when it comes to writing and living and loving. These people are my day-to-day, my constants, my soup of comfort. For their support, I owe them at the very least a few words on a page. Stories are always relational and the following people have helped me craft mine.

To some of my dearest friends: the Moon Sisters, Dana Langford, Bita Haidarian Nossa, Alejandra Mireles, and TSB buddies, I've appreciated your faith in me and your check-ins on this book! Shannon Kopp and Jami Latham, you are amazing tethers to the animals as mothers, as women. Jami, you make every project better. Gene Blalock, you remain a steadfast role model of animal love. Laverne McKinnon and Jamie Keane, there'd be much less clarity and joy without either of you to coach me through. Kristen McGuinness, I'm glad we've reconnected or this would have never happened. Carrie Howland, I value your hard work and feedback as an agent and as a fellow dog lover. Christopher Dale, keep going, but rest too. Thank you for the motivation. To the team at McFarland, especially Brian Duggan and Susan Kilby, I'm grateful you said yes to this book and for all of your help.

To my sisters, Kendra and Kelsey: There is no way to measure the impact you have on my life. It is impossible to think of a time without your presence, and power. To my nieces and nephews, I love you every day, no matter what, forever. Mami and Papi, there is literally no me without you. I have yet to find the right combination of words in any language to encompass everything I want to say to thank you, honor you, and reflect how much you mean to me. *Los adoro con toda mi alma.* To Fiona, Hamlet, Charlie, Bella, Sophie, Wally, Libby, and all the dogs to come: You got yourself a group of crazy, but you will be made family, and you will never be alone again. Matzah, I wish we'd known back then, but we didn't. For that, you will be a source of dedication and inspiration until I see you again and we get to do it right.

Eric. What if I left it like that—just your name and a period? Would you feel everything that little dot can stand for? Thank you for your love, championing, writerly guidance, and tolerance for all the dogs. Thank you for eating chocolate chip cookies and wanting to sit by a pool so that I could be more. Thank you for making me laugh. You were Ophelia's dad.

To my two daughters: That you knew Ophelia and that Ophelia knew you is a blessing I cherish. I would do nothing different if I had the chance to do things over again and avoid mistakes or be wiser on the way in. I would do it all the exact same because it means I end up with you two. You make me want to be the best me I can be because, quite frankly, you are worthy of nothing less. To be your mom is the best thing that's ever happened to me, to know that my story gets to be about your stories. I love you the most I can love.

To the dog rescuers, foster parents, volunteers, animal shelter workers, veterinarians, veterinary staff members, nonprofit warriors, activists and adopters, you are my people. I thank you for fighting on the front lines, for protecting animals and the love they have to give. You are everyday heroes. Don't forget to save yourself. Our well-being and the well-being of the animals we take care of are interconnected.

To those who attend 12 Step meetings and/or spend time at animal shelters, we know all about last stops. They're full of pain, but they're also full of hope. We spend time in the places many don't want to go. Because you are there, they are my favorite places to go.

And lastly, to all the shelter dogs who don't make it, to the ones I will never see, to the ones who will never know a kind hand or a good life: Sometimes all I can do is meditate again and return home to the Real Me with HP. What happens to you, in a very real way, happens to all of us, and it's safe to say, you deserved better. When I close my eyes and think of you, I hope you feel your significance and belonging. May you be tucked into a blanket of eternal peace and love.

Table of Contents

Acknowledgments   vii
Preface   1

1. Dog Love Is More Than Me   9
2. Dog Love Is Wordless Energy   22
3. Dog Love Is Acknowledging Feelings   36
4. Dog Love Is What We Focus on Grows   49
5. Dog Love Is Recess Every Day   64
6. Dog Love Is Receiving as Much as Giving   79
7. Dog Love Is a Clean Slate   92
8. Dog Love Is a Full-Body Experience   106
9. Dog Love Is Planning for the Unpredictable   119
10. Dog Love Is Daily Ego Adjustments   132
11. Dog Love Is Healthy Boundaries   148
12. Dog Love Is Saying Goodbye   165

Epilogue   177
Chapter Notes   185
Bibliography   193
Index   197

Preface

I bet somebody in your life has talked to you about rescuing a dog. Told you about all the homeless pets euthanized every year, and how you should "adopt don't shop." These are valid points, and the people who preach them can be very persuasive, emotional, and insistent about it, almost as if they're trying to convince you, because often they are. I know because I myself used to be one of those people. I wanted to propel you to adopt a dog because that dog was going to die. I wanted to engineer pity in you and persuade you to adopt a dog who was suffering. I wasn't asking about you, your needs, your wishes. I simply wanted you to go save a dog because those dogs were what mattered to me. Now, I still care a lot about animals, but I don't emotionally manipulate other people anymore with lectures about the selflessness of rescuing, even though there is certainly some truth to that. Because if we rely on emotional manipulation to get animals rescued, we will only reach people who can be emotionally manipulated. I want people who cannot be emotionally manipulated to adopt animals. People who are on healing journeys or seeking them, people who are already well or striving for more wellness, people who are balanced or in the process of balancing, people who understand that rescue dogs will be among the best companions on their path. Who get that dogs do us a favor by coming into our homes.

Don't get me wrong: I remain passionate about dog adoption and wish everyone would adopt a dog. However, what I think is missing in the animal welfare space is the legitimate fact that there is a selfish case to be made for pet adoption and that this is not a bad thing. This perspective is actually necessary to the conversation in order to reach the people we are not reaching. Because as far as I am concerned, rescuing a dog is a gift you give *yourself*. It helps us, the humans, to evolve. Adopting a dog captivates and clarifies so much in life. So rather than play into the human tendency to be needed or save the day, rather than feed the ego's desire to be important, I want to stay with what a relationship with an animal so purely delivers, which is love—the bigger emotion, the healthier one, the one that matters and changes us, the people, forever.

Love is the thing every dog, even the most traumatized, and each person, even the most traumatized, still has to offer. Love remains available even if everything else is taken from us or lost by us. I believe that it is a wellness journey we go on when we connect with a dog—that if we take a dog home assuming we will be getting as much out of it as the dog does, then we will be more prone to investing in them not only financially but also emotionally. Although this may sound like a bold claim to make, across the upcoming pages I hope to prove how adopting a dog can be that significant, and how it is inherently selfish at its finest. Sure, it is selfless as well, because it's also good for the dog, which to me is the greatest added benefit there is. But I'm writing this book to emphasize how dog adoption is primarily good *for you*.

• • •

My focus is on shelter dogs because they are the dogs I know, serve, and adore. But this book is for anybody who wishes to explore the love between a human and a dog, whether you are a person who took a stray in off the streets or you pamper a pedigree pup from a store. Even readers who don't have a dog can benefit from this book because *everybody* can benefit from dog love. Everybody can benefit from understanding how sharing a life with an animal is a gateway to self-healing.

It's perhaps easier to imagine this happening naturally when there is a cute, squishy puppy in your arms, a wee, wiggly body you have to protect and take care of. But when a dog is full-grown, large, or graying at the muzzle, a cathartic connection is still abundantly available and capable of the same potential for big love. Regardless of age, size, breed, or color, the love doesn't happen because a dog is perfect. If that were the case, both we and our dogs would be in big trouble because there isn't a canine or human (or any being) on Earth who can meet that unrealistic expectation. So if no dog or person is perfect, then how does it happen? How does the love form?

The answer is from bonding. The sort of love I am referring to in this book comes through bonding with our dogs. Not training, but bonding. Not to dis on training—I myself am a former positive reinforcement–based, certified dog trainer through the Companion Animal Science Institute. I respect dog trainers. I admire them and their mastery of behavior. We can still train our dogs! It's just that often dog training as we come to use it today demands a lot from dogs, forcing them to be less dog-like and more convenient for us and our human, modern world. What I will be delving into here is bonding as a mutual pact intended to reward both parties and therefore requires effort from both parties.

If we rescue dogs assuming they must be what we want them to be, they will surely fail and disappoint us. Equally, if we adopt dogs assuming something is wrong with them and it's on us to train them how to be right, we will fail them by unintentionally looking for their flaws in order to perpetuate our own bias. We can spend thousands of dollars on training, but if our relationship isn't solid, the training likely won't last. Dog training might be important, but dog bonding, I'd argue, is the priority. Dog training may offer benefits, but I'd say dog bonding offers miracles, the types of miracles that lead to a profound connection between you and a dog, which is what I believe we really want when we adopt them: We want the love.

So this book is a guide to bonding with a dog to attain that love, which ironically ends up yielding the best behaviors from the dog: not perfect, but right for you. Right for both of you. Bonding gives precedence to the relationship, not the results. Bonding acknowledges strengths and weaknesses; it is both an outlook and an action. Bonding responds to expressions of behavior by asking "What do you truly need right now?" rather than jumping to tactics that will squash the behavior or squeeze it into something more suitable to us. Bonding creates a love that is emblematic of how we wish to love, perhaps of how we were born loving. Maybe that's the most alluring aspect of bonding with a dog: that it can return us to our natural state. Because the love dogs give comes without any of the crap we humans lump atop it. And when all the unnecessary stuff is stripped away, when love is not suffocated by complications, not stage-managed, not packaged into intellectual candy bites, not overanalyzed, not expected to deliver the American dream or a lifestyle we think we need in order to feel fulfilled, not made into a commodity or a checkbox, then there it is— love as a simple emotion that offers us the chance to be the best version of ourselves, day after day, simply because a dog is around. It not only makes us love the dog for generating a feeling we've always craved, but it also leads us to love who we are when we're with the dog.

The magic of dog bonding is that the love you feel for your dog will be bolstered, but surprisingly, so will the love you feel for yourself. The two end up matching up, which makes dog bonding uniquely therapeutic for people. This is the way we should look at (and market) dog adoption: as an opportunity for healing because of and alongside an awesome friend!

If I had to sum it up: I believe *dog love equals self-love.*

Over the next 12 chapters, I will discuss the shifts we can take to launch the bonding process, to facilitate better communication with our dogs, and to nurture the love that will develop from an enhanced bond, which can deeply impact the rest of our lives. I understand if this seems like too much to put on a dog! But it's not going to be just your dog who carries the burden of initiation or who incorporates ways to constantly make the bond accessible; it's you too. It's both of you and what's in between you, which is bigger than either of you. Your dog's love will become a new lens through which you see yourself, others, and the whole world. Because how we interact with animals reflects how we interact with society at large, and how we feel within ourselves. Bonding with a dog ripples in, and ripples out.

So I invite you to sit back and get comfy. Maybe invite the dog up beside you as well, or you go sit on the ground with them. Work the muscles of your heart during the quiet reading of words and ideas. I will provide information on some principles and activities that make optimal bonding possible between a person and a dog. Although I will incorporate some of my favorite behavioral tenets, I will not leave you in the science of applied behavior or linger on methods intended to strongarm your dog so they'll heed your command when you think they should heed it. Instead, I will apply behavioral concepts in a way that enables more trust from and for the dog so that a loftier love can exist between the two of you. Any subsequent heeding will occur *because* of that. It's bonding with our pets and then the behavior changes, not vice versa. I will explain how to think about behavioral concepts so that they are applicable to us as well as to our dogs. When we understand how behavior works, behavior changes.

Bonding is a *we* modality. It happens in time, and in tandem.

The information in these chapters is scaffolded, step by step and mindset by mindset, building upon itself. My goal is to enhance your relationship with your dog so that rescuing dogs becomes not something you have to do, but something you want to do. Not only something to do for the dogs, but also something to do for yourself. Because you count too. And if we do not prioritize people, people who we need to adopt dogs, then the only humans who will be attracted to rescuing will be people who think they themselves don't or shouldn't count.

An over-reliance on adoption messaging that centers on begging people to help animals in desperate situations can be inadvertently dangerous. It tells some people to hurry over, swallow any anxiety they might experience, and put themselves last because that's "good," while insinuating that other people are "bad" for wanting to avoid desperate situations of stress, that they're selfish for putting themselves first. Rescue dogs are at the whim of all of this and the consequences of how it shakes out, when in fact they just want to live. They just want a buddy. Rescue dogs are just as good for us as we are for them. Rescuing a dog could actually be a putting-yourself-first type of move.

• • •

Preface

In this book, I use stories and photographs from my own life, featuring many of the foster dogs who revealed the most invaluable lessons I have to share with you. My family and I have fostered more than 70 dogs. That's more than 70 times I have said, "Another dog is coming today!" And that's more than 70 times I've been met with an incredulous stare by my family members. I will also use examples from the many mistakes I've made. After 15 years of working with rescue dogs—sometimes as a certified dog trainer, sometimes as a volunteer in animal shelters, sometimes as a professional working in the animal welfare nonprofit space, sometimes as a writer about animal advocacy, sometimes as a dog foster mom, sometimes as a Creative Grief Coach and Breathwork Facilitator for animal welfare people, and sometimes as a combination of all those roles at once—trust me when I say most of what I have learned has been in my home and in my life, not just in theory.

Furthermore, as a positive reinforcement-based dog trainer and a Family Paws Parent Educator (which means I specialize in families who have both kids and dogs), I aim to positively associate a person to their dog while creating positive associations *for* the dog. I will attempt to do the same here with you, dear dog hair-covered reader. I'm not coming to you as The Best Dog Trainer in the World. To be an extraordinary dog trainer, I believe one has to be in it all the time, be with the dogs, not only constantly furthering their own education and experience, but just as importantly, also aligning themselves internally, daily, with unlimited composure despite whatever those dogs do. Being an effective behaviorist requires a commitment to cutting-edge information, as well as the ability to apply those ideas on paper in the flesh, with the dogs in front of you. It's both a rooted-into-the-ground and an ever-reaching-out connectedness that makes somebody the kind of dog person who doesn't need to raise their voice. Who can walk into the kennel of an imbalanced, insecure dog. Who can bring calm to a reactive dog. Who can put behavior from a dog over their own internal story about that behavior from the dog.

I am coming to you as a thinker about dogs and a lover of dogs. Something comes to me and through me when it comes to dogs; I just know how to love them. Maybe I am not The Best Dog Trainer in the World, but I know how to be proactive about dogs, how to attribute the spiritual richness in my life to them, and how to value them.

• • •

We've all probably heard by now that having a dog at home promotes health in various ways, most significantly by increasing cardiovascular activity and decreasing loneliness. But research also shows that merely touching a dog can lower blood pressure along with the stress hormone cortisol, while stimulating feel-good hormones like oxytocin.[1] Additionally, learning the principles of behavior might seem dog-centric in this book's presentation, but the principles are not dog-specific. Having a bird's-eye view of another being while they learn provides wonderful insight for how to change our own behaviors.

Consider yourself warned: I have a somewhat new-agey perspective. You can go ahead and call me a woo-woo dog lady. But in a world where peaceful parenting has become a popular model for raising children (a concept that centers on the positive, respectful, mutual relationship between parents and children), I insist on advocating that the same kind of elevated thinking apply to our pets too. When it comes to dogs, we can prioritize joy and connection over results and control. In addition to my dogging ways, I am a Creative Grief Practitioner and a certified, trauma-informed Breathwork Facilitator. What does this mean exactly? It means I support animal people so they can reflect and intentionally make meanings out of their experiences and move forward in a way that works for them. It means their stories and lives become a creative exploration and I hold space for them. I also facilitate breathwork sessions, which refers to breathing practices designed to ground us, return us to the intelligence within our own bodies, boost energy, help us process emotions, and bring clarity to the mind. Breathwork can activate the parasympathetic nervous system so we can more deeply regulate and relax,[2] which is great for us and for dogs to feel when they are with us.

It is my privilege and my pleasure to weave all these different threads together for you. I hope you will feel by the end of the book that bonding with a dog is a precious endeavor. Prepare to find two bonding activities in each of the 12 chapters that follow—one exercise based on behavior modification for your dog, and another rooted in self-development for you, both complementing each other. I ask you to take into account that the dynamic between you and your dog is an extension of what is between you and *yourself*, that you let bonding enhance both, that you let the love between you surge and feel good. If our dogs are external representations of our internal landscapes, perhaps we can go so far as to consider that the very things you say to a dog are the things you wish to say to yourself. I hope the 24 exercises offered in this book act as figurative love-bumpers, designed to keep the love on track and away from the gutters.

I want you to be well so that the dog can be well with you. I want you to believe that adopting a dog can become a corridor to more wellness, and that it's the real reason why you should take a shelter dog home. I can't promise it will be easy, and in some cases it will be downright hard. But wellness and easy aren't synonyms, and a fair share of challenges are common along a personal growth journey. Whenever you get set off, wherever the question of sacrifice comes into play, there will be information, there will be confirmation, and there will be transformation. How we overcome obstacles with somebody we care about *is* in and of itself a path to greater well-being. Still, your feelings do not have to be entirely whacked out of balance just so a shelter dog gets a home. That is unfair to you, not to mention unsustainable.

The truth is nonbinary, even spirituality, even dogs. The truth is nuanced. So I must also add that I'm not here to judge if you decide you want to buy a dog. I am here, however, to offer alternative perspectives about pet adoption because, admittedly, it's what I believe in. It *can be* easy to adopt. It can also be welcomed when it's challenging. We can improve, make progress, and do better for animals and for ourselves. How we think about animal welfare and within animal welfare contributes to its evolution, for if the current ideology worked, wouldn't we find ourselves in a better situation by now, with emptier shelter kennels?

We need greater human wellness to provide greater animal wellness. The people who work in animal welfare, who adopt, and anybody in between cannot be overlooked, not if we want to help animals. This is how we can begin to make the systemic changes that are required in order to support all the beings involved.

As of the writing of this book, there are still too many dogs who do not end up finding homes. I cannot guarantee that every dog will live and get love in the end. I hate this, I rail against this in the night. I want it to be possible for every single dog to be safe, just as I want the same for every human being, and I stand by my idealism because I do not regard it to be a liability. Hope does not cost me anything. I do not propose to have the solution that fixes injustice, or to be the one who can make sense of why some animals (and some people) get such an unlucky break. I do believe, however, that looking at the natural world differently—as coexisting with us, as wise on its own and offering as much as people do—is part of the answer. For me, the way into this colossal shift in consciousness is through dogs.

In some ways, bonding with a dog is as simple as it sounds—taking long walks, slowing down, surrendering the struggle to constantly pressure the dog, and letting go of the ways we block peace for the dog and for ourselves. Ultimately, bonding will result in the willingness and ability to intertwine an animal into our lives because of how good the dog's love feels, so much so that it will hurt deeply when we have to brave the loss of them. Because a goodbye concludes every dog love story. That's how I got here. The goodbye that brought me to you. The heartbeat of this book, why I wrote it, why I believe it, why I know it.

My Ophelia. Perfect circle, O, no beginning, no ending. My first rescue dog. She was The Dog. With me through everything worth remembering and everything worth forgetting. Ophelia's love taught me how to be loved and how to love well. Her love opened me up to the dozens of dogs that came after her, to all animals, other humans, my husband, my children, to me loving myself. I am writing this book in the spirit of Ophelia. Every dog has the potential to be somebody's Ophelia, and if there is one thing I am absolutely certain of, it's that everyone ought to experience an Ophelia. The cornerstone of the kind of soul-level relationship between a human and a dog, between a me and an Ophelia, is the bond that built our love.

Something I want to mention because I would not be me, with my point of view and my voice, if I failed to say it: On top of my adoration for Ophelia and passion for shelter dogs, I'm a Russian-Cuban-Jewish interspiritualist from the border of Texas and Mexico. I self-identify as a mutt because I am one. I am grateful for my experiences and my family and my continued education, but it is this very muttness that drives my storytelling, my writing, and my advocating for animals. Muttness is baked into my personality. Belonging and bonding were never effortless for me, as is the case for so many rescue dogs. I understand them. I empathize with them. I am them. They are the ones who guided me into a vortex of self-love despite this reality about myself. If you can relate, I hope dogs might do this for you too.

If you are someone reading this because you are considering adopting a dog, I hope this book makes you feel prepared for one of the best things you will ever do for yourself, and like I'm holding your hand through the process. If you already have a dog, I hope you listen to them more thoroughly and to yourself. I hope the love is notched up a level, that it blows you away, because love is the only thing that exponentially grows. Welcome to your official guide to dog bonding and dog loving. Go on and be selfish about it. I appreciate that you're here, and I thank Ophelia for bringing us together.

1

Dog Love Is More Than Me

There I was on the bathroom floor again, having just binged, making myself throw up five times in a row, with my hand in my mouth up to my wrist. I'd been struggling with an eating disorder since I was 11 years old, and yet I was 25 and still in the same position, watching as blood shot out from between my teeth and into the toilet. Me with my head upside down, eyes watering, throat aching, purging out every bad part of me. The only difference this time was that I'd recently adopted a puppy, and as I wiped the food and saliva and blood from my lips, I noticed that there she was across the bathroom staring at me.

I am not sure how many days Ophelia had been with me before this night, before she stumbled into the bathroom and observed me at my very worst, before the switch went off inside of my head that sparked a desire to change. But suddenly, as I crawled along the tile floor, I wanted to take care of her. And I knew I had to be okay in order to do that. Suddenly something about living with this dog and the love being offered by her—her sleeping curled up beside me, her delicate nuzzling, our walks in the quiet morning—made me not want but *need* to get better.

It was Ophelia who loved me when I couldn't love myself. It was Ophelia who brought forth a piece of me that could receive her devotion. The piece of me that felt like I deserved her love, like I was worth it, like I could stop hurting and hurting myself. And I knew, I just knew, that if I loved her back, everything could be all right. It was Ophelia who taught me about the power of dog love, what it has the potential to do, what it can combat, what it can overcome. It was her love that made me begin my recovery, led me to my purpose and to the rest of my life.

Dogs love us even when we don't love ourselves. Lucky for me, I stumbled into adopting a dog, and it proved to be the only remedy that would allow me to heal. We choose the stories we tell ourselves, about who we are, about our past, about how things have to go in the future, and those stories can make us or break us. I wanted to change my story and the way

I was living, but I didn't know how. I kept searching, only to collect more evidence of my not-enoughness. Until Ophelia. Until my story became her story too.

Dogs witness us in our entirety, including our issues, dysfunctions, and flaws, the way we talk to and treat ourselves and others. Having this kind of a mirror may sound unbearable, but for me, it encouraged me to be honest with myself for the first time because regardless of what Ophelia saw, from the good to the not so good to the terrible, I knew without a shadow of a doubt that I was loved by her. We can trust a dog's love precisely because they offer unwavering support and warmth, making the truth about us tolerable, making the truth about who we can be seem possible. A dog's love can help us believe that despite it all, we still have value. To piggyback off Jack Nicholson's line in *As Good as It Gets*: "Dogs make me want to be a better person." It is inspirational, it is aspirational, it is a privilege, the love we get from a dog.

Ophelia sleeping on half of my face in July 2012. I was not super comfortable, but I would not dare move because she was there.

"I choose you," I began to say to Ophelia. And so I began to say it to myself.

Bonding with dogs is a practice in presence.

Based on more than 15 years of experience volunteering with animal shelter dogs, as a former dog trainer and Family Paws Parent Educator (which means I specialize in families with both kids and dogs), as a dog mom and a foster dog mom, I can safely say that we build the relationship

1. Dog Love Is More Than Me   11

Ophelia commanding the dinner table. Perhaps this was her form of exposure therapy for me as I recovered from an eating disorder.

we want with dogs through bonding, and that bonding starts in the mind. It is a decision we make.

How exactly? By choosing to believe that this approach will create harmony, we root ourselves in spending more time with our dogs so we can sync up. We choose to trust that a softer attitude toward them will bolster our interactions without undermining anything. We settle on bonding as an addition in our lives that helps us accomplish what we seek, whether we're bonding with a new rescue dog we're about to take in or reexamining the relationship we have with a dog we've had for 10 years, whether the dog is reactive or laid back. It begins by setting aside doubt and taking a leap into dog love.

Choosing to bond is not complicated, but it does require an agreement on our side to grant dogs the benefit of the doubt instead of assuming they are obstinate assholes. If our dogs are not being disobedient, then they haven't learned a behavior yet under certain conditions: No big deal, we just haven't established it together up till now. If we shift our perspective to be bond-oriented, we no longer live citing our dogs like we're cops on the lookout for what they do wrong. Instead, we understand that it's not solely on the dog, that we have a role in how they act, not by thinking about it in retrospect or apologizing after we get mad or making empty promises or feeling guilty later or hardening our hearts, but by admitting that how dogs act falls at least fifty percent on their people. We take some responsibility for the ways in which our dogs behave. There's no need to be tempted by shame here; blame is irrelevant. Accountability, on the other hand, is an opportunity, and it's essential to bonding.

This is a choice we can make as pet guardians to awaken, to come from a place of in-it-togetherness. This kind of connection is so much lighter to have and to hold. This kind of love upgrades our own wellness just as it demands wellness, cultivating more wellness for everybody involved. Bonding nurtures the type of dog who *wants* to "behave," a dog who cooperates and buys into what we ask of them, a dog who wants to strengthen the bond from their end too. Because bonding is contagious.

So sharing the load is the groundwork for bonding, and then a right-sized feeling of accountability sets in. On its own, organically, an awareness inside of us about who we are and how we are, how we cause this other being to feel, starts to amplify. This drops us into the present and activates our consciousness, or maybe it's the other way around. The point is, we discover that we can only bond in the moment. Thus, if we want to bond, we must be in the moment.

In order to have a close relationship with our dogs then, or perhaps because we do, we might find ourselves untethering from ruminations about the past and releasing the grip on the future so that we can slip into HERE NOW. Here is where dogs live, which makes them some of the greatest portals into Now. Here and Now is also where love exists. A synergistic dynamic can bloom once the human tendency to dwell in regrets of the past or try to wrangle the future is relinquished. Bonding with a dog keeps pulling us out of the not-now because dogs can't not be in now! How fortunate then are we to have dogs in our lives, to get to adopt one, to get to elevate our own awareness.

• • •

We can become more aware every time we pay attention to our breath. It really is that simple. We're breathing all the time anyway, whether we realize it or not; breath is happening for us and to us. By tuning into our own breathing, we embody the moment. For the people who resist mindful breathing or never want to take up a breathwork habit, if they have a dog they want to bond with, noticing their dog's breathing can do the trick.

"When I first meet a dog, my primary attention is on the dog's center of gravity and his breathing,"[1] renowned dog trainer Patricia McConnell shares. Before assessing behavior or addressing issues, before any training, it's the dog's breath she considers first. To follow McConnell's advice and focus on a dog's breath welcomes us into being with our own breath too, as that is the fallout of being in the now, where every breath actually exists. So with a dog around, there is an overlap available to us—a land where our circle and theirs intersect. We become a Venn diagram. Tending to their breathing is tending to our own. This can take us into a zone of greater awareness.

Certified dog behavior consultant Leslie McDevitt says, "Being present with your dog is a bit like meditating with him…. It doesn't matter what he is doing, just keep him in your awareness and let everything else go."[2] She goes on to describe how she believes dogs appreciate when we tune into them like this, and how they often respond by connecting more to us. Perhaps it's even an alternative to meditation, if meditation is not your thing, to sit and be, without closing your eyes, and instead to close in on your dog, and to sense how noticing them as they are is an act of well-being on its own. In fact, by doing nothing but getting quiet and still enough to notice, we can pave the trail for change[3] and healing over time. Somehow, someway, even if you're resistant and hesitant and doubtful, just by showing up day after day and getting present with your dog, it will shift you, it will do the work for you, through the average of all those times you sat in silence and noticed.

Another method for welcoming the present is to immerse ourselves in the senses. This kind of observing bypasses bracing, planning, making meaning, and tangling up in thoughts, and instead nurtures purely *being* in the messy, complex splendor that is full aliveness. No judgment, no evaluations, just feeling what is. Inserting a bounty of moments into our days where we pause to take stock of what we smell, touch, taste, see, and hear creates the opportunity to grow our awareness and truly be in our lives. I don't think anything we can achieve or buy comes close to the immersive equanimity of feeling through our senses. We might consider trying this for the love of a dog, but it will end up benefiting us greatly.

By simply choosing to bond, we keep in mind that our dogs are right beside us, and put down our phones and the multitasking and the buffet of thoughts that constantly threaten to ensnare us, and dial into the moment with them. The funny thing is that in providing for our dog's needs by committing to greater awareness, we tune into many of the same needs we've likely been ignoring in ourselves. Bonding is as much happening inside of us as it is happening outside with them. These majestic ambassadors tap us into living more consciously because dogs operate from and within presence, which can lead us toward a sense of More. It is how we can touch the More. And so bonding with dogs grants us access into the state of More.

Dogs are a pathway into More.

Bonding with dogs is opening up to a Higher Power.

Ophelia's love was the balm I never would have guessed I needed—I found that my challenge wasn't really about food, my body, or my weight. It was about the web of ways I felt about myself, my worth, and whether or not I was lovable. It was about realizing that everything I fought for out there was already inside me, and had been since inception. I did not intend to be overcome by something bigger than what the worldly plane had to offer. But Ophelia showed me it was available by simply loving me. Somewhere along the way, consciously or not, I must have decided to believe she could do such a thing. That she would love me completely.

When we bet on bonding as a way of relating, we begin to recognize that we are being led, that there is much we don't know. When we bet on bonding as a way of relating, we open to something greater than we are, to the invisible force of love, to what it might have the capacity to manifest. We have proof that invisibles work every day, like oxygen and electricity, but what is unseen still requires believing. What else is spirituality but a belief in all we cannot see? Dog bonding then is a conduit for faith. Faith can be a conduit for healing, for both the dog and yourself.

"If you expect total attention for your dog, you must give total attention to him in return. Connecting is a team effort,"[4] Leslie McDevitt explains. So we can choose to bond with our dogs and to be in love by paying attention to someone who is paying attention to us. That attention aligns us together in a shared awareness—two species finding common ground, communicating through the knowing plane, based on the many subtle movements that become recognizable between a human and a canine. A myriad of shifts, positions, and expressions get translated into feelings and sensations, wiring the brain synapses on the electricity grids that power our bodies and theirs, inside a shared home. It is beyond comprehension! But it happens.

When we choose to bond, we employ a faith that bonding will work, even if we don't like to call it that. And so dog love moves us into a spiritual experience. Because divine things happen to us when we love a dog. Divine, not as in religious, but as in the humble mystery to whatever power out there is greater than we are. Some call it Source or God or another name, but out of respect for all religions and as an homage to the 12 Step Program that changed my life, let's call this a Higher Power and shorthand that reference to HP like we do in the rooms of recovery. HP, as in yours, however, whoever, whatever you believe in or can stand to believe in. HP, as in an idea that can change and grow, wildly and intuitively, as you do. It is on the cutting edge of real life as it unfolds. HP does not have to be something fixed, rigid, or dogmatically assigned. It can be real to you, morphing, and wonderful.

If you struggle to come up with an idea of a Higher Power, I honor that. I get it. For a while, my HP was a giant tree. But dog love is such a radiant thing—couldn't it alone be evidence of a Higher Power? Dogs are in the flesh, but also consistently tuned into what is not tangible. Who else loves us as unconditionally as a Higher Power might but dogs? Could the love a dog offers be a spiritual solution to life's problems? I think so.

Our dogs hear us trying to be funny, telling the same jokes, whining the same complaints in defiant fits, see us picking our noses while peeing, procrastinating work, declining phone calls we should be answering, and still our dogs are enthralled by us. Their modus operandi is to love us without judgment. Isn't that what we always say? Isn't that what we come to dogs for, for the unconditional, God-like love? But unconditional love doesn't have to only be a dog thing, or an HP thing; it can be something we realize *we also have inside and can give too*. It can be a people thing. Our connection with dogs lets us feel into it, lets us love like that, and thus lets us access a More state, lets us become it, lets us dip into spiritual possibilities. Being with your dog can be its own form of prayer, maybe the only kind you can approve of.

I know, I know, you're thinking: *I picked up this book to get my dog to sit, and now she's talking about a Higher Power?* But it's the bigger gift! How bonding with a dog can be a path into the vast dimension beyond us, and how regarding dogs in this manner can get them to sit because it's not just about having a pet. On a personal level, it's another living being with needs and wants who affects our lifestyle. On a larger scale, it's evidence that a force greater than we are is constantly restocking, maybe even orchestrating, more love in our life. The outcome of dog love is the chance to deepen our spirituality and get closer to a Higher Power. There are many ways to live in faith, but this way, the dog way, involves so much joy and closeness, so much awe and silliness.

Okay, so um, no big deal, we're just going to get to know God now!? Yeah. Because your dog already loves your Highest You, the one that is always connected to HP, the you your dog sees you as. I'd argue your dog met that part of you when your dog met you, and that it is the wiser part of you, it is the you that drew you to that dog, that said *yes, yes, I'll take her home*.

Your Higher Self is your dog's best friend.

Bonding with dogs is the Real Dog + the Real You.

No dog comes ready-made or tailored for your home; they are not stuffed animals. Regardless, the act of being the Real You and admired by your dog despite any of your shortcomings will feel like an everlasting legacy. The real treasure is in you learning to love the Real Dog unconditionally, learning to live with the dog you have, not the one who passed away or your neighbor's dog or the famous pup on Instagram, because once we love another creature like that, as they are, we alter the way we love everyone and everything, full stop. This is how we align with our Higher Self. This is the You your dog already senses, knows, and adores. We get to be our Higher Self, an extension of our Higher Power, when we are bonding with dogs. So it's not only in the love *they* give *us*; we fall in love with ourselves, with how *we* love *them*. It is loving our dogs well as much as it is being loved by our dogs well.

With other people, experience has taught us that it's too risky. We've learned it's scary to love that hard. We've been disappointed. We learn to hedge and hesitate, cull and calculate. But we can rain our love down upon our dogs, loving as boldly as we've always dreamed we could, and delight in it. It doesn't feel terrifying or exposing. Hang out with a dog for one hour and I dare you not to walk away more enthusiastic about loving or more faithful about living than you might ever be in the company of humans. We can most feel who we are when we are loving another. And when we love our dogs wholly and holy, when we just give that love to them, so much more of it comes back to us. It is safe to love them. They cherish our big love.

Bonding with a dog proves to us that we are not here to produce and amass and earn and win, but to engage in this kind of love as much as possible. Even just going for a walk isn't just going for a walk anymore. We can begin to see it differently as we take dogs out of the large crate that is our homes, and take off our own chains to the computers, and enjoy and watch and let ourselves wander and let ourselves wonder, and show ourselves that we want to take care of another being, that we can be okay enough to actually take care of another being, and that other being can mean more to us than whatever trauma or negative patterns or fears or defects or goals or desperate need for praise we may be clinging onto. We bond for our dog's wellness, and bump into our own. We wind up taking care of ourselves as we take care of a dog.

This is what makes dog love radical. Bonding with them inevitably compels us to be kinder authors of the stories we tell ourselves about our lives, about the main character living them, the person we always wanted to be, the person we now get to be because dog love is part of the tale. So in a way, our dogs co-write our stories with us. And then, the whole story about who we are and how life goes changes. Your story can have a Higher Power in it, and a Higher Self in you, and a Higher Dog at home, and one day at a time, love will completely and utterly enough you. (Yeah, I used it as a verb.)

1. Dog Love Is More Than Me

Look, I wouldn't blame you if just regular dog training sounds way better than everything I am saying right now. We can pay a trainer, get our dog handled, and skip to the good part. (Or so we think.) It's tempting, result-oriented, and boxes can be checked off lists. (I love lists.) Yet here I am asking you to decide to bond and to believe that being present with your dog will outweigh any checkmarks on any lists because maybe you'll fall in love with life too? Bananas!

But I am, and it's true. Even though I think dog training is a great avenue to take when the relationship is solid, strengthening the bond should still be its guiding intention. Because bonding is teaching and learning together, not forcing a dog to do what we want when we want it. I'm not suggesting you merely visualize to manifest your dog's manners! But done without a bond established, training can tend to focus on commands and tricks, which can be diversions from what your dog is actually telling you in the moment, if only you were to pay attention and be aware. Teaching dogs tricks can unintentionally and unconsciously become "I tell an animal what to do," designed to impress. Commands are helpful if they help lead to desired behaviors or reinforce your connection or boost your dog's confidence. Otherwise, tricks and commands offer a shiny, sneaky way to give you an out from having the significant relationship with your dog that will really make the difference. It is about substance, not show.

When the bond comes first, behavior modification will be an inherent by-product of the relationship. The juiciest part about it is that a bonding dynamic between a human and a dog not only makes for better dogs but also for better people—as individuals, as parents, and as members of our communities. The tenderness we develop for our dogs, with our dogs, turns into a tenderness inwardly pointed at ourselves as the feeling the bond carries becomes a new standard we apply to the rest of our lives. As we offer an active, marvelous love to our pets, we not only begin to give it to others, we also begin to insist on that kind of love in return from others. And we can break through some of our hang-ups. When we believe in dogs, we learn to believe in others, in the world, and in ourselves. I don't mean to sound Pollyanna, but ironically, the more we bond with dogs, the less we need our dogs (or ourselves) to be trained and changed. The more okay we begin to feel about them and about who we are. The very stuff we do to establish a connection with our dogs *is* what makes us feel lovable and makes us recognize their lovability too. Then it's just love everywhere. I don't care if you call that force Mother Nature or God or Buddha or Jesus Christ, all I know is when I am left to my own human mind, I don't access it. But by opening myself up to More, I have learned to cherish who I am by doing what I did to bond with my dog.

Bonding with my Great Love, Ophelia.

Back to her because it always goes back to her. I figured out everything I'm sharing by living it. Not from my family, not from counseling, not during my studies to be a dog trainer, but from my very special Beagle mix Ophelia who was more than a pet to me. Before her, I lived with a raging eating disorder and had a knack for obsessing over people who did not like me (while ignoring anyone who did). I was an Olympian at self-judgment and self-disgust, duties that I performed daily, hourly, sometimes every freaking minute. Everybody was a variable shoved into that equation, to prove me right that I was wrong. Feeling bad was homeostasis.

But Ophelia loaned me her love when I had none of it for myself. She saw in me an ability to persevere. She saw in me the person I didn't yet see. Somehow, wanting to be who she saw and relishing each moment with her meant more than obsessing over my jean size. Time with her meant more than anything. It was magnificent to be beside her warm body pressed against mine, to allow myself the exuberant dropping in that is a dog's default setting. Loving her and being loved by her far outweighed the other end of the scale.

The inner connectedness between human and dog, between me and Ophelia, turned my life upside-down. But what's important here isn't me or my yearning to feel like somebody; what's important is the tricolored hound who waltzed into my life and made me stop needing to be extraordinary out there so I could feel extraordinary at being myself. Ophelia compelled me to discover that I was worth discovering. It wasn't an instant cure, but it was automatic. It was both the beginning and the end of something huge. She took me right to my Highest Self and the Source for that Self. I credit the undeniable spirit-level relationship I had with her for giving me the stamp of okayness I'd craved my whole life, and with granting me the burst of faith that my recovery was built upon. You might experience this feeling already, even fleetingly, when you do nothing but gaze into your dog's eyes.

Some of you get what it's like to end up stuck in your head. What a remarkable place to be. What a rotten place to be. Yet dogs live outside of their thoughts, and can gracefully escort us out with them if we let them. So dog bonding can mean a lot to people like me. As Ophelia's devotion got me out of my own mind, as our connection blossomed, it felt undeniably spiritual because it was no longer all about me. More than me became about her and me and our shared existence. Eventually, more than me became about purpose.

Dog bonding is not just the love a dog gives and gets; it is a force greater than us, calling us out of ourselves to get beyond ourselves. This idea is available to anyone who wants it because dogs don't care if you have a mansion or an apartment, if you're homeless or the Hollywood elite, what you look like or what the world thinks about what you look like. A dog's love is restorative because they will just love you to death. And if you appreciate them for it, they'll love you even more. That infinite, simple gold can become a constant feeling in your home if you live with a dog. That place where More Than You resides, not the buzzing brain, but Real You, the watcher, the vastness flowing under all the disorganized thoughts, the site of completeness, *that* can be where you live from. That sensation IS love! And it is also where the bond with a dog is born, where it thrives, and where the relationship never ends, not if a dog misbehaves, moves away, or even passes away. That kind of love is infinite. It stays forever if you believe in it.

Ophelia's love was—still is—my idea of a Higher Power. (Although Bono remains a close second.) Her love is my Goddess's guidance. Her love has inspired me to help another dog, and another, and another. And that's how my faith endures, it keeps growing.

> Hi, hola, woof! In each chapter, you're going to see a box like this where I am going to pause and tell you about someone I admire who has helped shape the animal lover I am today. Christy Schilling is the co-founder of Better Together Forever in Los Angeles. We met volunteering decades ago, and eventually brainstormed the first shelter intervention table we ran together. Since then, Christy has grown the Shelter Intervention model to create an incredible, supportive, inclusive, full program through her non-profit, supporting animals as well as the people who love them so that they can remain a family. Christy doesn't only talk the talk, she walks the walk tirelessly, dependably, and graciously. If there are angels on Earth, she's one of them. I'll be a soldier with and for her any day.

CHAPTER 1 EXERCISES

Are you ready? We're going to start by writing a letter to our dogs as a way to help us make the decision to go all in with bonding. Set a timer for 10 minutes, and just free write, pen to paper, fingers to keyboard, without stopping or editing. Write to them whatever comes to mind—whatever is in your heart, what you need, what's bothering you, what makes you laugh, what you dream of, what you're afraid of, anything. When the timer goes off, shake yourself out, and then write your dog's response to you. Another 10-minute timer, another stream of consciousness. Don't overthink it, this isn't to publish or impress. Practice awareness, practice meeting them in the now. You don't have to be a member of the clergy to hear them or to access More.

Then we're going to play a "Watch Me" game! You and your pup will practice checking in with one another by making eye contact. I recommend starting this practice somewhere with few distractions, such as your living room. Ask your dog to "Watch me" and feel free to point to the area between your eyebrows to clue your dog where to look. When they do, each time your dog meets your gaze, release a treat, and get a tail wag. That's it, that's the drill—just ask for their attention to come back onto you, their eyes to land on yours. I like eye contact to be a default behavior from my dogs. As McDevitt describes it, "The dogs offer these behaviors because they have a strong reward history for doing so. These are behaviors that the dog automatically gives you when he wants something from you or doesn't know what to do and is asking you for information. The stronger these automatic behaviors are, the more self-control your dog will show."[5] In order to condition default behaviors, we have to create the reward history. Looking at each other is so important. You can make eye contact—aka Watch Me—a default behavior by teaching it to your dog, and then by reinforcing him whenever he gives you eye contact whether you asked for the eye contact or not. We want our dogs to choose for themselves rather than always needing us to tell them what to do, McDevitt explains further. We earn default behaviors together over time.

So after your dog understands the Watch Me game inside, try it outside in the yard, eventually working up to taking it with you on walks. Your dog may have to relearn the game again every time you move locations because dogs don't generalize well. Behaviorologist James O'Heare describes this: "Dogs don't generalize these lessons as well as we might like, so you specifically have to cover them. That means carrying out the exercises in a variety of environments so that the dog learns that the same contingencies are in place even if the situation is a bit different."[6] Dogs not only act inconsistently among different environments, but also during different times of day. This might seem like a bummer that requires a lot of extra work, but it can also be regarded as good news. It gives us many more opportunities for practice.

In between Watch Me drills, watch your dog watch the world, watch the world together, watch as one. Patricia McConnell says, "Honing your observation skills is directly related to having a better-behaved dog, because what you do around your dog should be related to what your dog is doing."[7] It's all about how you see their behavior and your own. It's all about noticing and sharing the living world. Don't be surprised if you start to check in with each other more often after you regularly start playing the

Watch Me game. And every time your dog glances at you, smile, praise him, let him know you like eye contact in order to maintain that default behavior of connecting.

Share the here and now with your dog. Because here and now is a good place to be. You've got each other, in the present, in love.

2

Dog Love Is Wordless Energy

So, we've chosen to go all in. Now what? What comes next for this bonding thing to happen? Well, it feels like the right time to admit to you that I am not a perfect dog mom. I still get impatient, grit my teeth, and beg a foster to hurry up and pee in an utterly irritated tone of voice as I stand outside getting bitten by mosquitos. I am still flawed and flailing. But the love dogs give back to me regardless demolishes my moods and thoughts and invites me to keep trying again because the bond—however fleeting—is always worth it. Only beside a dog can I brave living despite what I know and what I don't yet know. And it isn't because of what dogs say, as they don't say anything. It isn't because of what I say to them, words that they hardly understand half the time. It's because of how being around a dog makes me *feel*. It's the energy of them, and the energy that goes back and forth between them and me.

When people tell me all the things they want in a dog, I listen. I do not judge, I understand. But at some point, when they're finished, I will inevitably, gently encourage them to scrap that list or put it in second position to one thing, and one thing only, which I believe is the most important thing: What is the dog's essence? Do you like it? Do you want this energy in your home? Does it match up with yours? This matters infinitely more than a dog's color, weight, or breed. Assessing a dog's energy and trying to ascertain what kind of personality they have (which they may or may not feel comfortable displaying in a shelter environment or until they know you better) will help you glean so much more information about your compatibility. That compatibility is everything. Your compatibility should be a match-up in vibes.

Bonding with a dog then is also based on *how* we do what we do, *how* we say what we say, and on what our own energy transmits. Dogs are masters in energy communication. They will pick up yours, and you won't be able to lie to them about it for energy cannot be faked. You will be able to read their energy too, if you want to, if you let them show you how.

Consider deaf dogs, who can pick up on and sense as many cues as

2. Dog Love Is Wordless Energy

dogs who hear.[1] They often know when to be afraid, when to defend themselves, when they are safe. Take your own dog: What happens when he or she jumps up on you, and you shout no? They get more excited, not less, right? Why? Because it doesn't matter what you say, it's your energy they're paying attention to, and when you're charged up, even if you're responding with "Down, Fifi, I said no jumping!" it is imparting excitement, albeit annoyed excitement but still it's engagement. You are turned up. And the dog will ramp up, despite your words. You could call your dog a dum-dum idiot head in a baby voice (not sure why you would) in place of whatever cute nicknames you have for them, and your dog will not pinpoint your mean name-calling. He will show you his tummy instead based on your sweet energy.

I can recall dozens of times when Ophelia came toward me and placed her lean face on my leg. She'd get up from whatever she was doing, wherever she was, and decide to find me because at that same moment, I was feeling lonely and small and didn't know who to call. It was as if she knew, almost as if she read my mind. In a way she did, but it was my vibe she was dialing into. We don't do this enough as people with other people—rely on what we sense over anything else. This is another indirect benefit to rescuing a dog, how you will have no choice but to get more skilled at intuiting frequencies, not so much what someone is saying but what they are not saying, as well as the state they're in. You'll be doing this with your dog, you'll be assessing where they're at, and it will provide you great insight to further recognize it in other beings, to heed the messages inside you that tell you to get closer or stay further away, to have compassion for what you sense over what is being told to you. It is a feedback loop that gets constructed between you and a dog, one that's read on an energetic grid based on vibrations, including what is unprocessed, withheld, denied, or protected, but still palpable. This feedback loop is made of an abundant account of wordless energy that you will not only learn and trust in, but will then be able to apply to the rest of your life.

"I love you, I am listening," I tell my dogs. And so I am telling myself.

Bonding with a dog is minding the mind.

We must pay attention to our thoughts because our thoughts create our feelings, which affect our actions, which determine our results, which always—and I mean always—confirm our thoughts. A culmination of thoughts put together adds up to the energy we emit. The good news is that since we're already being more present with our dogs around, it will be that much more possible to notice our mental and emotional states. Dogs can serve as external touchpoints to help us stay in touch with what we're thinking because our thoughts impact our energy, and our energy impacts them. They see through all the bullshit we humans are dazzled by—explanations, context, promises, gifts, words, words and more words—and instead they decipher the aura. But that aura is connected to how we think, a constant activity that we are often habitually far removed from and seldomly pay attention to.

When we are unaware of or asleep to our own thinking and fail to wonder with curiosity if a thought is true or what another thought might be that would serve us better, companies benefit. People who sell things benefit from us being in a trance, as do social media platforms. But it does not benefit us, the ones living lives while stuck in unconscious thoughts. Unchecked thoughts can become beliefs that control us. So mindfulness is not just about sitting cross-legged with our eyes closed and chanting, although that is a lovely thing to do. Mindfulness is a way of living. It can happen while you're washing the dishes and paying attention to how the water feels, how it sounds, to the temperature, how the dry parts of your hand feel compared to the fingers getting wet, to the soap bubbles making soft popping noises. Mindfulness is about recognizing with lightness the thoughts we have, the ones that flit by or stampede in or even the ones that are so seminal and so engrained, we barely hear them whisper. We can let them pass or pull them in to question, and then keep detaching from them, recognizing them not as facts but as there, as we return to feeling and being.[2]

A commitment to consciously acknowledging thoughts without getting caught up in them leads to huge dividends when it comes to how we feel inside, but also when it comes to how our dogs behave outside, because they will respond to our inner peace. So the progress we make with our dogs and the strength of the bond end up being equal in measure to our mindfulness. If nothing before has compelled us to gently observe our minds and then get back into the senses of the body experiencing reality as it is, perhaps understanding that it impacts our dogs will be the motivation we need.

I remember talking to a client who was baffled by her dog's unpredictability. She just could not understand why her dog was sometimes tolerant but sometimes went into attack mode around other dogs. But as we chatted, we identified that in their home there was a constant slew of new foster dogs, as well as guests traveling who would stay over. What I pointed out was that she herself was offering her dog an unpredictable life. She herself was upholding a frenzied, unpredictable energy, aligned with the anxious thoughts she herself was having about that all the time. And her dog was merely adapting to the frequency around her. This does not mean that the dog didn't have changes to make, or that she was absolved from going after other dogs when she did, or that it was all the human's fault. Of course the dog had work to do. But so did the human. If we want a good relationship with our animals, which to me is the point of having them around, we must recognize that we sync up.

Whether you are reading this book with the hope that you might be able to repair the relationship you have with your dog or you're preparing to adopt a new dog and would like some encouragement, this concept remains the same: Dogs are supreme experts at calculating energy and reacting to it. Connection and communication with them happens not in words, not in the concrete, but in the energy channeled between us and around us. Maybe you want to call this a sixth sense. Maybe it's just what love does. Regardless, it is imperative to include energy in discussions about bonding with dogs because what we think about, we frequently end up radiating in emotion, unless we are aware. And our dogs pick up on it. So keep checking in with your own energy while gauging theirs, and it will take you toward your dog, who will in return lean toward you, instead of maintaining a fraught relationship that requires you to pull a hesitant dog into your agenda of people stuff.

A solid bond is based on give and take. It's a *we* thing, not a you thing. We can choose thoughts that ooze an energy of openness. In this way, bonding with a dog is loving them enough to want to love them more. It is also loving yourself enough to want to love yourself more. But they can't love you more. They already love you the most. It's just how they love. It's why their energy is so delightful to be around.

Focus your mind, then get out of your head and into your life! Let this lift the ambiance of who you are because your thoughts make your energy and so does the amount of time you spend in them. Let bonding with your dog be a stamp upon the thoughts you're having, and let it raise up your feelings, your actions, and your results. Let your dog's awesome vibes bless yours.

Bonding with a dog is mirroring.

Dog trainer Sue Sternberg breaks down dog behavior as being primarily influenced by a trinity of factors: a dog's natural threshold, their person, and their environment.[3] To understand what threshold means, the words of Leslie McDevitt articulate: "All of us have a threshold. Beyond it, depending on our personalities, we might have a totally reactive response, or we might shut down and sit rocking in the corner sucking our thumbs. Each of our dogs has his own threshold, too, and his own response once he's crossed it.

Once a dog has crossed his threshold, he is too pumped, scared, or stressed to learn."[4] Working within threshold optimizes the ability for a being to absorb information. It is therefore valuable to identify and remain under that limit. Back to Sternberg—according to her, threshold affects who the dog is, sure, and although it may not be as malleable as we want it to be, we can keep our dogs under it, preventing them from reaching extreme behaviors. Yet the other two out of the three things that impact our dogs most we have an even bigger say in—their people and their environment.

People and environments emit a frequency akin to radio waves, projecting out a sense of who they are and what the space is like. They impact who the dog will be. When we take responsibility for our thoughts and beliefs (beliefs are thoughts we repeat over and over), for how they drive the essence of who we are and how the atmosphere around us feels, we step into a fuller expression of ourselves. Of who we want to be. When there is a dog around, there is someone responding to us and the environment we create. So in this way, bonding with a dog can help us realize, tune in differently, and consciously evolve.

Sometimes the dogs who test us the most become our best teachers because of the energy *they* radiate, which may reveal to us something about ourselves that we did not want to see. I have had this experience, and I want to mention it as part of dog bonding. It's not dog love's antonym nor its nemesis. You might yourself have a challenging dog. Or if you love dogs as much as I do, it's bound to happen to you in the future—if not in your home directly, then it'll be your mom's dog or a friend's or a lover's. One day, you will likely meet a dog you can't stand. Of the dogs you will cross paths with, these are among some of the most important. Please allow me to tell you why.

I stumbled into the world of volunteering at a Los Angeles animal shelter over 15 years ago. I was in over my head from the jump. The noises, the smell, the desperation, the trauma; it's a world of hurt in there. Combine that with the cuteness, the longing, the wiggliness, the camaraderie. At an animal shelter, you see and feel the whole wide spectrum of emotions. At an animal shelter, you witness the best in people and animals, and the worst in them too. Once I started volunteering, I became consumed by the shelter and spent all of my weekends there. I learned to survive the band-aid rip to the heart of finding out a dog I'd just been walking days before got put to sleep. I learned to survive the great abyss of mystery when I heard a dog I cared about got adopted, and I had no idea if it was to a good home. I learned to survive the reality of injustices that still haunt me. There were also many causes for celebration, like each time a wonderful person or couple would come in to adopt a senior pet.

I was only a few months in when I witnessed a Shepherd mix getting surrendered at the front desk: a sleek, skinny dog, so dirty she was gray, and only weeks later after a bath did I discover she was blonde. I stood there as her former owner turned her in and walked out the door without so much as a glance back. I watched the dog, could not look at the person. What I didn't know in that moment was that the dog would pick me. I began walking this Shepherd, networking her, and put my name on her, which was a way to identify that as a volunteer, I was doing all I could to get this dog out into a home or rescue group. I took pictures of the dog. She fell in love with me. I fell in love with her. So when I got the call from the shelter that she was going to be euthanized due to lack of time and space, I did not think much. I simply jumped into my car and ran to get her. I brought her home as my first foster.

Feebe was a dragon of a dog. Feebe had impulse-control and aggression issues. Feebe's threshold was challengingly low, to say the least, and in order to keep helping her, I had to study to become a dog trainer just to manage her in our house. Talk about rising to an occasion. I had no idea how to adjust myself and her environment in order to bring out her best behavior, but I needed to figure it out because her threshold was limited and her history riddled with neglect. She was, in short, a butthead who growled at every person she met and tried to pounce on every dog she could. My first instinct was to attempt to "cure" Feebe just as my clients would later hire me to do with their dogs after Feebe had inspired me to study and become a dog trainer. Many of us probably start there, whether we are dog trainers or pet parents or both: We want our animals to be less assholey, to get fixed up as if they're cars and we're some sort of mechanic.

But what stood out as most interesting to me, so

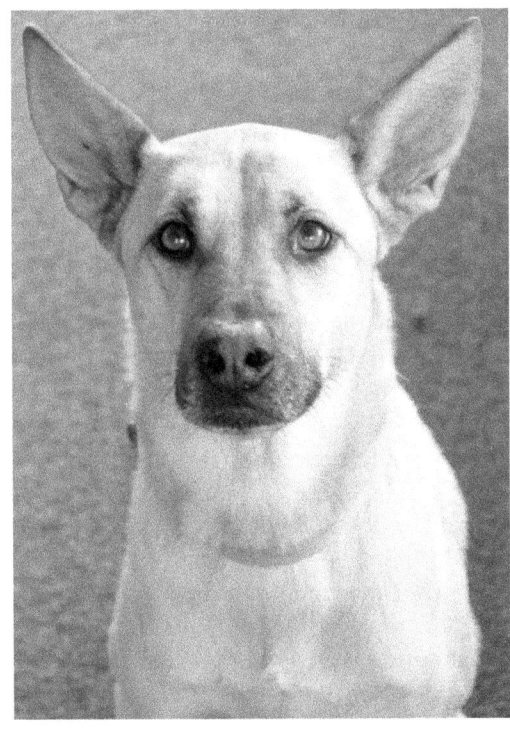

Earnest, complicated Feebe turning up the intensity in our home in the winter of 2010.

new to these sheltering and dog training worlds, was that the more I tried to implement the principles of behavior in practice as a dog trainer and as Feebe's person, the more I tried to force her and change her, the more she wreaked havoc in our home. Each difficulty brought on new difficulties, until opening my eyes in the morning and landing my gaze on her brought about intense feelings of frustration and disappointment. My thoughts about her were negative. That energy grew and grew, as I resisted and resisted, as I coerced and coerced. Eventually my thoughts about Feebe spilled over into who I was being, into what was between us. The blending of our energies together seemed to worsen each of our energies individually. All my negative thinking about her really did was add tanks of gasoline to the fire of a mismatched reality.

However, despite what we read in books or study in theory, our capabilities as humans get cultivated through experiences that are usually ripe with compromise. It was not until I teased out what I wanted from what I needed that I began to give Feebe grace. It was not until I spent as much time tending to my own energy and thoughts about Feebe as I did to working on Feebe, that things began to change. It was not until one day, before she lunged at Ophelia, that I found myself lunging at my husband. And I saw it clearly: *my* impulse control, *my* aggression issues. Feebe and I had synched up. I didn't want to admit it, but we'd singled one another out through familiarity. I reflected back to Feebe what was wrong with her. She reflected back to me what was wrong with me. And that was the basis of what lived back and forth in our dynamic. All the education in the world could not prepare me for a dog with such a nervous temperament, so vigilant, so beautiful, so defensive and insecure and needy and shattered. She had been through a lot. So had I. We were going to have to be something else now, independently and together because of our togetherness, because that's what it means when we make a commitment to a dog.

I learned to treat Feebe as the dog I believed she could become. I would literally envision turning my energy dial to land on a station that saw her for all the potential she had, and I held that vision for her despite anything she did or did not do. And you know what? It worked. She grew to be a better dog. But I also grew to be a better me. It meant I could turn that dial for myself too, or at least reckon with why I wasn't. I grew to interpret Feebe's actions through thoughts that were loving toward her and toward myself. I could, in fact, treat myself the way I wanted me to feel about me, just like I was doing to Feebe. I was now the kind of person who did this sort of thing for a foster dog, and I felt proud of that me when I looked in the mirror. In a major way, Feebe brought another layer into my recovery. I became a person of generous interpretations because of her.

Perhaps I think too much about dogs and spend too much time

with them. That's a fair critique. But I still hold true that one of the best things we can do is be aware of what we're conveying to the ones we love through our invisible signals, because those invisible signals convey messages, and those messages will teach another being that they can do it or that they cannot, that they will be okay or that they won't, that they need our scolding or that they ought to enjoy life and trust themselves, that they're enough or that they're exasperatingly inconvenient. This wordless exchange is going on regardless of whether we want to accept it or not. Recognizing that your energy is something you are responsible for, and that has significant influence on the creatures you're around, can alter the way your dog behaves, the way you go through your life, and the love that pulses around you. Because the truth is, you can't clip and edit to change somebody else's energy. Just your own. And often enough, that is what will end up doing the job.

Bonding with a dog is knowing when to ignore them.

There were doable actions that came along with changing my mindset around Feebe. I believed it was possible for her to adopt alternative behaviors, and at first, I held an allegiance to that belief over what she did. Was it somewhat fantastical, nearly delusional? Maybe. Nonetheless, it allowed me to ignore the behaviors I didn't like from Feebe. Instead of correcting or reacting, I ignored anything she did that bothered me. In doing so, I was only letting her know what I did desire, which were all the behaviors she did that earned her my attention.

Dogs (like people) will do what works to get them what they want. In the world of operant conditioning, a process of learning we'll talk more about in Chapter 4, behavior is reinforced due to the consequences that follow it.[5] Removing myself and all forms of reinforcement is considered negative punishment in this paradigm. One might consider that I was punishing Feebe in this sense. But I promise you, it's not what you think. I'd *never* recommend hurting a dog, so please suspend that interpretation of the word punishment for a minute.

"Punishment," in behavioral terms, is something that decreases the likelihood of a behavior. "Reinforcement," on the other hand, increases the frequency of a behavior. "Negative" means something is taken away, and "positive" means something is added.[6] There are already powerful, insightful books out there that further break down this behavioral terminology in detail, so I'm not going to pretend you need another one. What I want to explain is how removing a cherished reinforcer (*you*) can help decrease the likelihood of an undesired behavior (removing yourself to decrease a behavior = negative punishment *without* hurting your dog). This approach does not harm your dog. It does not have you in a tug of war battle with a dog. Simply turning away from your dog or moving your body to increase your physical distance can be a very loud message to your dog that what they are doing is something you don't like, that it leads to less of you. It is the same thing as taking a kid's iPad away because they did not clean up their room (therefore taking away something they like), which will probably inspire them to do what was asked of them next time (clean your room!) in order to have more access to an iPad.

This negative reinforcement is a noninvasive technique Feebe understood in energy. I wish Feebe would have understood me with only the application of treats, massages, and kisses, but that's not how things went. I used the removal of me when she behaved in a way that was hard to handle, and this removal was enough to get her to perk up and pay attention to what made me go away. We are often the greatest reward there is in our dog's world, so it's not just food or play that serves as reinforcement. By removing eye contact, voice (no words), and touch, we give a "talk to the hand" attitude. Blowing them off when they do something we dislike is a way we can communicate in energy clearly without causing pain. What matters when using this tool, though, the biggest teachable moment, comes *right after* we take ourselves away and emit a talk to the hand vibe, when the dog ceases the behavior we do not like and offers up another behavior, one we do like. Right at that second, that instant, we come back to them! We give them our eyes, touch, praise, and closeness again. We reinforce what we *do* want by giving it and them attention. The discrepancy between your responses is noticeable. Because what we want is to return to them! Under the conditions that are peaceful to both of you, you can, will, and do.

Behavioral scientist Murray Sidman calls out: "Positive reinforcement leaves us with something we want, or in a position to do or to gain something advantageous, with behavior and resources that occupy us productively and with feelings not of relief but of satisfaction. But the only good thing that negative reinforcement leaves us with is the feeling of relief; something bad has stopped or has gone away."[7] And he is right; positive reinforcement is always preferable. That is why coming back to our dogs *after* we remove ourselves can help both relieve them of the bad feeling (being ignored) and prevent our continual withholding (which becomes punishing to them and hardening in us). Yes, it sucks to have any badness in our dogs' lives. But we live in a time where I believe we put an immense amount of pressure on dog parents, terrifying them about what constitutes force, and pushing them to strive to do it perfectly. That standard of precision and the amount of guilt that follows when we cannot live up to those ideals are not conducive to our mental health, our wellness, or

2. Dog Love Is Wordless Energy

the relationship. It is not sustainable. In my experience, not being able to express our disdain out of an overcaution that it could be interpreted as punishing leads to pent-up frustration that ends up being taken out on animals eventually.

I would never and am not looking for an excuse to be nasty to a dog. But I am looking for a reality where we can have likes and dislikes, just like our dogs should be able to have. Where we can match up within parameters of gently expressing those likes and dislikes, which may factor into an adoption going well. There must be permission to let a dog know our displeasure (without hurting them) and hopefully that permissioning will inspire us to *want to* find the moment after we have taken away our attention, to come back to our dogs, to positively reinforce them, to end on a high note, to end on the love.

Love can be the culture of your family. But it must be real. It must be doable. Choose positive reinforcement every single time you can, yet do not subscribe to pressure in the name of perfectionism. Be force free every day, all day! There is no justification to add punishment. But we must be real to our dogs, with all our emotions, just like they should be allowed to be with us. And I do not believe removing a reinforcement falls in the same category as adding punishment.

So when Feebe would bark in my face, I'd turn around and give her my back. As soon as she stopped barking in my face, I'd engage with her again instantly! This is how a term like "negative reinforcement" can translate into something useful. This is how we can communicate clearly and deliberately to let a dog know what kind of energy is going to work between us. Because the thing is, the more solid vibe will win. It was either going to be Feebe freaking out that took over me, or my holding centered that took over Feebe. One of us would have the stronger energy, and as a dog mom who wants to bond, I dedicated myself to it being me.

In the end, I'm glad Feebe was more dog than I had bargained for, and I'm glad I had to search high and low for ways to help her. Because in order to do so I got to watch myself shift, I built my own confidence, I learned to manage my own expectations, and overcame my own propensity for negative thinking, overreacting, willful goal setting, and willful goal insisting. All of it changed, I changed, my vibe changed, and it massively impacted Feebe. I learned to read and relate to her improved energy as she learned to read and relate to mine.

Dog love flourishes because of the investment we make. The investment is what elevates who we are, as well as the relationship itself. Sometimes it's difficult and irksome, not uniquely because it's a shelter dog or a traumatized dog or an old dog, but because a pet is a living being. They all come with their own story, history, and energy. But even the dogs we don't

Feebe trying to be cute after terrifying the mail carrier with her lunging and barking.

get everything we want back from can improve through our love, and give us in return the feeling that we have improved through their love. Once we know through action and sacrifice that we're the type of person who offers love independent from how we're loved back, we become the energy we've always wanted to be. We get loved back in a way we need.

Feebe was never lobotomized, sometimes to my chagrin. She never became an easy dog, or a dog-park dog, or a non-dragon dog. But her behavior got better and her threshold rose, even if it was one percent, and the love between us blew off the charts. She lived up to her potential. It's one of the things in my life I'm most proud of, that we stuck by her until she died at sixteen and a half years old. That's right, she was a foster fail. My family and I ended up keeping Feebe forever because we knew we would do what it took for her to be the best she could be, and because we appreciated the sensation of her smooth, bald belly, and because we were consistently met by her exuberant tail wagging, even if we had to watch her closely, keep her separate from Ophelia often, and make sure she didn't eat our neighbor's cats.

Making the most out of the growth opportunities our dogs provide us allows the journey to be more profound. Eventually it gets to be more peaceful too. As for the dogs who will never be who we want them to be, there is still an enormous amount to discover. Proof: A control freak like me loved a dog with immense control issues like Feebe. What does this say about the power of love? I had to teach Feebe the same thing 500 times! But wow, did I rejoice when she got it after the 501st. And wow, did I rejoice when I realized I was the kind of person who would be there 501 times later, still tuning my own energy.

Bonding with Ophelia and Feebe.

As you can tell, once we officially adopted Feebe, it wasn't all roses and daffodils from there on. My husband and I argued about her more than anything. She was a high-octane dog, which I discovered was common among Belgian Malinois mixes. (She was a Maligator, you guys, I had no idea what that meant before adopting her!) Ophelia was attacked by Feebe three times. And still, we remained devoted to her. I wonder what this says about the power of love—that we can care about someone who could bite us. Well, I discovered that the energy of giving love to somebody despite the fact that they could bite us turns out to be among the most powerful factors in melting away whatever thing in them would make them want to bite us. You are absolutely accurate if you're calling me a hippie at this point, but I'm going to say it anyway: Love saves the day. Love thaws out everything else. Love converts into The Energy.

Feebe proved that it's not about getting "there," to some finish line that always moves ahead and is forever out of reach. It's not about arriving, which had been my addiction before her. She showed me that there is no "there"; it's about the work we do as we do it, the path is truly the best part. She taught me that dog bonding isn't about the finished product but the process of loving and being loved. In the 12 Step program, step nine is about making amends. I remember being very excited about step nine my first time around. Yay! I'd get to tell everybody sorry! I'd get to fly around the country, make calls, and write long letters pouring out my soul, my reasons, and my apologies. But what I have found over the years is that my living amends count most. Not the ones I vow or the big speeches I make, but the amends I become. The amends I exemplify. By relying on the wordless energy of being my amends, I behave accordingly, consistently. It's what makes the biggest impression on those I care about.

As for Ophelia, she was the only dog Feebe could ever live with, just the right amount of apathetic and above it all. But because Feebe was bigger, stronger, sharper and more intense, for a while, I blamed every negative interaction between them on Feebe. It took me a while to recognize that when Feebe and Ophelia disagreed or fought, it was not all Feebe's fault. I had no idea what shade Ophy was throwing, what messages she was emitting. I had missed dozens of micro dog conversations happening between them in their body language and in the energy they bounced back and forth between each other. I learned to stop painting Feebe as the rotten egg and Ophelia as the victim. In the end, Ophelia became more real to me, imperfect, allowed to be flawed. And Feebe became more than the summary of all her flaws and mistakes. We were a family. A family grows and changes together, not just one member, but all members. Feebe deserved us changing with her as much as the rest of us deserved to request it from her.

An "identified patient" is a psychological, clinical term used in family therapy to describe the role that a family member is given when they serve as a scapegoat for all of their family's dysfunctions.[8] It's an outsourcing of conflict onto one person, often a black sheep, instead of upgrading the entire family system, requiring everybody to adapt and pivot, so that the system is healthier for all. It is not easy to confess to you that Feebe was our identified patient for some time. I was mine in my family of origin, and thanks to Feebe, I began to understand what that did to me, and what we were doing to her by continuing to uphold it. I wouldn't be the kind of mom I am today to my human kids, if not for Feebe's colossal impact in highlighting for me how love is about committing to an inclusive arrangement, not about defending a scheme for blame. Feebe inspired me to tend to my own thoughts and energy so I could be more intimate and responsive with the ones I love. The identified patient can become a convenient way for other members of a family to avoid the growth work they need to do, and in this way they are not only harmed but harmful to everybody else because they leave people who need to change stuck. Every hard moment Feebe and I had together does not tip the scale compared to my gratitude to her for revealing these truths to me. She did not come into my life to be a shield. She was more complex and whole than I ever realized, and that meant I was too. We all were. We all are.

> It's easy to sum up Lori Weise as the Mother Teresa of the dog world, but that would fail to encapsulate her best quality, which is how down-to-earth she is. Lori has been saving animals since before it was cool. She believes in the human capacity for growth and potential, she believes in attraction rather than promotion, she believes in believing in others. On top of her own shelter intervention work and significant spay and neuter programs, Downtown Dog Rescue's Pet Support Space moves the needle even further, offering pet food, medical vouchers, and counseling support for pet owners in need. Lori does not hesitate to reinvent her energy in the name of community. She is fearless, investing in harm reduction and immersing herself where nobody dares to go.

Chapter 2 Exercises

This chapter's first exercise entails doing breathwork with your dog. Sorry, not sorry! Any resistance you experience is welcome. Go on and roll your eyes at me. But then sit beside your dog and invite that defiant energy into the breath. Breathe with whatever you feel, wherever you're at. It's impossible to breathe in the past or in the future, we can only breathe in the moment. And so breathwork helps deposit us into one mindful moment at a time. It's what we love about dogs, their commitment to the present, so now notice your dog's breath. Maybe lay a hand on their tummy if they like that. If not just watch the rise and fall of their breath. Let it transfix you. Then join them. Breathe in the quiet stillness as you sit beside your dog, and let this simple act benefit your mood, your day, your relationship. Interacting with a dog calmly on purpose is crucial so your dog correlates you with tranquility, not just with stimulation. As McDevitt puts it, "Teaching relaxation is the foundation for all behavior modification programs."[9] By this she means that behavioral modification and progress are not only supported by but may even come from relaxation, receptivity, and wellness. I urge you to stay there consciously breathing with your dog for however much time you can muster. Can your breathing match up with your dog's?

The next exercise entails engaging in a recall game with your dog. Start with a treat in your fist. (Side note: I hold treats hidden in a fist so that I am not teaching my dog to only respond to me when they see food in my hand. Instead they learn to target on my fist. Sometimes it opens and there's food! Sometimes it opens and unfolds into petting. They never know but are eager to find out!) Call your dog's name while he is distracted. Then wait. Maybe add a whistle or a kissing sound to get their attention, but resist saying their name over and over. When they spot you, crouch low, and offer a treat or scratch. Keep practicing until your dog understands, *Hey, when my name is called good things happen!*

We want your dog to buy in. We want you to have fun and make this exercise part of daily life so it is natural for your dog to come to you. Over morning coffee every other day of the week is great. As you play, as you wait, observe (without judgment) what you're thinking, and how your dog responds to you while you swim in those thoughts, in that energy. Observe curiously: What is your tone when you call your dog over? Does it get your dog to listen? What vibe do you convey if they don't listen? What signals do you demonstrate if you become impatient? What energy do you want to convey to your dog? What energy would get your dog to want to come over? What thoughts support the emission of that frequency?

Now be it.

3

Dog Love Is Acknowledging Feelings

We're assessing energy now, cool, but where do we go from here? By creating conditions that result in good feelings in our dog, behavior can improve as our connection remains intact (hopefully not the dog though; please spay and neuter your pets). Because if the bond is our North Star, then any need to rush the dogs or their changes fall to the wayside. Hurrying is unnecessary if we recognize how beings learn, and they learn what something is by the associations they make about it. Please rest assured: New associations can indeed take hold.

Many of the dogs I've met—shelter dogs, rescue dogs, but equally as many dogs from breeders—have negative associations that they live with and carry around like heavy luggage. It may be that these things were caused unintentionally, innocently enough, or have never been specifically identifiable by their pet parents. We can tell ourselves that this only happens when a dog has lived in a shelter or has had three other homes, as is the case sometimes with rescue dogs, but the truth is, people get puppies and bestow upon them (again unknowingly most of the time) many negative associations. Getting a puppy doesn't mean you get a dog without problems. It often means the problems the dog demonstrates were likely developed while living with you, and I say that in the least blaming way possible. Those issues can be dealt with just as the issues a rescue dog developed with somebody else can be dealt with. In both cases, these dogs have potential. Therefore, "new" dogs don't necessarily have better potential than "used" dogs.

I'd ask us to think about how old we are when we get a dog. Are we "new"? Because our dogs allow us to be who we are, one of the most important things we can do is let them be who they are as well. Dogs don't deny us an adoption. They never go "Ewww, she's messy" or "No, he doesn't make enough money" or "It'll take too long for them to be successful, I refuse to go home with them!" They dive in. They get in the car. They are at the whim of us. They meet us wherever we're at, no matter how we

3. Dog Love Is Acknowledging Feelings

feel, no matter how "used" we are, because to them we are worth it regardless. Furthermore, they are the ones with less power and less autonomy. As the ones with more power and more autonomy, isn't it our obligation then to grant them some grace? I am not insinuating that we can't want our dogs to learn things or that we shouldn't train behaviors we wish to train. But I am requesting it be on us to accept that they have associations, personalities, likes and dislikes. We should care about how they act because it is indicative of *how they feel*. And I very much believe we should give a shit about our dogs' feelings.

When we get good at caring about how another being feels, we get better at caring about how we ourselves feel. Flipped around, it's still true: When we get good at caring about how we ourselves feel, we enhance our ability to care about others. Again, dog bonding bumps up our own wellness. Because getting good at being with feelings can make all the difference in our lives. I won't pretend that we should smile away a negative association or act like it's anything less than disruptive when a dog demonstrates a challenging behavior. But I'm also not encouraging us to *solve* it right away. I am urging us instead not to give up on a dog because of it, and to start with merely acknowledging their feelings. Not dwelling on the feelings or making excuses because of them, but making space for them. Seeing behaviors for what they might represent could help us access information about our dogs and the emotions running underneath their actions, because emotion generates behavior. If we could begin by meeting emotions with understanding, I believe we could change our dog's associations and our own with more ease.

I'm not here to point fingers or shake my fists or make anybody feel guilty. But I am trying to suggest that how our dogs express themselves is directly linked to how they feel about something, and when we get caught up in changing the behavior, we sometimes overlook the reason it exists. In my experience, in order for a behavior to change and at the same time for a bond to grow, which I believe is really want we want with our pets, instead of only treating the symptom—what we see, the behavior—we have to first, or simultaneously, also care about how this other being feels. That is the behavior's cause.

"You're safe," I whisper every night to my dogs. And so I am whispering it to myself.

Bonding is the associations made.

The technical way to think about a positive association is that one variable increases as another variable increases. Conversely, a negative association means the value of one variable decreases while the value of another variable increases.[1] In dog terms, the difference might look like your dog hearing you open a bag of Bully Sticks (an easily digestible chew treat) and running into their open crate because they know that is the only place they get those Bully Sticks. That would be a positive association. Conversely, if your dog resists going into a crate because in the past they've been shoved into it and yet you still force them into it because it's the only way to get them to go in, this would be a negative association with the crate.

Sticking with the crate example, I like to pair being in the crate with a treat-filled Kong (a rubber toy with a hole in it for food) or chew toy for my dogs. In fact, it's the *only* time my dogs see these items. If high-value chew toys exist exclusively when they're apart from you and in the crate, you might find your dog rushing into their crate as if they're asking you to leave your own house! This is because of that positive association they have with you leaving and them being in the crate, an ideal scenario. As a dog trainer, I went into homes all the time where dog guardians wouldn't enforce limits. Kongs and Bully Sticks and bones would be all over the floor. And I'd want to pull my hair out. That's the equivalent of leaving gummy bears on the ground for toddlers or cell phones lying around for teenagers. You wouldn't do that, would you? You'd know that would make them act badly. Constant access to items designed to have value not only takes away the significance of those items, but also takes away their use for you to reinforce behavior through positive association. It's shooting yourself in the proverbial foot. Then your dog won't listen to you—why would they?

High-value activities like Kongs or Bully Sticks should be associated with your absence. These items should come from you and end with you, deliberately paired with the crate so that being in a crate feels awesome to your dogs. That yum will go away as soon as the crate door opens and it will return the next time the door closes. This is how we keep those activities meaningful. Furthermore, by pairing a happy, "Crate time!" voice with the enrichment activity, your dog will learn that the crate is fun and that you leaving is a good thing. What a lot of people do is tend to rain their excitement onto the dog when their dog is coming *out* of the crate. But that teaches the dog that the crate is not a desired location, and that coming out is way better. Instead, think about how your dog might feel. When the dog is let out of the crate, I recommend being completely calm and neutral, as if somebody turned your power button off. I call it *the Dead Robot Effect*. Any joy should be expressed when they're going into the crate!

Associations are not exclusive to canine behavior. This is a behavioral principle across all species, including human. Examples of those? When

3. Dog Love Is Acknowledging Feelings

your partner expresses gratitude for the chores you do, you will likely do more chores; when your partner says, "We need to talk," you probably avoid them because you have a negative association with the phrase "We need to talk" having led to arguments in the past. Associations take hold due to feeling safe or not, due to it having gone well in the past or not, due to no harm coming or a perceived or real threat correlating with an event. Associations occur during situations, in the moment, but they are also built up after, in between experiences as a being processes and links up thoughts and emotions about what would transpire if they were in that position again. When we're bonding, we want our dogs to have faith in us, in the world, and in love, so it's important to remember the level of safety they feel as they do something, which will linger afterward. Feeling safe is often predicated on the opportunity we give our dogs to make their own choices instead of being forced by us. That alone has a huge impact on the associations they make to whatever it is we're asking them to do. So the associations they build that we are a part of will either work for us or against us. A dog's level of safety, therefore, ends up impacting us down the line.

Here's another common real-life example: A dog struggles to walk on a leash. That might be because as a puppy, the leash was put on that dog who was then dragged around in order to learn how to leash-walk. Some dogs might have a threshold that could tolerate that, but others perhaps would be adversely affected by that association. It felt unsafe for them to be pulled around, when what they needed was to be lured or given choices, offered touchpoints of empowerment and confidence so they could feel safe as they learned to do this new going-on-walks thing. In the case of a dog who developed a negative connection between the leash and going on walks, he may now resist, go noodley, drop to the ground and refuse to budge.

From a place of empathy and understanding, I'd deliberately create a positive association where the negative ones exists. So for example, a dog who hates being pulled around on a leash, and who has learned to associate that as walking and now won't walk, can be given time along with slow, laddered exposure to having a more positive experience while on a leash. Laddering allows learning to be a process. Let me explain further: Maybe as step one, that dog would get the leash clipped on and drag the leash around the house behind him without being pulled by a person at all. Maybe step two would be standing in the yard and keeping hold of a slack leash, and whenever the dog moves forward, following him so the leash doesn't go taut. Step three could be that we move bit by bit, little by little, and begin walking a short distance on our block, avoiding the need to pull so we can create a new association that will turn this dog into a walk aficionado. How long will each step take? As long as it takes.

If you're reading this thinking "Ugh! How boring! How slow! How irritating! I can't do it!" then welcome to the club. I don't mean to burst your Michael Bublé, but everybody feels that way. The point isn't for you to be stuck because you have those feelings nor to gloss over them; the point is in this point itself! Acknowledge that *you* feel this way, own it, understand it, and be gentle with yourself by caring about how you feel. Then perhaps get curious about what negative connotations you have around slowing down and doing less-stimulating activities or letting things take time. Start with you, in you! Let bonding with the dog help you! Maybe there is a way to create a positive association for yourself as you impart the same onto your dog. Maybe you're put out by the notion of changing associations for them because this is an area of growth for you, an opportunity to juice the joy out of making a new association for yourself around doing something for the well-being of your dog.

Again, if you're reading this thinking "She's nuts! It's a dog! Animals are not the same as us!," I want to encourage you to dig deeper here too. To wonder why that's your reaction, why that's your association. To wonder, what if we looked at our animals more expansively? What feelings lie underneath our desire to make them not equal to us? What if our feelings don't weigh more than theirs? What if when looked under a microscope, feelings from different beings look identical? What if a dog's feelings are as real and round as ours? If we are the ones who benefit from the unfair power dynamic, isn't it our duty to bring the possibility of new and improved associations into the relationship? Because here's the thing: When it comes to doing what we want them to do, if there is something your dog hesitates with or refuses, the dog can't do the work of intentionally changing their associations to what we're asking. We have to decide to do that with them. This is yet another area where we can become simpatico with our dogs and enhance our own state of well-being by caring about theirs, learning to optimize how we both feel as we live our lives together.

Bonding is Classical Conditioning.

Remember that this is not a terminology book, so I won't do the all-out scientific thing, but since we are talking about associations, and because I want you to have the knowledge you can use to bond with your dog (and yourself), allow me to give a little spiel on classical conditioning, also known as respondent conditioning, because it's one of the ways associations can be altered.

Classical conditioning is a learning process that links two events or variables together.[2] Think Pavlov. The basic premise of Pavlov's experiment

3. Dog Love Is Acknowledging Feelings

was that when a dog was exposed to food, the dog began salivating, which is referred to as an unconditioned response. It's a reflex that happens without any learning. Pavlov would then ring a bell and the dog would produce no effects. But after he introduced ringing the bell *during* the exposure to the food, the dog began to salivate due to the food while the bell was ringing. And eventually, the sound of a ringing bell caused the dog to salivate.[3] What does this have to do with anything? Well, classical conditioning involves using a stimulus that produces a behavior so we can borrow the relationship between the stimulus and the behavior and associate it with an unconditioned stimulus so it too can lead to the response. Just like the food caused salivating, which makes food a "conditioned stimulus" that produced a reaction because the subject learned to associate it with a given outcome (eating food = yummy, feel good tummy).[4] Salivating became a "conditioned response," which was transferred to the bell by adding the bell into the established association between the food and salivation. Eventually, salivating began to occur at the sound of the bell alone.

Are you still reading? What this proves is that pairing a stimulus with something not previously associated to it can change a dog's behavior (and yours), and that it can be done without compromising the dog's positive association to you. Because when classical conditioning goes down, events get linked while the dog is doing what he's doing. It focuses on the emotional reactions that drive behavior. We can use classical conditioning to shift a dog's *feelings* about a situation and to achieve a new response by shifting their emotional state. We do it by pairing an activity or situation with stimuli on purpose. (Note that this might also shift your emotional state as you do it!)

Behaviorologist James O'Heare's workbook on dog aggression breaks down in greater detail how emotional reactions can be learned through respondent conditioning by pairing associations to a stimulus that was previously neutral. "When fear is a motivating force behind aggressive behaviors, we need to find out what elicits the fear and we need to change that emotional response,"[5] he says. That means addressing the motivation behind a behavior. That means what is required is caring about how the dog feels. As two other dog trainers and canine behaviorists who have written books together, Karen B. London and Patricia B. McConnell, illuminate about a behavior technique and form of classical conditioning: "Counter Classical Conditioning (CCC) is a process in which your dog learns to link something she loves with the thing that used to scare her, such that she begins to feel good whenever either are presented."[6] This is classical conditioning applied in training terms, but woven with compassion because it features the cause and not just the symptom or effect, aka the behavior you don't want.

It's important to focus on desensitizing your dog through classical conditioning by making sure you expose your dog to low-intensity versions of whatever scares or upsets him. There's no need to saturate the learning. The timing in which you present the conditioned stimulus is also significant; CCC is very much a timing game. You don't want to inadvertently reward an undesired behavior. So getting in there, paying attention (i.e., not being on your phone) and working with your dog *before* an undesired response begins is key to changing your dog's feelings and the association. It's not about training a particular behavior. Can classical conditioning be applied dog by dog, case by case? Yes, most of the time. Is it easy? Not necessarily, as it can be a trial-and-error, timing-based, highly attentive process that you would need to give yourself some grace around, too, which in and of itself would be a wonderful by-product of doing this work with your dog. How long will it take for a new association to take hold? Again, it will take as long as it takes! The joy is in the doing of it, not in being done with it. And you'll know when this has happened because you'll be implementing Chapters 1 and 2, connecting spiritually to your dog and banking on the energy between you to communicate what you need to know. Classical conditioning can be a tool to use with your dog that conditions higher levels of patience and tolerance in you.

Each dog (and person) is an individual, which means they will each have their own experiences and ideas about what is good or bad, what has proven to feel scary or safe for them, and how long it will take for that to shift. Dogs can feel a myriad of things. Oftentimes what is unknown to a dog is unsafe unless we go about exposing this something to them while intentionally making them feel safe as the exposure occurs. We don't get to decide the associations another makes in their minds, but we do get the chance to notice which responses don't serve them (or us) and then do our best to try to build new, more positive associations to replace negative ones. Hopefully, by working with our dogs strategically, we can inform their behavior and enhance the bond at the same time.

• • •

Sassy was a Beagle–Jack Russell Terrier mix we took in as a foster when she was 11 years old. Walking her was tricky. Her reflex was to growl at other dogs and instigate drama. I tried to stop her by hiding behind trees or crossing the street, which are fine avoidance moves; however, I knew the power of classical conditioning and I knew Sassy loved baby carrots. So I used that knowledge to my advantage. I decided to take a baggie of carrots with me on walks. When other dogs appeared down the street or around the corner, *before* she got riled up, I started creating a positive association to seeing other dogs by feeding her baby carrots.

3. Dog Love Is Acknowledging Feelings

We use food a lot in classical conditioning because food usually releases feel good hormones. I did not ask Sassy for a "sit" or anything from her, I merely let her gnaw on carrots in my hand while dogs passed us. In fact, baby carrots only existed on walks, and they took a lot of time for her little old lady teeth to chew up, which kept her busy. Chomping on carrots far outweighed wasting her energy grumbling at passing dogs, until eventually the grumbling atrophied because she began to associate baby carrots, her ultimate snack, with the sight of other dogs on walks. It became a positive experience. With time and repetition, dogs walking by us on the street cued a boost in Sassy's mood. She'd turn to me for carrots, demonstrating that her association had changed. Barking at other dogs was no longer practiced.

Sassy a few months after becoming a new addition to our family. It was like she had always been part of us, just waiting to return home.

If this seems inconvenient or even, dare I say, below you, I want to acknowledge how you feel! And you could pay somebody to do classical conditioning for you; that is valid. But I am still going to nudge you to consider being a part of your dog's learning because at the end of the day, we're the ones who live with our dogs. Hiring a dog trainer certainly helps, yet we have to carry the torch when the trainer is done, so whether we accept it now or later, it's our bond that will make the difference and cause the behaviors to sustain or not. Please do not misunderstand me: It's not easy to be a dog trainer. It's an incredible profession that requires persistence and wisdom, and we often need their help! But I'm also saying nobody knows your dog more than you do. You *can* learn and try, with a trainer to help you if you can swing it, but also without one. Just like parenting experts have great information yet we have to trust ourselves as parents to know our kids. Besides, what we practice as we teach a dog in this way is valuable to our own lives: How to slow down, cultivate the skill for conditioning, trust another to get it while trusting ourselves to get it while trusting the process of classical conditioning. So much trust.

After the baby carrots drills, I began to pinpoint areas of my own life where I had negative associations and, thanks to my practice with Sassy, figured out how to change some for myself. How to give myself my own version of baby carrots. For example, instead of plopping myself down at my desk and writing for hours without giving myself much credit for it or much of a break, I bought myself a beautiful hat. The hat made me feel fancy and altered. I wore the hat when I wrote, and eventually the good feelings the hat gave me associated with sitting down to write. These positive emotions spilled over and gave a boost to my work, pulling me out of the writing slump I'd been in. In sum: Your participation, your intentional construction of positive associations as something you offer your dog (and yourself), is a generous gift you can give that not only recognizes feelings, but also gives those feelings room to move and permission to change at their own pace. Classical conditioning is love in action.

Bonding is continuity in order to develop loyalty.

What we frequently do determines who we are. We can be something else then, if we want to, by changing our consistent actions. Consistency comes effortlessly when it's an old behavior we've been practicing, but it's tougher when we're creating an alternative response, and maybe toughest of all when we're replacing an old reaction with a new one. When we help our dogs change their responses due to holding space for their emotions, we recognize that we alter not only their behaviors but also the emotional signature associated with each behavior. Thus, each time we ourselves choose to act differently, especially when it doesn't feel comfortable or etched in a pattern, we must also endure shifting the emotional autograph associated with the behavior. It takes courage to release what we know, but each time we practice, it gets easier to endure the discomfort for next time. It engrains the new behavior just a little more, despite how awkward it feels at first. Titration involves slowly adding a new element in so that neutralization can continue to be achieved amidst a new mixture, so that we don't blow a nervous system out of the water.

Love grows when we value reliable behavior not only from dogs, but also from ourselves, so that we can count on one another, regardless of how difficult those reliable behaviors might be to establish in either/both of us. There is a hefty dose of listening required in reliability. Listening builds the readiness to depend on as well as be depended on, so in its own way, simply listening consistently will foster the bond. This can be a revolutionary thing for those of us who have a history of feeling like an outcast or alone, who have been repeatedly unseen and unheard. What if there are negative behaviors that stem from a plea to just be seen and heard? What if by listening we can nurture instead of fracture connection, and employ a method that changes behaviors? What if giving a listening ear makes us feel heard?

Taking it further, I describe a growl as a dog's way of saying "Please don't make me bite you." Growling is a natural warning signal from a dog because they cannot speak words. It's us humans who squash expression too often in dogs and in ourselves. Many dogs have been punished for growling, even though the fallout from that can be escalation; if they can't warn, if we're cornering them and not listening, then we're pushing them to go for a nip. If we take away dogs' warning signals, they will just go for the bite next time.[7] Those same dogs get relinquished to animal shelters all the time, and they literally die for it. But it was not their fault that somebody taught them not to use one of their natural forms of communication, that somebody punished them for using a caution sign to show how they feel.

Dogs come with thresholds, limitations, and capacities, just like we do. I'm *not* suggesting we let ourselves get bit. I'm *not* suggesting we dismiss or giggle in the face of true behavioral problems. But we can remain calm and hold onto our center no matter what, especially if a dog is in an escalated state, and hear them. Having a dog is signing up for a long-term relationship that involves work, like all relationships. When we decide not to get pissed off at the job or harbor unfair expectations, we break through to the other side where love flows.

Our consistency and theirs can merge to form the solid ground we walk on, to help us both feel safe. This is how loyalty is created, how we earn the type of Lassie-style love we dream about. By giving them some control over their environment, we give loyalty to them. If a dog is asking for space, please let them have it. If a dog growls, step away and heed the warning. It's not about your dominance or the need to smack that warning growl right out of them. It's about thinking of what they might be feeling and honoring their requests, just like you insist they honor yours. From there, you will watch their behavior change along with your own. They are as alive as you are, so both entities must be seen and heard, be permitted to have feelings in front of each other. That is how any reflexes and reactions that come from feeling unsafe will deescalate, allowing for your dog's cognitive brain to remain online as you interact with each other. It does the same for you and your brain, too—keeps you under your own threshold.

If we want big love, we must listen to our dogs as much as we require them to listen to us. Most beings seek somebody to count on, somebody who stays for them. If you can be that to your dog, they will do whatever it takes to be a best friend to you, to be a dependable presence in your life.

A typical Sunday walk for me as I pushed seniors Sassy and Ophelia in a dog stroller, paying no mind to the snickering neighbors.

3. Dog Love Is Acknowledging Feelings

Bonding with Ophelia and Sassy.

Caring about how someone feels holds them with compassion in real time as they change. It meets displays of aggression with tenderness, and that's not just for behaviorists to partake in. Emotional associating means something was learned and linked together. What's great about that is if something was learned, it can be unlearned. It can be linked differently by riding the obscure wave of timing, through consistency, and with the permission to go through it.

Having Ophelia by my side made everything bearable—when I broke up with a boyfriend, when friends left me out, when I didn't get the job. She cared about how I felt, I cared about how she felt, and we felt together. By the time Sassy came onto the scene, Ophy was roughly 16 years old. I believe Ophelia passed the baton on to Sassy, that Sassy was the exact dog Ophelia could entrust to take over loving me and our family. The moment Sassy's Tootsie Roll body walked into our house as a foster, we were all smitten. She loved my kids so much I think she believed they were hers more than mine. She and Ophelia were great buddies. The day Ophelia died, Sassy stood at the window at the backdoor howling for an hour. There was nothing there. There was everything there, outside, in the air. Ophelia had merged with Mother Nature.

Because when Sassy first arrived, weary and unsure, it was Ophelia who offered her a positive association with our home and with us. After she'd gone, Sassy bravely yet bashfully took Ophelia's spot in our bed, as if she was linking the loss of her sibling with our warmth, support, and embrace. She was as sad as we were. She mourned Ophelia as much as we did. Okay, maybe not as much as *I* did, but the point is, after Ophelia's death, I took care of Sassy, who took care of me. I went from feeling everything with Ophelia to feeling Ophelia's profound death in my life with Sassy. At first, I felt guilty, but I let myself feel that while accepting small sips of Sassy's affection. Because the relay race keeps going. We continue onward and go forward. The love wand keeps moving past, held to another hand/paw. That's what Ophelia would have wanted—for me to have love, for me to love dogs who would love my love.

Dogs give me positive association to living. Ophelia was the first to show me that. Sassy carried it further down the line. I'd like to think they discussed it over pie, two senior hound mixes similar to an episode of *The Golden Girls*, plotting how to condition me to be okay with another dog in my arms in order to get over the loss of the dog who had been in my arms for so long. Ophelia, who broke in my arms.

> Sophie Gamand is a photographer, an artist, and an animal chaplain brimming with great talent and great capacity to care. She takes people behind the scenes, revealing the lives of shelter dogs while also befriending those dogs, bringing their plight to the doorstep of those who would prefer to never visit a shelter. Somehow ranging in emotional depth from devastating to joyful to funny to beautiful to aching, Sophie captures and confronts the marvel of animal connection through art and activism. With her chaplaincy, she also manages to make others feel seen, supported, and celebrated. Because of Sophie, dogs who have been discarded or disposed of can be viewed as what they honestly are: Works of stunning creation. She invites the people who care for them to know that they are masterpieces too.

CHAPTER 3 EXERCISES

Chapter 3 ends with an experiment to help you better understand classical conditioning. Hang a chime on your doorknob before you go on a walk. Every time the door opens and closes, let it ring. Watch how soon the mere sound of the chime makes your dog rush over to the door. Don't be surprised if your dog starts ringing the bell with her nose or paw. If you want this behavior to continue, reinforce her for it with praise, a treat, or that immediate walk!

For the second chapter exercise, track some facts down like a scientist: When does your dog exhibit a reaction? What's the behavior? Can you identify the trigger? Can you intuit or describe the emotion you recognize underneath the behavior? I'd like you to pick a notebook (or a half-used notebook, doesn't need to be anything special) and start to collect this data. If there was no timeline, could you describe the behavior you desire in place of the behavior you dislike? Can you think about how you might attain that desired behavior if you were to pair the situation with a new association by creating a different emotional experience? (Food works great for this.) Could you keep notes on even the slightest of improvements so as to encourage yourself and your dog, so you don't give up before a new conditioned response takes hold?

Feel it out. Feel together. From a place of love, from an acknowledgment of feelings, from listening, we can set our dogs up to feel good about life with us. In doing so, they set us up to feel good about life with them.

4

Dog Love Is What We Focus On Grows

We're applying classical conditioning. Does this mean we can be done now? Nope, let's continue to prioritize bonding by cultivating the type of relationship where our dog chooses to behave in a manner that suits us both. If we understand that our attention is a form of reinforcement, why wouldn't we pay way more attention to what we love about our dogs and to their catalogue of preferrable behaviors? Let's focus on the stuff they do that we like!

This switch alone can make dogs feel good around us, like they should make decisions because we're there to applaud them for making the ones we agree with instead of singling out the ones they shouldn't have dared to try. How else could they know what we want from them unless they try a variety of behaviors? I personally want my dogs to feel like I'm cheering them on, like living with me is similar to living with somebody who is always holding up an encouraging sign during a marathon. Because if that is who I become to my dogs, doesn't it make sense that they would *want* to keep the relationship going, to maintain my natural loving gaze and praise, and therefore to be the best version of themselves in order to get it? It means they're allowed to take a crack, make an effort, endeavor, test and experiment because I'm going to give them clear information about those behaviors by focusing on the ones that result in a yes from me. The no's won't be a big deal. It doesn't have to be scary for them to get it wrong, and it doesn't have to mean they're wrong. They just won't get much from me when they act that way, so why would they keep those behaviors in their repertoire? Do I want to hold up and put emphasis on the times they get it wrong or the times they get it right? Which of those two scenarios creates a more secure dog? And which creates a happier me?

We waste an enormous amount of time and energy engaging with our dogs when they're doing things we dislike. Humans have it backward. We think that's when other beings need our input most, our correction, our force, and our lectures. But all it does when we spend more time on what is wrong than on what is right is keep our dogs in the dark about what to do, while teaching them at the same time that doing things that get a rise out of us will garner our complete and utter attention. They don't learn what they *should do*, but rather that acting out is the way to own us entirely, even if it comes with a spiral of negativity that often leads to insecurity.[1] It's too risky, too miserable to live in a loop of negativity at home about who we are and what we have or don't have to offer. It leads to limitations in our dogs, and to limiting beliefs in us about them.

So it's on us, the people, the ones doing the reinforcing, the ones who have the minds that get to wonder about what we are doing, with the consciousness to think and reflect and look at results and work to decode what might be causing them. The ones with the power, who get to come and go from our homes, the ones with options. When we concentrate on what is wrong, we become addicted to searching for what is wrong. We begin to live a life where we miss a million right moments a day, where we overlook a thousand delightful behaviors from our dogs, where we might say we are ready for love, but we never *feel* ready for love. It is feeling ready for love that gives us the sense of it, that fills us up with deserving and optimism and hope. Paying attention to what is wrong is love repellent, but paying attention to what is right is love magnetic. So why would we squash love within ourselves along with our pets? Why would pointing out every wrong choice inspire better behavior? How can we improve our inclination toward love, seeing with 20/20 vision to constantly seek the good out, spot it, and grow it?

Positive reinforcement is presenting feel-good responses to your dog for behavior they do, knowing that it will increase the likelihood that they'll do it again. Food and play are obvious reinforcers, but as we've already discussed, so is petting them, talking to them, being close by, even eye contact. McConnell and London claim: "To think this way—proactively rather than reactively—requires training yourself, but it will save you endless amounts of time and frustration. Once you learn to ask yourself 'How can I teach her to do what I *want* her to do?' rather than scolding her for doing something you *don't want* her to do, life will get a lot easier. After all, if you don't teach her, how else will she know what you want?"[2] This shift in outlook can change your entire life.

Honestly assessing how often and for how long we focus on our dog when they're misbehaving or being punks, and comparing that to how much attention our dog gets when they're resting on a bed or simply watching the birds outside, can tell us a lot. We tend to ignore our dogs when they are relaxed or quiet, giving them no feedback, giving nothing at all actually as if it's not worth mentioning. But that's some of their best behavior! That's when they need the note—*More of that please!* Whenever they're in a desirable state of mind or acting in a way you'd like them to continue, they need reinforcement to further get the message that they're good and lovable and loved. When we give ourselves to our dogs only when they're acting out or being annoying, it's confusing. Most dogs are downright confused by when they get the most valuable reinforcement ever: us. And the confusion can lead to an overall sense of uncertainty that permeates the air they breathe because they don't know what to do and may even become afraid that whatever they offer will lead to punishment. Our dogs need to understand how to behave to get us because what they want is us! They need clarity around what we *are* asking from them, not a worrying list about what we're not asking from them.

Focusing on the behavior we want to strengthen is predicated on the assumption that the dogs can learn through love and change through love, and will thus choose behaviors that are beneficial not only to us but also to them, the type of behaviors that earn them praise, food, attention, fun, joy, and more love. It implies that we want them to feel secure enough to make choices because we've committed to being there to highlight every time they make a good one. We're going to catch the good ones.

The inevitable outcome of this way of relating is that they believe in us for believing in them. I don't know about you, but I want to be believed in. I give it, and I get it in return. "I believe in you," I exclaim to my dogs. And so I exclaim it to myself.

Bonding is operant conditioning.

Operant conditioning is intentional. A dog learns to do something in order to obtain or avoid a given result. We teach our dogs a behavior that they perform voluntarily, not through force, and that behavior will either increase or decrease based on the reaction they get for performing the behavior. Operant conditioning requires dogs to be able to make choices so they understand the difference between getting a reward and not getting a reward. Karen Pryor is a behavioral psychologist, known as the mother of clicker training. She describes operant conditioning as giving an animal a chance to win and control at least a little part of their world.[3] She acknowledges that it takes effort, it takes thinking, and it takes a tolerance for trial and error. "You have to 'wing' it and use your imagination,"[4] Pryor advises. It's not about getting it perfectly or sitting down at the keys and immediately playing like Mozart. You have to earn the damn thing. Most of us have to practice piano to get good at it. Using a reinforcement marker (such as a clicker) is useful in operant conditioning. Pryor describes reinforcement with a clicker as, "not only rewarded their dog, it changed the owner's attitude. People discovered that their dogs were smarter than they thought, and lots more fun. The attitudes of the dogs changed, too."[5]

Using a clicker or whatever reward marker you want (even an exuberant "Yes!" works) will positively reinforce your dog and you at the same time. Keep in mind that your words, touch, proximity, and smiling eyes, as well as food and play, are all effective reinforcers just like a clicker could be. Your attention is an extremely influential gift that you should give to your dog at the appropriate time, as a consequence of a behavior you want to strengthen, or when your dog is in an appropriate frame of mind. "Every time your dog is in a physiologically relaxed state, his behavior reflects that state,"[6] Leslie McDevitt writes. I am not suggesting you go touch your sleeping dog (please leave them alone). I am suggesting that just noticing right then how wonderful they are, and feeling it in you about them, positively reinforces you for having this dog. And it will impact how you treat the dog subsequently.

When it comes to changing how we pay attention to our dogs and to changing their behaviors, we can totally outsource this to a dog trainer, and that's fine. But if we want a love story with our dogs, I'd encourage us not to farm out this part. I believe that the doing is the bonding. The bonding comes from the doing. It comes from learning a new thing, feeling frustrated at how hard it is to learn a new thing, messing up and trying again. When bonding with your dog, anytime you feel your frustration or impatience or exasperation growing, it is okay to stop and get back to it later or tomorrow. You get to practice self-regulation as you work with a dog, yet another wellness boost from your time together. It is also normal for your dog to get frustrated when learning new things, so at least you'll be in it together.

Being intentional with how we respond is new for many people, getting ourselves accustomed to knowing when to engage and when not to. Repeatedly interacting with our dogs mostly after they exhibit behavior that we *do* like will say everything that the words and actions we've been using to deter unwanted behavior never got across. Operant conditioning strengthens or weakens a behavior because of what follows it,[7] so we don't ever need to add punishment into a dog's lives. Adding pain to an animal's life is never justified, not to mention entirely unnecessary when not getting a reward is enough of a message for a dog while still maintaining the bond between you.

Punishment does not uphold connection. Punishment is a relationship shredder. It requires no special training. It is not skillful to be mean. Furthermore, apart from lacking in morality, punishment is most often

4. Dog Love Is What We Focus On Grows

carried out in order to get another being to do what we want when we say so or to stop being who they are. But if our own wellness is contingent upon somebody else being different, we are sourcing out our own wellness too. Someone who is well understands that they are responsible for their own wellness. Someone who is well seeks to communicate without inflicting pain because they perceive how it would risk their own well-being and that's not a risk worth taking. They understand that what they do to another, they are in essence also doing to themselves. And so they strive for another way. Thus, we can gauge our own wellness based on how we treat the animals in our lives. How we treat animals is akin to a billboard sign on a highway, blinking the truth about what is inside of us. So it is not small or trivial, the use or not use of punishment. It says much more about a person than just how they act with a dog. As Murray Sidman puts it: "Negative reinforcement produces lives of desperation, stamps out ingenuity and productivity, turns joy into suffering, trust into fear, and love into hatred."[8] That applies not just to the recipient, but also to the punisher.

I do believe, however, as I referred to in Chapter 2, that taking ourselves away from an undesirable behavior is a non-reinforcement technique that works without inviting cruelty or abuse. It simply entails withholding reinforcement around less-preferred behaviors. An example of operant conditioning and positive reinforcement is giving your dog a piece of cheese after you ask for a sit and he sits. Your dog performs in a way you like and he gets something fabulous. By committing to giving dogs our feedback when they're doing the things we want them to do more of, we can cleanly communicate with them and let them know what we prefer, what we need, and what they do that is awesome. We will know they hear us because how they act will change. We will see it in the behaviors they do more of because anything your dog does more of has been reinforced by you!

But when your dog lunges at the door as your friend rings the doorbell and you yell "No!" to your dog (using your voice) and you try to move him away (touching your dog) and basically do a whole jazz routine that inadvertently showers your dog with attention, you are reinforcing your dog to bark at the door when your friend rings the bell. How do you know I'm right? By asking yourself one question: Has the behavior stopped? Has it increased or continued? What did your response actually do in regard to how your dog acts? So what should you do in that scenario instead, based on what I'm saying? I'd advocate for you to walk away. Give your dog not you. He barks and lunges, you walk away. The key is the nanosecond he stops barking, when right then you give your attention back to the dog and reinforce his new choice, letting him know, *Yes, I want quiet! Yes, I want calm! Yes, I want you to come to me and leave the door alone!* And yes, this does mean you will have to ask your friend to be patient and wait a second because your dog is learning. In this example, not only is your dog's behavior being addressed, but you are also choosing to stop reinforcing the dog when he is in an agitated, revved-up state of mind. You are taking care of him, regulating him, regulating yourself with him, being the strongest vibe in the room and holding it, which is one of the most loving things I think we can offer somebody. Plus, you are prioritizing his needs—a family member's needs—over a friend's in that moment.

This simple, pure, but not always easy pairing of your feedback is the animal way because they don't rely on words like we do. Yet operant conditioning is not particular to dogs. This behavioral tenet applies to the human world all the time, such as when an employee who goes above and beyond gets a pay raise or a picture framed on the wall in acknowledgment of her work, making this employee want to continue working hard (positive reinforcement). But we don't offer bonuses when an employee is late over and over again, do we?

One bump I've experience around this kind of learning is that people tell me they don't want to bribe their dogs in order for them to be well behaved. But I think it's all about how you look at it. It's not bribery to be a positive person who reinforces positively a dog's positive behavior! Do you remember how you talked to your dog as a puppy, or if you adopted an older dog, can you imagine how you would talk to a puppy? Why is remembering that your dog remains a tiny puppy in their soul bribery? He's the same soul who still wishes to be met with softness no matter how many years have gone by! Why isn't that just love? Whether the dog is four or nine or 13, his soul is still the soul it was as a puppy. Why don't we want to reward our dogs when they're behaving the way we want and when they're in the state of mind we like? Why do we forget their need for our gentleness, or act like they no longer warrant it because of gray whiskers? Why are we more prone to giving them our anger when they're doing what displeases us? Why do we think that works? What does the evidence show—that it does or does not motivate their behavior to change? The way we treat our pets can become patterns, further entrenching how we treat our kids, our employees, and one another. Much is on the line.

Here's a tip, a clean form of reinforcement I suggest that mostly goes over well with dog moms and dads: Use your dog's kibble. Let them "work for" their meals instead of just feeding them for free in a bowl. That's kind of the opposite of bribery, isn't it? Do simple stuff with them like ask for a "Sit" or "Down" or "Watch Me." And here's an even bigger tip: Whenever I'm working with a dog using food, I hold the food in a fist so the dog learns to target on my fist. My fist comes to mean *I am talking to you, pup!*

Sometimes there is kibble or a treat in my hand when the fist opens up, which I'll release to reinforce behavior I've requested or a behavior the dog has naturally offered that I want to capture. But sometimes the fist opens up into soft petting. I never have my hand in a fist otherwise, so when I do, my dogs know we are conversing, and they pay attention because it always leads to something good for them. This also means they don't only perform a behavior if they see a chunk of food being held up in my fingers. Instead, they regularly check to see if my hand happens to be in a fist, even when we're not working.

So my dogs cue onto me. I take that as an honor. Especially because my dogs help me put on rose-colored glasses due to the devotion they inspire for me to focus mostly on what I want more of, and pay less attention to what I don't like. We will see what we want to see. I want to love others into life and be loved into life by them when I'm around them.

Bonding is understanding the full fallout of punishment.

As Pablo Picasso went through a Blue Period, I went through a Hound Phase and fostered a rotating door of Beagle mixes, approximately 25 over several years. (I have a type.) As a recovering bulimic/anorexic/compulsive eater, I always want more—more cake, more weight loss, more accomplishments, more hound dogs. But every dog is unique and every dog we took into our home required me to train my brain again to emphasize what I wanted, and not to dwell on what I didn't want or didn't get or didn't have. It had to be this way in order for me to help more dogs; otherwise, my home would have been a constant barrage of whatever new thing was going wrong. But by looking for and catching what I wished to reinforce in my fosters, I was able to bond with all of the Beagles we helped and reside pleasantly alongside each one of them until their adoptions.

I learned from them not only about the power of individuality but also about the power of focusing on what I wanted more of as a confidence builder. Despite each dog's uniqueness, the irony was that every dog we took in thrived through positive reinforcement. Their self-esteem remained intact or bloomed because we refused to succumb to punishment. Sidman describes that positive reinforcement "does control behavior, no less than coercion does. Positive reinforcement is preferable because it can teach us new ways to act, or can support what we have already learned, without creating coercion's characteristic byproducts—violence, aggression, oppression, depression, emotional and intellectual rigidity, destruction of self and others, hatred, illness, and general unhappiness."[9] As I've pointed out, by simply removing reinforcers you can let your dog know when you don't prefer something they're doing. Think of that, of what it means, how not only through treats and Frisbee tosses, but anytime you talk to a dog and interact with them, you are in essence saying, *Do more of what you're doing!* If your attention can be used intentionally to reinforce a dog, then using your attention unintentionally when your dog "misbehaves" misses the mark, but then grows their behavior, but then punishes them for it, establishing a cycle that likely creates anxiety, doubt, and distrust.

So there is no need to punish. It was on me to prepare myself for how each new foster would make things a little different at home. I would walk into the situation with eyes open, knowing every single one of them would not know how to live here, would mess up and do things I didn't like, would summon me to adapt and plug in anew, and that we'd be at odds in some way. So it would be my job and my privilege to help them adjust to our lifestyle, to pay attention to their good traits so that those would grow, and not to get swept up by what they did that irked me, for how would that help them, really? And how would it help me, really? What I'm getting at is that I don't only foster for the good of the dogs. I am not a saint. I also foster because fostering makes me better at loving—others, myself, and my life. Shelter and rescue dogs are my weights, my bootcamp. They are the gym that builds my love muscles, the muscles that allow me to live with more positivity, replenish all of my relationships, surge my outlook, and elevate my well-being.

Dogs give me the chance to focus on what I admire, appreciate, and applaud. Foster dogs teach me that love is mixing the feedback of another being's needs into the recipe of my life to find interconnectedness again. Fostering dogs shows me that love is perpetually morphing, in motion, not static. We can either look for what we don't want and live a life aiming to coerce it out of existence, or we can look for what we *do* want and increase it through deliberate positive attention.

• • •

We can even experiment with behavior, and with how to alter it. There was the time I actually reinforced behaviors I did *not* want, like with our foster dog Whiskey, who would howl at the mailman. I put howling on a command by positively reinforcing it instead of fighting his tendency. This made it possible for Whiskey to learn a howling command and to then howl when it was more appropriate and less scary for the mailman. This meant I had to provide opportunities for him to howl throughout the day, but not when the mailman was around. It also meant I had to keep reinforcing him for howling at the right time so he knew when to howl and when not to howl. My point is, it's all right to figure out what works for you, which far outweighs constantly scolding a dog for something they do, which usually teaches them to hide the behavior from you and to avoid you, but not necessarily to stop doing it. With Whiskey, I wanted him to feel how good a boy he was, not to feel like he was the culmination of everything I deemed wrong with howling. Nobody deserves to live like that: to feel bad and scared and unsure. Truth was, the me who was still—and will always be—recovering from an eating disorder needed to know that goodness as much as Whiskey did.

Whenever a foster demonstrates a problem behavior, before trying to fix it and instead of getting angry, I've learned to ask myself: Am I somehow accidentally reinforcing these behaviors instead of more desirable ones? What am I conveying from my end of the conversation? Are there more ways I could positively reinforce this dog, sharpening my ability to positively reinforce others and myself along the way? Is there an opportunity for me to grow and step into more wellness here? Can I experiment with and get curious about how to approach this? There is not just one way to utilize operant conditioning. I implore you to explore and tailor it for your dog, yourself, and your life together. Make it support the unique signature that is you + your dog. Nobody else is an expert on the relationship between you. What's at stake if we think there is only one way and it doesn't end up benefiting us and our dogs, if a trainer tells us what to do and it doesn't work out, is that we may end up resorting to the sort of punishment that adds pain to a dog's life (technically this is called positive punishment and it includes responses like screaming, spraying a dog with a water bottle, shock collars, and God forbid smacking). These reactions tear at the fabric of connection.

Punishment causes more problems than it provides solutions for, especially when it comes to love. Common side effects in dogs (and people) are escape and avoidance; vigilance and heightened fear; neuroses, depression, and anxiety; apathy, shutting down, and suppression; illness and hatred; violence, aggression, and counter-aggression. Coercive tactics breed coercive behaviors.[10] Using punishment amplifies in us the very defects of character that dogs are here to help us overcome. It makes learning hostile and bonding impossible.

When I reflect on my own intense self-punitive nature, how I obsessed over what I did not like about myself, how I punished my body, how I tyrannically singled out every one of my mistakes while dismissing every positive thing I'd done, I see how all it did was bring me a surplus of shame and a struggle for joy or the feeling of worth. We punish because we believe it will change things, but it hardly works to change anything. And even in the cases where it does work, its drawbacks are so numerous and probable, not to mention that they usually appear later.[11] The use of punishment might reinforce us in getting our dog to stop doing something in a moment, but any counter-control, desperation to escape, rigidity, or incapacitation we've modeled will show up at another time, seemingly disconnected to the punishing event when it is actually not. This is how loops of mistreatment and chastisement, abuse and pessimism continue, and how they are perpetuated in families. And then it festers inside of us.

But dogs can help lift us out of those cycles. Punishment moves us further away from seeing the gems that are already here now, from letting ourselves and our dogs enjoy today's blessings. There is no inspiration or happiness or harmony or love when life is filtered through a hurtful, neglectful, or punitive lens. It didn't breed change or growth in me or for me when I treated myself harshly. It created an aching heart that kept from me everything I wanted and needed. It spoke of something more than my behavior. Similarly, if you follow the chain of a tethered dog up into the house behind him, you will likely find problems and trauma in that house. A chained dog speaks to something more than the chain.

Mastering positive reinforcement with my dogs enhanced my confidence and made me feel like I was in general a less destructive participant on Earth. It feels good to feel good about who we are and how we treat others. It impacts how we act toward ourselves. Plus, not only is an alternative to punishment smarter, but it's also more efficient, so I also felt smarter and more efficient to boot! Sidman says, "The other changes that take place in people who are punished, and what is sometimes even more important, the changes that take place in those who do the punishing, lead inevitably to the conclusion that punishment is a most unwise, undesirable, and fundamentally destructive method of controlling conduct."[12] When we utilize punishment, it's not the dog's unlearning or their "bad behavior" that keeps us stuck and unhappy. It's that we chose to punish at all. It's what it does in us, to us, when we rely on it.

Bonding is honoring power ... yours and theirs.

Needing to have more power than another or stepping on top of the power of another is a trap because if it can happen at all, it can happen to us. If we do it to animals, we leave the door open for it to be done to us. Understanding how to relate to dogs, how to adopt them and love them without needing to have power over them, doesn't mean chaos and anarchy, dog fights and dog bites, and it isn't just for hippies. We can teach and model, demonstrate and learn, grow and change together, while honoring the value intrinsic in us and in our dogs, in all living beings.

How do we do this exactly? I like the Premack Principle, which states that highly preferred activities can be effective in reinforcing less preferred behavior.[13] (Huh?) We can tie a low probable response to a higher probable response. (Still huh?) We can give dogs the opportunity to engage in an activity *they* want under conditions that reinforce a behavior *we want*. We acknowledge and respect both sides. (Got it!) This indicates that one being does not have more value than the other, or needs that matter more.

Leslie McDevitt described it as, "Using the Premack Principle and letting the dog do what he wanted to in the first place allows you to become the gateway to the environment. The dog learns that being attentive to you is not in conflict with doing other activities; being attentive to you is the way your dog gets access to the other activities. In this way, your dog becomes patterned to pay attention to you even in very distracting situations." By knowing this principle, you can set up conditions that are this *and* that, not this *or* that, making you a teammate instead of an obstacle. To my previous point about how conflict can itself become addictive, McDevitt adds, "There is a strong reverse psychology component operating in this principle as well.... The more you tell the dog to do what he wants, the less he wants to do it!"[14] By removing the friction, resistance, and tension that power plays provide, all this energy becomes available for bonding.

An example of how I used Premack in action was when, in order to encourage our foster hound to stay beside me when we went on walks, and with an intention to enjoy our walks, I built in sniff breaks for her because she liked to sniff (she was a Beagle after all). She was constantly pulling me so she could follow her nose. The intervals I built into our walks gave her time to be a dog and analyze scents like she was wired to do, like she loved to do. Rather than me being bothered that she wanted to explore the outside world, the world she only got to visit when I decided to grab the leash and take her, I

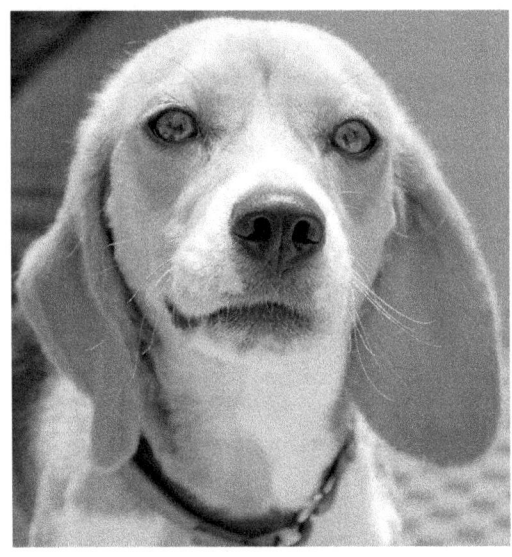

Shiloh, a one-year-old Beagle, saved just in time from a Los Angeles County shelter the day she was to be euthanized due to overcrowding in 2011. We only fostered her for eight days before she got adopted.

developed a cue to let Shiloh know when she was "free" to investigate and let her nose lead us. Our strolls stopped being a battle. Sniff breaks reinforced the walking as she began to trust that I'd given up on fighting her for doing what was intrinsic, and would instead provide opportunities for her to do her favorite dog hobby.

"You must meet your dog's needs in order to get the performance you want from him. Dogs need to sniff. Dogs need to greet other dogs. Dogs need to look at things. Dogs need to be normal,"[15] McDevitt highlights. So I'd reinforce Shiloh's walking beside me by giving her sniffing time every five minutes or so. Sure, this meant our walks took a little longer or were a little shorter if I was pressed on time—but it's quality not quantity that matters in a relationship. Her reward for walking beside me and not pulling was to smell, to get to the dog thing she innately very much enjoyed. She needed outlets to just be a dog, the kind of dog she was.

The Premack Principle is a method of operant conditioning. Here is an example of something that happens often when we don't realize how learning theory works: A person is playing catch. They toss a ball, tug toy, Frisbee, or stuffy, and the dog runs after it and brings it back. The reward for returning it to us should be an immediate rethrow of the item! But too often people do a very peopley thing and talk instead. "Good boy! Now sit … sit and I'll throw again … sit … blah blah blah," they might say. But why would the dog want to bring that toy back to us next time when we basically withheld playing after they fetched for us? In this example, we are failing to reinforce the desired behavior. The good news is, it can be corrected easily. In human terms we might think we're being supportive by pausing the game to talk, but in dog terms, we're not. We're signaling that they didn't do what we wanted or that it's not worth them trusting us that they will get to do what they want if they do what we want. It's the consequence that follows a behavior that reinforces a behavior.

So if a dog returns a ball to you, throw it right away as *the reward* for the fetch in order to reinforce fetching! Otherwise, you'll create a hiccup that wouldn't have occurred had you been clear from the start. And then there could be a whole scenario to deal with of trying to "undo" the behavior we don't like, which often leads to scolding the dog or getting mad at the dog, and basically giving them more attention for not fetching because we didn't originally reinforce their decision to bring it back in the first place! Being intentional prevents extra work, avoids potholes of negative behavior, and maintains our alignment with what we do want.

Recognizing where to use Premack Principle can aid in our own wellness by propelling us to take the path of least resistance. It can help us be transparent with ourselves, as well as reflective. To ask: Why am I doing what I am doing and what do I hope for? This drives us to fan the flames of love, and to commit to gathering the kindling that is the basis for its fire:

looking for what is good, what is abundant, what is a yes, what is joyful and pleasing and right in each moment, what we can surrender our agenda for when it comes to another's desires. Instead of waiting for certain outcomes, for things to be different, for more power or more control, this way of interacting with our dogs lets the present be good enough. Let's them having some authority be good enough. It doesn't make us complacent, but it does allow us to focus on the behaviors we want to increase, and ends the disillusion that through wrestling we will end up happier or more in love. It lets us have happiness and love *now*, and it lets our dogs have it too, fortifying the bond, and fashioning us into people who build solid relationships through constructive feedback, through enjoying life and searching for all the ways it's already terrific. Everything we want, we can feel our way into with our dogs if we turn our attention toward it. Any lack can grow through a fixation on lack. Why pay attention to what is not, when there is so much that is? See what more comes when you make this switch, not only for your dog but for your whole life.

Bonding with Ophelia and all those hounds.

The greater I fell into the vortex of animal welfare and fostering dogs, the more I'd smell of other dogs, and the more I worried my love was being spread too thin for Ophelia. There were times she protested by eating my lipsticks or shoes, and it was never the Target-bought flip-flops either, but the expensive shoes, because she had good taste. But I knew it would not be productive, conducive to learning, or strategic to yell at her for being destructive. So what did I do? I threw the chewed-up heels in the trash and kept my closet door closed for a while. I let her feel and express herself, and I let us legit argue. Because secure love is strong enough to withstand true feelings. She was the most important relationship of my life; we had to be able to be authentic and known to one another, on both ends. It made our love even more life-changing.

A few hounds into this phase, and Ophelia became the most incredible tour guide for foster dogs, a welcoming face, a cool friend. She was my assistant, or more like I was hers. A new hound would walk in and she'd be like, "Water bowl is there, we sleep there, poop there…." My connection with Ophelia was the basis of my understanding for all the new dogs who came home to us. It helped me communicate with each hound, let me tap into my gut intelligence and their individual traits, and was the catalyst for me to focus not on what challenged me about each dog, but on what they did that I loved. What about their personalities I adored. Each dog had their own irreplaceable heartbeat, their own hurdles to overcome, and each affected

Couch invaders, Ophelia and foster Beagle Whiskey, wondering if there's a treat in there for them, in November 2011.

me and my family every time, no matter how easygoing the dog was. But I kept focusing on what I wanted to strengthen in them and in myself. I kept walking the dogs and they kept positively reinforcing me to be beside them. Sometimes we heal inside out, and sometimes we heal outside in. Sometimes we heal by talking and thinking, but sometimes we heal by taking action.

I think with dogs around, we get to do it all, we get to feel it all, and not have to feel alone while we do.

> Brittnie Battle is an advocate, rescuer, and Director of Outreach at Casa Transports, a nonprofit that serves as a bridge between overflowing Southern shelters and Northern rescue groups who have homes waiting to adopt. Not only will Brittnie crack you up as you help animals together, she will tell you the truth whether you want to hear it or not. She is a bridge herself—between wishing for progress and getting things done. She is an unstoppable force with the skills to tackle almost any project and the type of humor that combines out-of-the-box ideas with boots-on-the-ground organizing. Brittnie is the sort of person who focuses on solutions, then does what it takes to implement the steps necessary to carry them out. She can move mountains. Find yourself a rescue friend like her.

Chapter 4 Exercises

Call your dog over to you and reward them for coming with a light massage (operant conditioning!). Notice their favorite spots. Where does their body relax? What are you doing and where are you doing it when they loosen up into receptivity? Does your dog's mouth turn up in a smile or their muzzle go slack? If there are areas of your dog's body that when stroked cause them to tense up, freeze, stretch their eyes (aka whale eyes), or watch you from the side with a sense of caution, stop touching them there. Those could be clues that your dog dislikes being rubbed in that area, or might even be experiencing pain. As you massage a dog, oxytocin releases in your brain. (Classical conditioning! Different types of learning can occur simultaneously.)

Exercise two involves playing tug with your dog and teaching the "Drop It" command by tucking a treat into your fist. In the midst of playing tug, present your fist hiding the treat, and let your dog smell the food. They'll buy into the value of dropping that toy. "Dropping is a great thing to do, I get food," they'll seem to think. Open your fist, offer the treat, and immediately give them the tug toy back to keep playing. Double reinforcement! Eventually you can phase out treats, and the reinforcement for "Drop It" will be playing tug again. Keep noticing what your dog is doing when you give them attention, and be mindful about what you are reinforcing. Perhaps on your next walk, you can give your dog some sniff breaks for walking so nicely beside you. Continue to choose positivity. Choose joy. Choose love.

5

Dog Love Is Recess Every Day

Moving on from conditioning and learning and theory entirely, let's play! If our outlook is that almost anything can be a game, if we make the ways we wish our dogs act at home opportunities for flooding them with amusement, the relationship will surely bloom. Bonding with a dog should center around having a good time! Your dog can be like a walking alarm clock in your life reminding you to have fun. To take a break. To have adventures like you did as a kid.

Having fun and having a good time is essential to our wellness and our dog's. It can't be 100 percent work and commands, constantly worrisome or serious. Play is often so undervalued and ignored that it atrophies. But play is where imagination takes over thoughts, where inventiveness takes over restrictions, and where intuition meets glee. Play is the sweet perfume of responding to self. It is an adult-made dilemma that we keep ourselves in cages, hold ourselves back from fun, justify a propensity for discipline, and deliver a performance of who we think we should be most of the time as if these are battle calls for growing up. Maturing does not have to mean the end of play. Maturing does not have to equate itself with the death of merriment. Maturing does not have to end wonderment or silliness. How many problems could be overcome if we let ourselves enjoy life more?

Play brings respite from self-consciousness. Not all dogs (or people) like to play the same way; therefore, it's essential to pick up on how your dog likes to play. Play brings an escape from our ego-driven lives.[1] It brings stress relief, a departure from what drains us, and a sense of fulfillment because play revolves around listening to ourselves and to whoever else is involved in the immersed amusement. Because play often requires a buddy and dogs are readily available to us, coupled with the fact that they're just so good at entertaining themselves, they inevitably teach us how to goof around. By giving dogs more outlets to play, we can upgrade their lives while also upgrading our own. When we bake more play into our days for them as well as with them, we take a page from them and allow for an

Hound dogs on patrol: Ophelia and Fonzie, yet another Beagle foster we got the chance to adore in November 2010.

increase of fun for ourselves, even if it's through a small act like zooming around the backyard simply because it feels good to zoom! More play can enhance our well-being and lift our mood while improving our physical health, even as far as decreasing symptoms of type 1 diabetes.[2]

Play is about leaning into the offbeat, the thump in between rhythm, the space where we aren't encouraged to go as grownups, where most of us don't go, a land of no work and no results. Play is adventures, not agendas; interactions, not theories; social in the flesh, not social media. Play is dogs, and dogs are play. My friend who is a math teacher told me once that math is learned between student and teacher not only through the lessons, but in the space in between their bodies and minds, in the air that holds the moment where she shows a child something and the child picks it up. I'd argue that the same magic transpires while playing. During play, we sense when backing off is needed, we can tell when it's too much, and we can tell when the fun needs to wind down a notch. During play, we can learn to build in a pause and reset, just like dogs do naturally during healthy play sessions.[3] We can teach dogs who don't know that it's okay to stop how to deescalate, shake out, take a break, sniff some grass, or come back to us to regroup.

There are times when issues arise because we're too on top of our dogs. We're too scared of play, afraid of the unpredictability of joy, the wildness of fun, the vulnerability of feeling good. Inevitably our fears can suppress us until what we're left with is boredom. When there is boredom, there are problems. Boredom is one of your dog's greatest enemies, and yours too. But play is its antithesis. Play is a preventative model. I am a way bigger fan of prevention than intervention. Boredom makes us restless because its very existence means we desire to engage, and aren't. In fact, whenever a dog is demonstrating behavioral challenges, my first questions are: Is the dog getting enough exercise? Is he bored more than he is stimulated? Do we need to add another walk in the morning or toss a ball in the yard to get some energy out? Is there an enrichment project we can add into the mix? Where are openings for extra pops of fun? More play can be woven into life, and it shifts the concentration away from needing to change the dog.

"Let's have a good time!," I propose to my dogs. And so I propose it to myself.

Bonding is all in the nose.

An easy way to give your dog some fun is to give them a chance to use their nose. Dogs process what they smell, see, and hear (in that order[4]) by submerging themselves in the sensory information they pick up on. Dogs have an estimated 50 scent receptors for each one a person has.[5] The area of their brain devoted to analyzing smells is 40 times larger than ours.[6] "Dogs have about 220 million scent receptors, while humans can boast only about 5 million,"[7] Patricia McConnell states in *The Other End of the Leash*. She goes on to say, "Dogs can detect some odors that humans can't notice until the scent is 50 times more concentrated." We haven't yet even begun to comprehend all the ways they (or we) can utilize the power of their nose.

Humans talk and bank on subtext, but to relate to a dog it would behoove us to activate the pure, seminal, organic endeavor of sniffing. Scent drops us into memory, into a feeling state, not a thinking one. Scent affects our attitudes, our emotions, and even the health of our brains.[8] As I've stated, canines process smell first, then visual cues, and last on the totem pole is what they hear. But it is entirely too easy for humans to get caught up in our words and expressions, to move too fast and explain too much. To bond with our dogs, though, we must shut up. Thus, this natural dog way of living can boost our wellness because to connect to a dog is to be all about the nose, and less about the content of our minds. To be less distracted and dazzled by our own soliloquies. To be engaged consciously with scent, which involves losing ourselves in what we discover in the real world, in amusement. Think of how we teach our dogs what the things they do mean when we could be responding to what is. For example, McConnell illustrates, "Have you taught your dog what *bark* means? After all, it's just a noise you're making, and the noise itself has no meaning until you've taught your dog what it is."[9] Your dog does a normal dog thing, like bark, and you react to it by shushing them, providing meaning for what barking is that your dog didn't have before you, rather than getting curious about what they might be barking at, maybe even using your own sense of smell to try and identify it. In this way, we and our dogs mold one another, the relationship itself defining each of us within the loop of reactions. But what if we instead exchanged molding and defining for being fully in a moment together?

This is just one way that words shrink scent when they take over an experience. Here's another: Think of how we use one word in so many different ways at so many different times in daily life. How do we expect our dogs to know the difference in meaning and context, for example, when "Okay" can mean so many things dependent on how we use it? Okay as in yes. Okay as in, I'm feeling all right. Okay as in, fine, whatever. How many version of okay do we have? We teach dogs words and they labor to understand the meanings, yet we are often unaware of how we use those words and which meaning we're upholding. While our dogs live trying to decode what we might be telling them, it is not terribly unlikely for the meanings of our words to lose their significance due to the lack of clarity around them. Unless we are going to speak impeccably clearly to and around our dogs, we should consider abandoning speech a bit more and relying instead on the untainted way of connecting with dogs through the reality unfolding in scent and senses.

One of my favorite dog-centric activities is nose work. You may have heard of scent training before. This canine sport allows for dogs to seek out and find specific scents that are either planted by you or explored freely by them, and the act of it can be done indoors or outdoors.[10] Born out of search-and-rescue work, scent work realizes that this kind of communication and activity comes organically to dogs, and that it helps to keep them mentally healthy to be able to do it. Folding this into your repertoire for bonding with your dog offers them so many fun moments, while also allowing them to burn energy and stimulate their minds. Sure, you could take a formal class on nose work and even compete with your dog in this manner, but you can also incorporate scent training into your home by keeping an empty egg carton or box on hand, tossing a treat into it, and letting your dog stumble upon it and figure out how to open it.

As your dog gets better at playing this way, you can set up the equivalent of scavenger hunts for your dog by laying out dozens of empty boxes for him to explore, waiting until he identifies the one with the specific scent, such as a piece of food or your kid's shirt or a lavender-soaked piece of cloth. You can reward him when he finds it. Or it might be more meaningful to toss your dog's kibble into the backyard (if you have only one dog) and let him work and track through the grass for his morning meal. This uses far more energy and brainpower than feeding the dog in a bowl. This allows him to utilize his natural abilities to smell, scavenge, and forage.

Using our nose more when we're around our dogs gives us the chance to be quiet so that it can be about that animal-connected way of assessing the world. By just taking a walk and telling yourself "I will pay extra attention to what I smell on this outing," you may be able to supercharge the bond. What might we pick up on and take in from our surroundings if we take a pause from putting so much onto our environment, if we stop numbing out through our analyses or intellect, thoughts or speech? What if we dealt with what was present, what was being offered, what was coming toward us, rather than adding our interests and opinions on top of life? Relying on scent entails meeting the moment, meeting nature. Humans could benefit a lot from decreasing our dependence on what we say. Through spotlighting what we smell and investigating it fully like a dog, with our dogs, we light up and use different areas of our brains.[11] This can lead to an expanded worldview, a deeper use of our capacities, and a feeling of more cohesion—that we are practicing healthy habits to thrive and be well.

Bonding is decompression time.

Not only does play entail an embrace of silliness, it also brings with it its opposite, which is rest. Play demands inhibition through built-in opportunities to take a pause from excitement. With dogs and with people, we must recognize when to be a team and when to be an individual, when to duck and when to goose. This makes play extraordinarily useful to both you and your dog because part of fun is the other side of its coin, which is decompression.

When dogs are first adopted, decompression time is vital. It is the most important thing we can offer a dog when we bring them home, whether from a former foster home, an animal shelter, a kennel, or a rescue group. Decompression time involves coexistence within the borderless realm of compassion. It entails offering your dog safety and warmth, a space where all her needs are met, but without any expectations, where she can process all she's going through without the added pressure of being the center of your attention. It may seem odd to include decompression in a chapter about play, but I'd argue it's essential because one facilitates the other. Our dogs will not feel comfortable playing and being free with us if they've never been given time to settle in and get comfortable in the first place. Our dogs need to be able to play and to rest, both equally. Letting a dog be is the beginning of play. Letting a dog free off the hook of expectations allows them to trust us enough so they can show us their goofy side. A dog does not always need the stimulus of our affection and petting, our grabbing and gabbing, and sometimes they downright don't need anything from us at all other than to have their basic needs met and to grant them space. They need to process and move through on their own timeline so they can acclimate through a transition.

When bringing a new dog into your home, decompression time allows a dog to get into their right mind. Because the fact is, you're in your element but they are not. Their future depends on you giving them this chance to adjust, to shed and shake off what has come before, what they may have lost, and to reset. Decompression time acknowledges that a dog doesn't know who you are when they settle in with you. Nothing is familiar. To them, every smell is something new about somewhere new, and they don't know if it is good, or how they are supposed to behave here. They are in the dark, and they feel it, although there's a wide range of how much, depending on how and who the dog is. So instead of looking for an out, looking for reasons to return the dog or bail on the adoption, reasons that will always be plentiful during the awkward decompression phase, we can instead spend all our time and energy laying off and letting them lay low. They don't know you. You don't know them. Please understand this.

Patricia B. McConnell and Karen B. London co-explain: "When we asked people with experience in rescue what they think new owners need to know, the most common response by far was 'to be patient.' You may be prepared to enter into a close and emotional relationship with your new dog the day you bring her home, and you probably have expectations of who she should be, but your adopted dog has no such mindset."[12] What an important point—that our human state of mind, and where we enter a relationship from, are not necessarily what we're going to get back from another being, at least not right away. Another being who hasn't been living our same life, and who may not be as close to the goal line we envision as we are. A being who might be coming in with weeks or months of accumulated stress or fear to detox and unwind from. We cannot assume everybody wants the same thing, or moves at the same pace.

McConnell and London go on to say, "Think of how you'd feel in an unfamiliar place surrounded by strangers; if you're like most people, you'd need some time to get comfortable." Gifting them this cushion of comfort can make all the difference in terms of who the dog will be and how the adoption will go. Dogs, like people, need time to form social relationships.

Some come from relatively isolated backgrounds, or have had no formal training to teach them manners. A natural tendency might be to cower and inhibit themselves, become overzealous and eager to please, or anything in between.

Regardless of how they walk in, give it time, let them breathe, and let them—at their own pace—test out the theory that it is safe for them to show you who they are while figuring out who you are too. Often we want a dog who is our best friend, who is perfect in our home three hours after adopting them. But this is a grossly unfair litmus test because it's impossible for them to achieve it. Furthermore, it is reflective of how we treat not only dogs, but also other people. It means we don't fully recognize a sentient being before our eyes, but rather see an answer for us, a magical fix we want, or a cute cartoon character come to life for our pleasure. In reality, a dog becomes the answer, the magical fix, and the cute cartoon character only through our involvement, our sacrifices, and our efforts to bond over time. Only a loving lens makes us look at another in those ways. Giving our dogs time to decompress when they need it (not exclusively when they're first adopted) is a significant act of bonding and a significant sign of our own wellbeing. It allows us the open space to meet and fulfill our own needs instead of making it a dog's job.

• • •

Ophelia and John Goodman, another of our hound fosters, doing their Beagle bays in the yard in May 2010. He lived with us for five months before getting adopted.

5. Dog Love Is Recess Every Day

I am a big proponent for dog crates. It's not because dogs are den animals (according to McConnell and London, they are not[13]), but because they can be taught to enjoy their crates as a comfortable, manageable space where they can let everything go and chill. Chilling hard makes playing hard later more possible. I think of crates as "leisure locations," not sad cages. They are a space where a dog's security can bloom, a designated area that increases the likelihood that your dog will rest and stay out of trouble when you need them to but cannot supervise to ensure. I think of crates as spa time. (Within reasonable expectations. I do not recommend leaving a dog in a crate spa for an extended amount. No more than four to six hours of the day.)

Impulse control is learned through adequate decompression time, as well as during play. Please note my choice of word here—learned. This means impulse control is something to teach, not something to expect from a dog either. A dog's mother might be the first teacher of impulse control, as are any littermates your dog had as a puppy.[14] Their mama responds when teeth are too sharp, bites are too intense, and behavior is too rowdy. This can inhibit and model a lot for a pup. Ideally, a dog's siblings and parents let them know when their behavior is too much, when they've got to scale it back, and thus impulses are curbed in the process. But after that, it's human dog parents who must keep the learning going.

So instead of getting mad when a dog can't control themselves, consider that they may require more input and support. Through mindful play and mindful decompression, their impulse management can improve. For those who need more impulse control support, here is a teaching game that is one of my very favorites to play, which I call Magic Mat. You roll out a yoga mat and lure your dog onto it. The goal is for all four paws to be on that mat, and bonus points if your dog is in a sit or a down. If your dog gets up, simply lead him back calmly onto the mat and reward him for returning (operant conditioning, people!). The point is to let him know you want him *There*, so don't call him to you or give him any treats off the mat. Once he's staying on, begin to gradually work with his ability to wait. He's going to want to get to you or the treats he knows you have, especially if you're holding food in a fist like we talked about before. You will start very small, counting to two seconds, then five, and slowly work up in time, strengthening his ability to tolerate staying on the mat. Each time he controls his impulse to run off or after you, you will return to the mat and give him a treat. He will learn to understand that wanting and waiting is what earns him the reward. We need to give the dog many chances and a lot of time to figure this out. Once he gets the game, either we can gradually increase the time we make a dog wait on the mat before releasing the treat on the mat, or we can begin to increase our distance from the dog before coming back to him to reward him. I don't recommend working on both time and distance simultaneously, as that commonly results in confusion and overwhelm. You might only be able to take one step back, then two, before your dog starts to move.

When a dog succumbs to their impulses or gets off the mat, it does not need to upset you—it is information. A data point. It lets you know the dog's current threshold to work from. If it's two seconds or two steps away, master that first, stay there before pushing him too quickly past his current limit. Slowly, you will saturate his tolerance and be able to take three steps back or add a second in time. If your dog is unruly at the jump or leaps off the mat at any point, simply wash the moment away and start over later.

"Remember that if your dog gets fresh, you raised your criteria too quickly,"[15] McDevitt puts it. An error from your dog can be seen as nothing more than an indication to lower the pressure and take it down a notch. Again, there is no rush, because the relationship is the prize. It's being established and nurtured as you play Magic Mat together. It won't come at the end of some arbitrary goal. The way I look at it, it's my job to help my dog learn, which should be a gradual process. Every time we increase the dog's waiting time or add another step away, every time we return to the mat to release a reward, the dog learns to control his impulses and to have faith that good things will come. Your dog will buy into waiting as the greatest thing of all.

You can play this game for the rest of your lives, until you can roll out the mat, get him on there, go take a shower, and return to find him on the mat waiting! (Note: I am not suggesting this is an outcome to work toward, but if you wanted that, it would likely take a long time.) The point is to have fun and keep playing. Five minutes a day of Magic Mat is a fantastic way for your dog to earn his meals, and will help you increase your awareness of each other. As you play this game, your dog will learn your tells, your subtle body movements, and the most minuscule physical communications that reveal your next move. And you will learn your dog's, too!

This implies that when you play this game you refuse distractions, including your phone. Because this game is a significant, potent way to supercharge the bond. You will build up the muscles necessary for relaxation, unwinding, and strengthening the trust between you. Magic Mat is a great way for your dog to believe that you will come back to him and for you to believe that your dog can control himself even when he wants something. It's a great way to practice uber focusing on one another. Your tolerance of him wanting and waiting may need work too. Teach your dog to wait. Teach yourself to let him wait. You will learn to trust that he can bear hard feelings and cope without jumping into action, and he will learn to trust that despite time or distance, you will return, and each time you do it is wonderful.

In my experience, this game works in concert when dogs play with one another. It teaches me to read my dog better, cultivating my ability to intervene when my dog's warnings signs are clear and his impulses seem out of whack. This means I am more prone to redirecting him and securing his attention when he's playing with another dog and things escalate even a bit. Because that is my job as his dog mom—to keep him safe and balanced, make sure he has fun, but also that he takes breaks when necessary.

Last but not least, Magic Mat keeps me as my dog's favorite playmate. Our dogs need us to play with them. Other dogs should never be more valuable to them than we are. It's not always about outsourcing their play at dog parks or doggie play dates. Teaching our pets that other dogs matter more lessens our influence and reduces the substance of the bond we share. McDevitt advises, "Self-control games will help a dog focus and connect without overstimulating him."[16] When we play Magic Mat with them, it's connection and not just stimulation. Play can also be about getting in tune with one another, in flow, and reading each other.

After you've been engaging in Magic Mat for a while, don't be surprised if your dog freaks out every time he sees you roll out the yoga mat. He will learn to love this time with you focusing on him as he focuses on you. He will love controlling his impulse as a part of your special play sessions, and it might beef up his listening skills in general. Also don't be surprised if after Magic Mat drills, your dog needs a nap in order to process the experiential learning of wanting, waiting, and winning. Who knows? Maybe you will even nap alongside him.

Bonding is handling identity with care.

All dogs are about the nose, but perhaps the hound is the most intensified version of that. "When Beagles and Bloodhounds put their noses down to the ground, I suspect that the rest of the world fades into oblivion,"[17] Patricia McConnell said. I must admit that I agree with that sentiment. I've loved every hound in my Hound Phase, but man, do they have a stubborn insistence to smell every single blade of grass. I guess I can relate. But they also come with silliness and snuggles, things I need more, and need to be more like. The Hound phase period of my life culminated in a foster dog named Sherlock, a laboratory test subject who'd been freed after he was considered "spent" or out of use, having been stuck in a cage smelling bleach for his entire life, only taken out to be poked and prodded, known as the number tattooed in his ear. He'd been robbed of everything natural to him. Beagles are docile, friendly, and kind. What we love most about them is what dooms them more than any other breed to scientific experimentation: It's because they let us.

Animals are not equipment or machine pieces to be tested on, used, and tossed aside. They have souls. Sherlock came to us knowing nothing, having no idea how to live in a home or in the world. Yet he exemplified the significance of a dog's fluidity, how when entering a new environment, a dog is not only trying to figure out who you are but also who *they are* now in relation to you. Which is to say, a dog's identity can shift based on who they're with. Imagine then how scary it can be when a dog is rescued. It could be exciting, but also possibly horrifying if they end up in the wrong hands. A dog's ability to conform is like how you were in high school when you were Goth, then Hippie, then Jock, but more intense and as if you never grew out of it. And yet because their identity is adjustable and adaptable, we can still help a dog like Sherlock after all that was done to him: by strolling in sunshine and smells, by playing gently, slowly, and following his lead, letting him be startled at first by every joy that had been withheld from him for his entire existence before coming to us.

This is another reason why the bond triumphs—it's all about who our dog is with us, and who we are with them. Sherlock learned how to enjoy, how to be a cherished pet. He learned how to rest without worry, without the possibility of hands reaching in to pull him out and do bad things to his body. He learned to fully have fun and fully decompress, which is amazing if you think about it—that he was able to learn all of this after having been harmed whether he kept his guard up or let it down.

Sherlock, a Beagle Freedom Project survivor, after he was freed from living as a test subject in a laboratory and came into our home for rehabilitation.

There are so many ways to play. Some involve more of your time and energy than others. With Sherlock, we bought a hula hoop from the 99-cent store and ordered a kid's tunnel online. We taught him how to jump through hoops and dash through that tunnel. We built a mini agility course in our own backyard. It was engaging and confidence building, a way to blow off steam for Sherlock and for us. Agility is one of the most healing things you can do for your dog, for yourself, and for you two together. It is deliberate fun and does not have to be for competition! There were ways to be playful that required less activity, too, such as when I'd sit outside with Sherlock to sketch him as he sunbathed. I'm not an illustrator, but so what. It was a fun way we could get on the same page, be on the same wavelength.

Whenever we humans spend less time on technology and focus instead on imagination, creativity, or IRL connections, we improve our bonds as well as our own cognition.[18] These sorts of activities are good for us! Time with our dog provides us these sorts of outlets. To boot, play is akin to making deposits in the relationship with a dog that will likely pay off in better behavior from that dog down the road. "Play is a great way to strengthen the bond, teach useful skills and exercise your dog's body as well as her brain,"[19] McConnell and London summarize. Bullseye.

If you foster a dog, the dog who got comfy with you will not be the one who goes into their new adopted home. They will revert to a more shut-down, unsure version of themselves when they are with unfamiliar people in a strange environment. They will spend more energy trying to figure out what is going on and piecing together their new identity than exposing their full personality, until they develop the same caliber of a bond, the same level of positive associations, trust, and connection with the new group. It simply takes time. That is a requirement. In a world of quick fixes and ten-second entertainment reels, giving things time is medicine for our brain, heart, and spirit. It is always worth it even if we fail to find our footing right away.

Bonding with Ophelia and Sherlock.

Sherlock's only interactions before us made him petrified of the world, like an adult baby. He arrived completely shut down, so his decompression phase was more intense than it was for other foster dogs. We let him take his time, forgave potty accidents instead of pulling or pushing him to go outside, gave him space to hide and cower and stay away from us. We let him be, let our focus stay on our own lives and less on him. We let him figure out that we were good, that this was good for him, and let him come out of his shell at his own pace. I trusted that his need to smell and romp and be what he was made to be would emerge and take over, that it would override all those years he'd lived harmed and hurt, used for mankind.

We earn our dog's devotion by being benevolent leaders who try to understand them half as much as they try to understand us. Dominance would never have worked with a dog like Sherlock; he'd only known dominance his whole life and it had destroyed him. Laboratories rationalize testing on animals. They say it is to make medical advancements for humans, to help children, to protect us from products, when mostly what it does is shield companies from lawsuits. Animal studies fail to be applicable to real humans in anywhere from 50 to 99.7 percent of the cases, yet animal testing remains the backbone of an entire industry that continues to treat animals as if they are nothing more than appliances.[20] Sherlock's story gave me a shaky, inky feeling about how far people can go to justify cruelty. But his rehabilitation and his ability to change set a new bar for what is possible, for the kind of hope that holds a planet together. When the time we share with our animals is full of playfulness and fun, we can inspire our dogs to be their best selves while they inspire us to live with more joy. To let go of whatever we think dominance might give us, for it pales in comparison to the love we can share.

I played with Sherlock and it helped him shed his identity as a subject. I offered scent work to Sherlock and it helped him relinquish his life as an object. He proved every theory I'd read in every dog training book about how dogs thrive as part of a pack because he'd never had a pack before coming to our home. He also proved how dogs have a phenomenal ability to reinvent themselves, collaborate, and brave living again. Whether or not they should formally be called pack animals, as dog trainer and author Jean Donaldson puts it, "Dogs are an intensely social species. They are genetically not very well prepared to be alone for any length of time, let alone all day every day as is frequently the norm in our society."[21] Could it be that it's harder than ever to be a dog? Could it be that there are more "issues" with dogs because they struggle to fit into modern society as we know it, as we've made it? They're not the ones who invented AI, but they will have to deal with the fallout and repercussions of people having AI, of humans choosing to spend more time in a virtual reality than in the real world with them.

Neglect seems to fry a dog's brains—not to have stimulation, companionship, a pack to build an identity with and within. Dogs live in communal frameworks. Dogs tend to uphold what is good for the whole in order to maintain the whole, yet they don't ignore the self or stop going after what they want, for what serves them. Even Sherlock never lost his capacity to adjust to a new group, to redefine himself, and to learn how to seek out love, despite having previously submitted to a life of learned helplessness. O'Heare describes learned helplessness as, "When an animal is exposed to uncontrollable and severe aversive stimulation, they will frequently abandon efforts to escape or avoid it and will not be able to learn escape or avoidance behaviors, even when these options become readily available. Learning is inhibited, and behaviors tend to be suppressed."[22] This level of defeat and dejection is heartbreaking to witness, but it is also completely life-changing to overcome. Sherlock's healing entailed him learning how to be a dog, something I could not teach him but Ophelia could.

Ophelia modeled for him how to play, how to sleep deep, how to be warm inside of a snuggle, how to dream. Ophelia ushered in his adjustment. In fact, Ophelia helped each and every one of our foster hounds adapt to our life. She adapted the pack for them, and I'd watch in awe, how she brought out their playful side, rested beside them, how she related and taught each dog what a friend feels like within the confines of who they were. It allowed them to be somebody new. And it encouraged me as a pet parent to ask myself, one hound at a time: Do I let my dogs be who they are? Who am I to my dogs? Who do I want to be? It prompted me again and again to look at Ophelia and thank her for signs she knew how to read, for the smells she knew how to interpret, and for the way holding her in my arms was both play and decompression at the same time. She was constantly an exercise in impulse control for me, as I wanted nothing more than to squeeze her tight and never let go. But I couldn't do that. I had to love her and release her.

I don't think Sherlock would have come out of his shell without Ophelia. I don't think he would have decompressed with more ease or played with more frolicking joy had it not been for Ophelia. I would have never broken out of my head, my scale, my smallness, or my self-imposed cage if not for her too. She was his key, and also mine.

Shannon Keith is president and founder of Beagle Freedom Project, with a mission to end all forms of animal exploitation through rescue, campaigns, and legislation. She is an animal rights lawyer as well as a documentary filmmaker, so she knows a thing or two about what it takes to affect real and lasting change on a wide scale. Shannon reaches across the aisle of her own values to enable conversations with animal testing laboratories around the world, offering to take animals they no longer use for research, to rehabilitate them, and care for them until they are adopted. She turned a former facility into Freedom Fields, a BFP sanctuary where animals can be loved into happiness and wholeness! Shannon changes laws as well as lives.

Chapter 5 Exercises

Your first exercise is simply to reinforce a spot that's just your dog's, whether that be a crate or a gated area, direct your dog to their "leisure location," and shower them with treats there. Let this be the best place ever where cookies rain upon them! Hanging out here is a nice timeout for your dog, a way to build in rest. Pair it with a chew toy and be upbeat leading your dog in there, but neutral when they come out. (The preference is not you, but going there!) Play classical music while they're in their leisure location to up the chilling ante. Whenever your dog chooses that spot on their own accord, acknowledge their ability to be alone and be okay. Then go take that time for your decompression too.

Second, here's a scent activity you can do at home. Set five paper cups upside down, and put a treat only underneath one of them. Mix the cups up, invite your dog over, and let your dog sniff, track, knock cups down, and find the treat. Get creative with new challenges and smells, whether you use boxes instead of cups or whether you add 10 more cups to make it more difficult. Observe your dog and note the exuberance they express when they do nose work, use their inherent talents, and get to do it with the one they love to play with most: You.

Bonus exercise, if I may? Play Magic Mat!

6

Dog Love Is Receiving as Much as Giving

Having fun is easy, right? Well, not necessarily. We think loving dogs is about giving to them constantly and that that's the most difficult part about having them, but I'd argue that the bigger challenge is receiving from them constantly. Receiving all that giddiness and goodness. Because once we start playing with dogs, once we are deep in bonding, we become aware of a dog's allegiance to joy, which is infectious. And what I often see in the people I work with is the instinct to pull away from too much enthusiasm. It is vulnerable to let our guard down and receive. Receiving is wild; it cannot be manipulated and it is not predictable. Furthermore, underneath receiving is a spirit of deserving, of knowing we should be happy. That it's not irresponsible to be happy. That it is safe to be happy. That it is safe to let in love, feel all that love, and see through eyes of love. This chapter is about letting your dog love you. What monumental freedom, to let ourselves love another with the whole heart and to be loved that way in return. When we live bravely like that, happiness can ripple out into the rest of our relationships, strengthening the currents that make life meaningful.

We might think it's impossible to laugh and roll around on the floor with a dog in order to prepare for a Zoom meeting if we believe we have to prove ourselves and earn our right to be here, if we think our objective should be a dog's obedience and our own hustle. I still hear too much about "being the alpha," an idea that blocks the beauty of give and take in exchange for an illusion of control. Dog packs have structure, it's true, but as I touched upon in the previous chapter, the "hierarchy" can adjust depending on who is in the mix. A pack is a social and relational model more than a set pecking order. Dogs change themselves and their roles according to alterations in the pack's dynamics, whether that be caused by a member that gets inserted into the group or another setting. "The fact is that behavior is 'context dependent,' meaning that all social animals

Ophelia and Timmy shared dog beds like an old married couple. Timmy was a 2011 foster hound pup.

behave differently in different environments,"[1] London and McConnell illuminate. Dog owners tend to think of dog packs as having one fixed alpha and then everybody else, but in reality canine hierarchical social structures are more complex and nuanced than that; they can be in flux, and can be impacted by new additions as well as new environments.

6. Dog Love Is Receiving as Much as Giving

To step into the top dog role, one must receive their role as a peacekeeper. "The irony is that dominance is actually a social construct designed to decrease aggression, not to facilitate it,"[2] says Patricia McConnell. True "alphas" deflate problems in order to maintain peace. Their power seems to correlate with their ability to mediate. McConnell describes status as ranking within the group, while dominance is a relationship between members because one has more status than the other. And what gives them that higher status is "'priority access to preferred, limited resources'—nothing less, nothing more."[3] It's about who gets what first, not some head game. A high-status dog in a hierarchy does not waste time questioning or justifying their value, denying themselves pleasure, or needlessly overreacting. The natural alpha is a "quiet, confident dog who is secure in his place in the world and seems to feel no need to prove himself."[4] This should be us as dog parents! This is the vibe that merits respect, whereas the use of force exposes a lack of power. Wasted energy is a cost. We, the humans, should be the ones managing and mitigating friction, turning down—not turning up—conflict. People's misconception of what makes an "alpha" contradicts its actual nature in the canine world. For you as a dog parent to "be the alpha" is for you to maintain tranquility for your dog and for everyone in your orbit.

Sometimes when we feel our worst our dogs are there to love us the most. Along these lines, sometimes when our dogs act the worst they need our love the most. I do believe we can love someone so hard that their hearts soften, and ours do too, simultaneously. Eventually, what happens to two soft, melted hearts but a melding? However we react to a dog's behavior is a demonstration of how we respond to our own behaviors. So the questions become: Why would we want to dedicate our energy to making our dogs (or ourselves) feel badly, feel punished, feel scared, feel dominated, and feel unsafe? Why not live with a melted heart? Especially when we can use that same energy to reinforce something else, to gently redirect toward a new behavior, avoid a problem, and cleanly communicate through support. How is ensuring that another being (or ourselves) feels disgraced ever productive or fruitful? It's okay to feel anger, to feel the full scope of all emotions, but as we've discussed before, by ignoring the small behaviors we don't prefer and by not treating everything like a big deal, the small behaviors we dislike will deteriorate on their own, having not been reinforced. The takeaway here is how in giving grace to your dog, you also receive it for yourself. You can be a top dog by giving grace.

We all have limited amounts of time in our busy, ever-changing lives. Adopting a dog and loving a dog is a responsibility, albeit a wonderful one. But we must ask ourselves if we want to use the resources we have at our disposal to oppress and dictate, knowing that will make a mark on the rest of a dog's behaviors and our own, or if we want to use those same resources of time, energy, and attention to bond, to benefit them and ourselves. This reflection can move us into the driver's seat of our own lives. It can empower us to let in more jolts of joy if we want to. In my dog coaching experience, people may initially resist allowing it to be that simple. They tell me they will be taken advantage of, that it will make them feel dumb to be so soft. I marvel at the meaning people decide to make—that it's dumb to be kind. Is it dumb to give our dogs the benefit of the doubt? To assume they don't understand what we're asking from them, not because they're stupid or bad, and not because we are, but because we are different species who communicate in different ways while sharing life together? Is it dumb to receive love and friendship? If that is dumb, do we want to be smart? Is it a win to be smarter but unhappier?

"You get to feel good," I remind my dogs. And so I remind myself.

Bonding is spending more time outside together.

We have a bad habit in animal rescue of enforcing our ideals on every dog and pet parent we encounter. Although I personally love nothing more than sleeping in bed with my dogs, I know from firsthand experience that not every dog is the same, and that sleeping in bed with people is not the best for every dog. Every dog does not need the same privileges, does not benefit from the same privileges, and may not even consider them privileges in the scope of how those access points affect them overall. Same goes for time spent outside. Some dogs need to be outside a lot more than others. Some want to work, or feel more comfortable in nature. We whip ourselves into a tizzy in rescue, asking potential adopters how long the dog would be outside, when the fact is not that it is not that dogs should be outside less but that we should be outside more! People should be joining their pets outdoors, in the sun, feet on grass, in nature with their dogs. Going outside is a great way to bypass pecking orders, "alpha" notions, and a tendency to live in the dichotomy between examining every single thing our dogs do as if they should live under our microscope to completely ignoring them otherwise. Getting into the habit of being in the elements more often is in and of itself an enjoyable act for the worthy. Being outside is receiving. The fresh air. Who you see. The whispers you hear inside of you and outside of you as you fall into the trance of a walk. The natural world works on you as you show up for it. Nature is an equalizing force.

Ask yourself if there are ways to include nature more into your everyday life, and share it with your dog. Allow your dog to gift you this. Perhaps picnics are possible during your lunchbreak instead of eating at

6. Dog Love Is Receiving as Much as Giving

your desk, perhaps grounding yourself with feet on the dirt can do something for you, can invite something to come to you, that you don't need to earn or strive for. Perhaps just tossing the ball with your dog for a little while will merge you with Mother Earth. Perhaps loving the ecosystem by spending time in it is receiving its love enough so that you can feel the truth, which is that you are a part of it.

When you share the phenomenon of the outdoors with a dog, there is often a leash that connects you, a literal tie between you two that carries messages back and forth. If you tense up, your dog will feel it through the fabric, and respond accordingly. If you are distracted on your phone, your dog will feel it float down the nylon and take advantage of the opportunity. Moving in the open air presently together, though, is bonding in and of itself. In fact, whenever we take in a new foster dog, the very first thing we do is go for a walk so that the new dog can share this positive experience with all of us in the most straightforward, enjoyable way.

When it comes to stepping into an agility ring, McDevitt suggests, "Both of you feel totally connected, grounded, and ready to read each other's mind as a good team should. Massage, visualization, breath work, circle work, self-control games, structured toy play, and other warm-up activities will help you and your dog prepare to step into the sacred space together."[5] But this should not just be for a competition or an agility ring. This could be how you and your dog face walks, face the day, face going outside, face being a family unit at home. Or to put in different words, life itself can be an agility ring course for you and your dog.

Because how you do one thing is how you tend to do everything. Dogs are not some things on the side. They are how we approach life, and the standards which we apply to our relationships and reactions. Dogs are the practice; they are the Meditation. The starting point from which we relate to our dog is the starting point from which we relate to anything that affects us. So nothing really begins or ends. Even a walk with them begins before we step out the door. That's one of the coolest parts of having a dog, how in this way, they bring the outside into indoor spaces. Not only through the bits of nature that they carry on their dander and the way they—as animals on four legs—so fastidiously connect us ecologically to Mother Nature, but also mentally speaking, if your dog is not listening to you in the home, and if you are not listening to your dog in the home, if you are already reinforcing behaviors you don't desire such as jumping, nipping, chaotic energy, or pulling you out the door, then you are giving into inside what you will receive outside. Before setting a toe outdoors, staying in control of ourselves, rather than focusing on controlling the dog, will help our walks go more smoothly. Regulate yourself through the breath, mindfully clip on that leash when your dog is sitting or calm, and begin to invite in the connection you want to carry down the road: the kind of connection McDevitt describes.

Tuck your phone in your back pocket, slather on your sunscreen, and participate in the experience with your dog just like you would if you were going to a concert with a friend. That concert would bond you, wouldn't it? You'd both know how it felt to pay the ticket price, hear the band play a particular song, how the bass sounded, who you saw rocking out, the taste of what you drank. Let each walk with your dog be like another show you're attending with a dear friend. Let yourself be immersed, let yourself constantly look to someone who is looking to you within the pocket of an event you're sharing. Be outside, really *be* there, and soak it in. Your dog is doing that and benefiting from it—your dog is at a concert! If you want to influence how the walk goes, then join them.

And if the walk doesn't go well? No need to give them ire and whack at your bond. If your dog is being a punk or you are, change directions. Change course. Turn around and go home. It is quality over quantity so that you can build a relationship off of enjoyable interactions comprised of intimacy and joy, not bad habits or negative associations. Lucky for both of you, you can always go outside again.

Bonding is a cycle of give and take.

In order to take things in stride, it helps to love the dogs we have, not the dogs we wanted. The lie is that they are not enough. The lie is that we are not enough. The lie is that through fear and intimidation, we will get what we want. The lie is that only when somebody is how we demand them to be will we be okay, so our well-being is outsourced and in their hands (or paws). But the lies only work if we don't know better or question them, if they were put on us and we don't begin a healing journey of our own. In order to have another reality, a reality that leads to greater wellness, we might have to give the things we did not get and create integrity by challenging the lies. It is through opening ourselves up to our dogs, by going gentle, that we uncover the lies, expose them, and gift ourselves what we haven't yet received, which is the truth. We receive it by giving it, and because of dogs we get the opportunity. Bonding means we don't neglect to give them the tenderness they seek. And because we provide it, we do not neglect to give tenderness to ourselves. Becoming the people we wish to be then is not about giving nonstop and forgetting ourselves; it's not only about what we put out. It's also about what we take in because we recognize that giving and receiving are opposites sides of the same coin.

The trap in rescuing dogs is to tend to give give give. But that out-of-balance fire hydrant of giving fails to restore us and resource us, and it causes us to give with less potency, less vibrance, and less wattage in the love bulb. We cannot shine at 150 watts if we never plug in. We cannot offer steadiness and comfort if there is not a give and a take. We cannot pour lemonade out of a pitcher that isn't getting refilled with water and lemons. If you've never felt comfortable receiving as part of your lifestyle, if being loved up was not practiced as a habit or even allowed in your world, filling up can be terribly uncomfortable. But maybe that's why this dog—*this dog*—is yours. Maybe they are here to help you as much as you help them. Go slow and gradually with yourself just like you would with them. Take in small sips and get used to receiving. Consider that the part of you that has been squeezing a torniquet on the love you get back, that has felt like it's too risky to be happy, that has stopped the flow in, was the part of you that cared the most. That part of you was working hard to protect you and it was wise, but it needs your dog's love desperately now because it's ready. Restraint and withholding dodges free and flowing and feeling good. All that can be taken away. But if you don't enjoy it when it's happening, you never get to have it at all. And if it is the standard we apply to ourselves, is how we treat ourselves, what do we think we will be able to give to others?

Behavior is linked. Behavior is a chain.[6] How we respond to a behavior may affect the other behaviors displayed afterward. Reacting to a dog by towering over, forcing, or generally being displeased by the dog's actions and personality as a way to try and change them will taint the actions they offer you moving on from that response. It will impact their personality and choices, and not for the better. Just like letting a dog's love in and letting it do something to you will enhance wellness into the chains of your behavior. Your

Found dog Gilda delighted and surprised us with her quirky love.

readiness to either completely surrender the term "alpha" or redefine it to mean peacekeeping will impact the connection you have with your dog and yourself. Because you are going to get back what you give to them. You are going to give back what you allow yourself to receive from them. Who you are to your dog is a representation of who you are to you.

There are times when we must use cues to teach our dogs. Cues can be verbal, but also based on scent, touch, or another indicator. Dogs are individuals so they pick up what they pick up, and also get to decide what is scary or aversive for them. Sometimes the cue we use to implement a desired behavior becomes a "poisoned cue" when, through the exposure, we inadvertently welcomed a negative association. We'll know this is happening because our dogs will meet us with hesitation, appeasement, or resistance to the behavior we're asking of them or trying to teach them.[7] This can be maddening if we don't stop and question if, despite our best efforts and reinforcements, there has been a negative association or "poison" involved. When our dogs regress, it's on us to cease using the cues we've been using and to go back to the drawing board. We are creative enough to find other ways to teach our pets, and resilient enough to deal with what is, not to insist on what must be. Ironically, when we do that, when rigidity thaws into fluidity, we end up getting what we had been insisting on because we don't need it anymore! The dog doesn't have to do xyz in order for us to be okay. We make ourselves okay, receive what we most want by giving it to ourselves, and lay off the relationship.

There are times when I see someone manhandling their dog and being rough, and my first instinct is to want to reach for the dog, to step in, to save him. My second instinct though is to wish I could hug the person whose internal self-voice must be so gruff, so nasty, so harsh, that they have to take it out on a dog who has less agency. Dogs are balls of energy who pick up, respond to, and endure whoever they live with. It's why people can be unkind to a dog and the dog will still come back to them. That is nothing to boast about or make fun of. It's the dog's default wiring for love. It's *their* brag, and perhaps our call to change. Dogs are in a continuous state of being affected, like landing pads, like arms wide open. Most of them are tasked with clearing the runway and uncluttering, so they can receive again, so they can give again. Dogs are portals for healing because they expose us to the very give-and-get cycle that love is. If their person is cruel to them, they will still offer love, hoping against all odds that it may reach the human heart. They are experts in modeling for us what the bliss of giving looks like, taxing us to be brave and let love in. Only once we do, can we then give love. Only once we stop splattering our desires onto the canvas of the bond can we receive more to give more. Eventually, the joy will come from loving, not from demanding we be loved, which is precisely when love will rain down upon us.

Bonding with dogs is structure and satisfaction.

Although I am all for abandoning authoritarian relationships with our dogs, we can still be solid, structured, and secure for them. Bonding should instill good manners, even though our response to bad manners may be more relaxed than "alpha" illusions promote. Because manners and relaxing, when strung together, prevent rudeness from growing so intense that your dog becomes first a jerk, then a problem, and ultimately a pariah. If we give dogs everything they want without asking for certain conditions in order to produce it, we might ask ourselves if we're doing that because we have a hard time affirming ourselves. This is a pendulum swing I caution to watch out for because though it may keep us comfortable, it deprives them of building confidence. If every dog is an individual, then we must set up a structure in the home that suits each dog specifically, that allows for their optimum satisfaction and well-being.

Clingy dogs, nervous dogs, shut-down dogs, rescue dogs, purebred dogs, all dogs require certain things based on what their needs are at any given stage in their life. And they grow, they grow up, they change. They are not fixed entities, just like we aren't either. It's case by case, but structure almost always generates success. Routine allows a dog to feel safe, and to feel empowered enough to make decisions. McDevitt describes, "That is why clear rule structures are necessary for anxious dogs. They need to know what is happening next, and they need to know they are safe."[8] Reliability is the solid ground that helps imbalanced dogs thrive, not more allowances or spoiling.

All of us creatures, including dogs, need a container for how we act, walls in place to let us know when we've pushed too far. Structure is not a naughty word and it's not the same thing as coercion. As I've stated, I am not a fan of punishing dogs, but I do recommend a warning—whether word or sound—to let your dog know when you don't like something they're doing. By using a quick, clear cue that is never violent, cruel, or punishing, known as a "no reward mark"[9]—something neutral that is just between you and your dog (I advise against words like "no" that you use a hundred times a day)—you can give them feedback that they will understand. I like to use "Nu-uh." You might do a simple finger wag, which is another option, subtle yet effective. Whatever the warning you decide on, it will come to mean, *You're not going to get a thing you want if you keep doing this,* or *I don't like this, it's going too far,* and it allows for a teachable moment because the second your dog goes from doing whatever less desirable activity they've been doing to offering up something you prefer, that will be when you pair the desired behavior with a reinforcer (play, petting, treats, praise, attention, etc.), like we've already discussed. A no-reward mark is another tool in your tool box to help you be heard, just like you hear your dog.

Dogs naturally look for what is right—it's us who tend to look for what is wrong (as described in further detail in Chapter 4). So by simply identifying when something is not best for them through uttering a phrase or sound that lets them know no reward will be following, they will learn to heed the warning in the same way you'll heed their growl. And when you reinforce a desired behavior that just displaced an undesired one, you give your dog a loud *yes!* message, which will make them perk up, take notice of what works, and alter their conduct. That structure leads to a satisfaction in them, so please do not mistake my affection for dogs as a prescription to lose all rules and form, because rules and form actually allow for your dog to feel good about themselves. Where I see a lot of people drop the ball (pun intended) is in the follow-up. Don't gloss over the shift in your dog's behavior because you're so utterly relieved that they finally stopped yapping, scratching, or whichever irritating thing they've been doing. If we want our dogs to believe in us, we have to believe in them. So it's normal to want to ignore and disengage when your dog finally stops doing something you dislike, but it is a baller move to give them another shot, to bet on them again out in the open, to show that you know how to deal with annoying behaviors should any resume. Being there to congratulate your dog when they replace an unwanted reaction with a better behavior that you endorse allows them to have a reference point that carries so much weight.

Gilda was a shy, skittish, stray gray Terrier mix my husband found running in the streets. He knows me well enough to know he could not come home until he caught her and brought her with him. She was a nervous dog and would whine in the crate when we put her to bed at night. I ignored any and all whining with no me, no feedback. But the second she quieted down, I'd gather my courage and acknowledge the voice in my head that screamed, *Finally! She shut up!* and I would remember what I had wanted to forget, which was that she needed the note from me on what *to* do. So I'd enter her room, presenting her with my serene attention for ceasing to whine, for being quiet. Would she start back up again? Sometimes. But I held firm in pairing and repeating my reinforcement. Silence led to me. I believed she would get it if I leaned on the structure of new bedtime manners and I believed in the satisfaction she'd feel when her quiet brought her my temporary companionship. I had to care about her more than I cared about getting the tranquility I wanted immediately. I had to care more about her looking forward to learning with me than to the sense that we'd completed some assignment.

It took practice and certainly messing up along the way. But the goal was not a perfect outcome every time. It was her and me growing together, aka bonding. This was how we put desirable behaviors like not crying in the crate on rotation. She began to absorb what was going on and to trust me. She grew more confident as she learned what *to* do. She learned to fall asleep with ease. I did too.

Bonding with Ophelia and Gilda.

Gilda struggled to be seen and touched, to receive affection—incidentally, issues I understood all too well. But she worshipped Ophelia and immediately relied on Ophelia's stable strength. We had a lot in common, Gilda and me. To be honest, though I was her benevolent leader, I needed Ophelia's strength too. We had a word for tender kisses, Ophy and me, something we ended up calling *tangerines*. And when I'd ask, *May I have a tangerine?* Ophelia would kiss me. One day on her own accord, Gilda crawled over, following Ophelia's lead, and she gave me a kiss too. And under the sun, I received it.

I gave Gilda a terrific foster home because Ophelia was my home, and this meant I deserved a terrific home. I was able to give it because I received it. I don't feel good when I forget this, when I'm base and rude and pulling and pushing and rushing and taking advantage of a dog's weakness or confusion or lack of power in comparison to mine. I feel terrible being that person. And I deserve to feel good. The way I treat my dogs allows me to receive more good feelings. What I think, say, and do around them, to them, gives to me as well as to them. That is, in my relationships with them, I give and receive to myself from myself. If that's not well-being, I don't know what is.

Watching Gilda's shyness melt away due to my family's love was like being inside of a flower as it bloomed. She learned to enjoy receiving affection. My job as her foster was to get her ready for a great home, and I did it. Though I wanted to give everything to this shy, shut-down dog, to heal her I had to let her love me too. That ultimately built her confidence.

"If a reactive dog learns to feel confident about something, he is less worried about that thing and therefore reacts less to it,"[10] McDevitt expresses. Low-intensity exposures that went well boded for less anxious responses from Gilda. I didn't prevent her from ever feeling uncomfortable because I could not rob her of the opportunity to give *to me*. To let that puff her up and build her self-esteem. To risk the discomfort that is baked into giving. Gilda's timidity morphed into friendliness as the restrictions she'd placed on herself to protect herself disassembled, like mine had. Ophelia broke us both in for love.

My idea of love before Ophelia had been limited, bound to a sense of scarcity. I was a cactus. I only needed a drop. More felt too scary, too untamed, too reckless, like too much. By the time Gilda came into the picture, I understood this and could hold space for it. Both of us craved ample nourishment, to be tended to, to widen our capacity for allowing in plenty. To release the tourniquet that promised safety and smallness as a semblance of control when really it just caused us to withhold from ourselves. Thanks to Ophelia, love became a connective force, abundant and infinite. I received it cheerfully and gratefully because it came from her. I took in her love and it did not drown me, oversaturate me, spoil me, or trick me. It was the structure I counted on. It nurtured me so I could have more love to give.

> Jenny Franz founded and runs Better Together Dog Rescue in Massachusetts. The thing with Jenny is this: she is unendingly loving and lovable. She extends that magnificent light onto the dogs she saves and the people in her orbit, whether they be volunteers, adopters, or fellows who collaborate with her. Jenny is the new face of animal rescue—the type of hilarious, hopeful, hardworking human who does not compete or tear down others because she's too busy having a good time making a difference. For Jenny, it's about doing good and doing it in good company. She is community-minded, nonjudgemental, radiant, and effective in making rescue dogs the best pets one can ask for in the Northeast. She is the equivalent of a human Golden Retriever.

CHAPTER 6 EXERCISES

This chapter ends with a request: Throw a party in honor of your pet's "gotcha" day. That's right, celebrate the adoption and accept presents for both of you! We normalize birthday parties, anniversaries, engagement parties, and baby showers. It's high time we gather for this kind of love, emphasize it, and host a whole event around it that is as extravagant or casual as you wish. The bond with your dog is something real, something to spotlight, and something to share with others. It merits your community showering you with gifts, an air of festivity, and you and your dog in the center of that merriment, receiving praise for your love. Their adoption story is as much yours as theirs. It can be *your* "gotcha" day too.

6. Dog Love Is Receiving as Much as Giving

Exercise number two is a two-parter and it begins with rolling around on the ground with your pup to just receive their love (and tangerines) before a work meeting or an important call. See how that lift of joy works on you, works in you, and how you show up for the gathering because of it. Note how others respond to how you show up. After the call or meeting, go walk a new path or trail with your dog. Whether there is rain, snow, or sunshine, go outside, be with nature, in the wonder as you wander together.

7

Dog Love Is a Clean Slate

You may be thinking, *I'm unnervingly receiving pleasure, what more do you want from me, lady?!* I want you to root for your dog but also to forgive them entirely when they fall short. Bonding with a dog must entail allowing them to be imperfect, with room to screw up. When dogs mess up, we can forgive them. When we mess up with our dogs, we can repair with them, just as we would with other humans. Conflict resolution is part of a dog's makeup.[1] Goodwill is more advantageous to them because it makes them and others feel safer.

As Norwegian dog trainer and canine ethologist Turid Rugaas put it:

And then they became best buds. Ziggy was one of Ophelia's favorite hound foster dog siblings.

7. Dog Love Is a Clean Slate

"Those dogs that are able to develop communication skills with other dogs, and that have not lost their signals because of us, understand each other and need never be in conflict with others. Wolves and dogs try to avoid conflicts. They are conflict-solving animals. It is usually we, the human species, who tend to create conflicts between our dogs and ourselves."[2] We can—and should—take a page from the dogs we live with and follow them in forgiving with greater ease, responding with greater mercy, and repairing relationships whenever there are problems. Being conflict resolution oriented brings relief, clarity, ease, and restoration to our lives. It doesn't mean we tolerate abuse or overlook grievances; it means we spend more energy creating solutions than dwelling on trouble.

What's so fascinating to me is that mending after a mess-up with a dog is done in the present, through the way we are being, ideas which we've already discussed before. Anytime we bring what just happened that we didn't like along with us into the next moment, we are confusing our dogs, and we are, in essence, punishing them and ourselves by not letting go. Dogs are more inclined to move on. We could benefit from that same slipperiness of fault, from forgiving and being forgiven with less effort, so that we can get back to enjoying life together in real time. Words don't mean as much to our dogs as how we show up to a moment with them. Our dogs forgive us when we screw up. They render their love as something we can stand on, something that doesn't go anywhere. The least we can do is give that back to them. We can set down the swell of antagonism inside of us. We can choose to hang up perfectionism, giving them and ourselves a break. We can wipe the slate clean because that is the natural path to move forward. It is also the path to love.

Practicing pardoning ourselves and others, releasing indignation and bitterness because we hold union and harmony in higher esteem than we hold a need to prove someone else wrong or wield power over them, reflects an enormous amount of healing. Do we think we have to heal first and then we can forgive? Is it first the chicken or the egg? What if we can heal by prioritizing apologies over reasons to be exasperated, and replace exactness with forgiveness. Neither our dogs nor ourselves will ever be flawless. Peace and coherence can be more valuable to us than whether we are right, and when it is, that is not a sign of complacency or weakness, but of connection. The bond between you and a dog does not in any way, shape, or form have to be perfect for you to stay in love. Dog love is constructed around the idea that you will miss each other and misunderstand each other, and that the best you can do is try to keep the interspecies dialogue going. The bond outweighs the dog having to be the way we decide they have to be, and that also lets us be who we are. This alone allows me to look at my own self in the mirror with different eyes, eyes that accept the woman standing before me even though she is not all the things I expected of her or deemed ideal. Ironically, the more I love myself, the better I feel. The better I feel, the more I do in the world and the more I am. The more I forgive, the more I heal.

I have made and continue to make tons of mistakes. What matters most though, I've found, is how I handle those mistakes. When I struggle to love myself through them, I can love my dog. That catches me. Because the more kindly I treat my dog, the kinder I feel about myself. The way I respond to my dog in the face of her blunders is directly correlated to how I deal with my own, and how I deal with my own faults determines how I deal with other people's faults. So it's not just about me and my dog; it spills out and over. It's all interconnected.

"I forgive you," I pledge to my dog. And so I pledge it to myself.

Bonding is setting them up to succeed.

Dogs can learn a lot. Scientific studies prove they are as smart as toddlers[3] and have the capability to count, to deceive, and to comprehend on an average more than 150 words.[4] Sometimes their learning will involve redirecting or reassociating through games or reinforcement. But at other times, the answer will lie not in them changing or learning anything, but rather in our own acceptance of them as they are and setting them up to do well as they are. When we insist our dogs have to be a certain way, that pressure can produce a hostility between us that is not conducive to things working out or us working in unison. As one of my favorite dog behaviorists Leslie McDevitt puts it, if your dog is doing something other than paying attention to you when you'd like them to, it might be time to rethink your training plan instead of correcting the dog.[5] By putting all our efforts and energy into creating a healthy bond, things have a better chance at being fulfilling for the both of us, individually and together.

McConnell and London break down how to see the dog and not the story when they describe what a newly rescued dog would benefit most from: "What your new dog needs most of all is the same thing a person needs—to be accepted and respected for who they are, to be 'heard' and understood, rather than be labeled."[6] These dog experts go on to talk about providing a safe and stable environment for a dog by letting them tell us who they are right now, understanding that "your dog will grow and change as time goes on. Do all you can to see him for who he is NOW, not who he was years ago or who you think he should be."[7] The energy of constantly criticizing and persuading a creature to be other than how they are is rooted in dismissal, in rejection of who that being currently

7. Dog Love Is a Clean Slate

is. It confines us to either convincing or being disappointed. We can't always force another to become what we decide they should be. Change is something that may come, or may not, but it will be discovered together and must be mutually agreed upon. Sometimes both a human and a dog change in tandem, and sometimes the dog changes a lot, but sometimes it's us who have to change most. Maybe because of a dog's limitations or maybe because of our own expectations, but in the end it might be our own acceptance of the dog we have, and not necessarily the dog we want or the dog we once had, that will facilitate a good relationship. When a dog is "misbehaving" and what we solely wish for is a way to absolve ourselves of the situation, we may want to reconsider that the challenge is to love them no matter what. Ironically, it is this very acceptance that allows for the most change to occur. And ironically, if we can gift this to our dogs, we can gift it to ourselves.

The 12 Steps taught me that we cannot alter something we resist, for in that resistance we waste our energy pushing against. In that resistance is a lack of listening, a deprivation of hearing the messages we need to hear, which will cause us to fail because the deprivation prevents us from figuring out why it means so much for this shift to happen, why we are so attached to the outcome. What would happen if things didn't change? That answer is important to our understanding of why we're doing what we're doing, and it may need to be the focus instead. Acceptance is a phenomenal teacher. Resistance, on the other hand, refuses acknowledgment. A denial of acknowledgment often blocks the very shift we want from taking hold! Resistance denies progress. So changing behavior starts by forgiving its existence, by accepting it as it is. This is not the same thing as condoning a behavior we dislike. What I'm talking about is being loving despite imperfections, failures, mistakes, and flaws. From there, we encourage growth. By learning how to acknowledge our dogs for who they are, we can call in who they could be, and we indirectly inherit the ability to do the same for ourselves.

Why am I harping on this? Because sometimes what we're asking from our dogs is a distraction, covering up something we actually need that we're not aware of. Quite frankly, often what we truly need is something our dogs cannot provide us, are not made to provide for us. If we are not careful, we can get caught up in having expectations of our dogs and get stuck being upset that they don't deliver them. Yet if we took a moment to tune in to ourselves instead, we might be able to better understand that what we seek is perhaps deeper than dog behavior—we may crave attention or approval, a sense of control, or something else entirely, but something we must give ourselves, we must seek or create. Clarity can bring truth and help us stop unintentionally turning a dog into a punching bag for what we find frustrating about our life. Then we'll be able to instead achieve what we want for ourselves, or accept that it's not possible.

If when reading this there's a sinking feeling, a knowing that we've perhaps been doing this to our dog, we can forgive ourselves. We can

Hunky blonde senior Labrador Ruffalo stealing our hearts (and lemons) when we fostered him during the pandemic.

7. Dog Love Is a Clean Slate

start the process of uncoupling so we can discover what we need by asking the simple question, why? Why do I insist on this from my dog? Why do I obsess over it? Why do I demand they behave a certain way? Why do I want this change in my dog, what feeling do I think it would give me if I got it? Because that feeling is what you *really* want—to be important, to be free, to feel lucky, to have power, and so on. A feeling we can give to ourselves any time, instead of deciding we have to wait for a dog to be perfect so they provide it for us. In fact, nothing outside of us needs to change for us to access a feeling we desire. It's inside us right now.

Another way to state this is: In the relationship with your dog, wherever there is heat, wherever there is a story that the dog does this, or is so that, the area where your dog is deficient or is the cause of your discontent, I invite you to pinpoint that exact spot. Review the narrative, the one you have on deck ready to share with anybody who will listen, the story wrapped in a neat bow about why the dog is so dissatisfying to you. Do you experience any sensations in your body as you think of it, and where? Got it? Great! Because that right there—underneath that—is everything you have been avoiding. The story about your dog is a shield for the feelings you have there. Your body gives you the map. That spiel about your dog diverts you from whatever subject you need to face in yourself in order to grow and reach your next level of wellness. The story about your dog is convenient, it absolves you of your part, and it's probably delicious to tell. It is satisfying, there is a payoff in sharing this tale! That's how you know it's a ploy. But when you set that story down for even five minutes, you will be able to access into yourself—not so you can feel bad, but so you can feel, period. Feeling brings insight, accountability, and intelligence. It connects you to your own needs. It's no longer using the dog to stay away from knowing yourself or who you want to be. It's shortening the distance between those two because you let the dog off the hook, and instead you let the dog lead you out of the dark, into the light of what's really happening. It's forgiveness, times two.

Forgiveness is clean energy. It lets things move. There have been many times with my own dogs where I've had to identify their thresholds, understand what sets them off, and surrender to preventing those triggers instead of trying to change them. Acceptance preceded any training we did so that we could keep our bond, so I could protect the love between us. There were times I had to do this same thing for myself. None of this was possible for me without first forgiving whatever behavior I was examining. There have been many behaviors my dogs and I have changed together, but there have been just as many I've had to resign myself to recognizing as part of them, or part of me. Because it's not about the answer that I think will solve why I feel uneasy and fill the hole inside of me; it's about the hole that's there, and why

I can't be with the unease, why I can't just listen to what the unease is telling me and lean into the hole. It is my choice to either be upset or meet my dogs and myself with love. To either focus on trying to force things to be otherwise, to bend things to my will, or allow our potentials to rise, adapt when things don't pan out, and forgive the realities that do not exactly go the exact way I exactly want them to go. For me with Ophelia, it was always more valuable to me that we were close. The priority was not for her to be different but that we felt good with one another, that we both knew we had us. What tremendous relief it has brought me to extend this to each dog that crosses my path, thanks to Ophelia, the one who revealed it to me.

Once we accept and forgive, we can recognize that privileges are easier to give later than unwanted habits are to undo. Setting a dog up to succeed may look like not giving them access to the couch, but rather petting them tenderly when they are on their own dog bed. It may look like them going in the crate when you leave the house. It may look like leaving them in another cushy room when you have guests over. And when we do not yet know a dog well, keeping things basic and better-safe-than-sorry helps us ward off bad behaviors from happening in the first place. As London and McConnell say: "If you are unsure about what might happen in a particular context, it's okay to avoid the situation until you're sure how to handle it. Don't put yourself in the 'hope-and-fear' zone ('I hope it's going to be okay, but I fear it won't be.')."[8] This is a reminder that prevention is a "powerful, active training tool and not a cop out."[9] Behavior modification is not the only solution. We can also prevent problems, and develop systems that reduce anxiety and stress. We may not have as much to forgive if we can be consistent with a dog's structure and routine.

How do we know if our dog is ready for more privileges? If we look at behavior as data, it can tell us a great deal. New responses from us get different results from our dogs, since how we behave influences what our dogs do. So we can get curious about experimenting with how *we* act and see what we get from them. But we can't bond with a dog and resent them at the same time; those are antithetical ways of loving. Instead, we can behave in such a way that an apology is not required after the fact. We can forgive our dogs, root for them, and keep bonding, as an alternative to punishing them, resisting what is, and making each other miserable.

Making the forgiving switch is not only for our dogs, then; it is also for ourselves. It is an act of tremendous self-care, of living and behaving esteemably. I like to imagine a balance scale, the kind with two plates suspended at equal distances from a fulcrum. I whip it out whenever I'm assuming my dog is rebelling or defying me or I'm spiraling about something they did that I don't approve of or if I'm simply feeling trapped in blame. I visualize placing my gut reactions, the most base and raw ones, on one side of the scale, and on the other side all the actions I could take that would get me to what I hope the aftermath would be, to the kind of dog I wish to share a home with and the type of relationship I wish to cultivate. I ask myself which side is heavier. By weighing as if on a scale what I resist against what I desire, I actualize my agency. Even not choosing is a choice. Whatever I pick will get expressed through my behavior, which will have an effect on my dogs. But only I have the mental ability to know this beforehand.

Our interactions with our dogs can either be bonding tools or vehicles for our suppressed emotions to seep out. If you've outweighed yourself and prioritized critiquing them over the good of your connection, welcome to the club! If you do it again, it's all right! As we've discussed, none of us are perfect, and dogs are immensely forgiving. But we can become more aware, accept their imperfections and our own, and transform from there. I know that being aware can feel difficult, unbearable even, because than we have to look at what might feel ugly. But guilt and shame can be overcome—especially when we realize that, as Karen Pryor tells us, "Guilt and shame are forms of self-inflicted punishment.... As a way of changing behavior, guilt ranks right along with flogging or any other form of delayed punishment—it is not very effective."[10] We don't deserve to be chastised any more than our dogs do. Plus, guilt and shame don't work. They're not efficient forms of motivation, and do not allow us to make headway.

So it's never too late for a perspective shift. That scale is in our minds waiting to be utilized. We can restore ourselves back into well-being in large part due to the portal of dog love. By deciding that what we want is what is best for the relationship, we can let that trump everything else. And so we forgive. And so we act accordingly. And so we—as the lovable version of whoever we are today—can set our dogs up for success by loving who *they* are.

Bonding is extinction bursts.

Whenever we set out to stop an undesired behavior in ourselves or our dogs, whether or not we replace it with a preferred behavior, we must start by becoming aware so that we can prevent the undesired response from being practiced and repeated. Before a behavior fades, though, often an extinction burst happens, which is a term used when a previously reinforced behavior reasserts itself and increases in intensity, peaking, before it goes away.[11] It can be maddening to endure or witness an extinction burst in real time. You've experienced them in your own life undoubtedly, like when you hit the button for the elevator, and it doesn't come. So then you push the button 80 times in a row. Only after smacking the button over and over again (which is a spike in the frequency of the behavior because the reinforcement, aka the elevator's arrival, has suddenly stopped working) would you finally succumb to taking the stairs. If the elevator stayed broken, every day might be more of the same—you attacking the elevator button—but you would likely gradually resort to the stairs a little faster each time. Perhaps by the end of a week you wouldn't go to the elevator at all and you might go straight to the stairs, ultimately changing your behavior due to the repeated end of the reinforcement you'd been expecting. This is a human example of an extinction burst in the works.

Here's a common canine example: If you've at any point opened your dog's crate door because he was crying, he will probably assume crying will get him out of the crate when he wants out. Thus, if you were to decide crying will no longer work to get him out of the crate, he won't simply understand that and comply immediately. No, his cries would intensify and crescendo at first. This is why I highly recommend not opening the crate door when a dog is crying or barking to begin with, and instead waiting for them to stop before that door opens. But if that's not how it went down originally, then you must teach them now that silence = the crate opens. This sort of strategic pairing speaks volumes to your dog in terms of what will work for them and what will not. It's similar to a toddler wailing and then getting the candy they wanted that made them have a fit in the first place. If you decided tears won't work anymore, wailing will turn into a full blown tantrum before it extinguishes. As a parent—and I mean as a human and dog parent myself—staying calm and committed to your intention greatly helps in these situations. Making sure to respond to any progress your dog (or kid) demonstrates also helps, as it mindfully pairs the reinforcement of your attention with alternative behaviors you want to move toward, the ones that take the dog further from an outburst and closer to relaxation.

When you're working on a behavior you seek to change, make sure it's the right time and environment for learning to take place. And when extinction bursts happen, employ forgiveness to help you get through them. For an old behavior to disappear and a new one to take hold, it usually gets worse before it gets better. It may help to plan on this.

Just like I suggest that we prepare for our dogs to mess up and annoy us, I also suggest that we prepare for extinction bursts to crop up when we go about altering a behavior that's been on rotation or engrained. This doesn't make a case for avoiding behavioral changes, nor does it make a case for dread; it's more like a mindset of knowing what we might be in for, so we can go about shifting our dogs' habits deliberately with an attitude of patience and support. Extinction is not necessarily a fast or permanent process.[12] It does not hinge on immediate gratification. The more I delve into dog bonding, the more I see that patience is a requirement even if we're feeling restless and racing. We must simply return to our breath, like in meditation or yoga, and choose to love our pets anyway because the extinction of a behavior will probably not happen in a single session. However, I believe it indirectly benefits us to be tested like this. Impatience may be holding many of us back from living happily, freely, and with more wellness. Making time our friend is something our dogs can teach us.

Ophelia in the summer of 2021. Was she watching me? Judging me? Bored with me? She and her buffet of emotions were all okay by me (photograph by Casey Chapman Ross).

Stay consistent and optimistic. If you're modifying behavior and at first your dog's reaction gets worse, perhaps consider gratitude. Because it's a sign that the behavior is on its way to changing, clawing to hang on before it eventually lets go. Forgive your dog for taking his path and his time, instead of yours. And forgive yourself too for wishing you could orchestrate the whole process. What if patience sits right underneath our desire to rush, so close, all it needs is for your impatience to flare up so it can finally let go too?

Bonding is appreciating senior dogs.

I'm obsessed with senior dogs. Perhaps nothing touches my heart as much as a gray muzzle. I'll go so far as to say that I'm shocked every time I go to the animal shelter that there isn't a line around the block for the senior dogs in the kennels. Because senior dogs have seen it all, done it all, still have as much love to give yet less energy to punk out. They are like moving pillows. They offer a more chill version of companionship, but continue to learn and grow. I believe every old dog that is lucky enough to live into their golden years merits a warm place to lay their head at night, full stop.

Senior dogs push us to be more forgiving, to release heartbreak, resentment, and failure. They motivate us not to dwell in anything beyond the magnificent forever that is today. They make us strong enough to bear watching their decline and still live with lightness, to invest for whatever time is left—a week, a month, a year—and to get on with loving. My family and I have fostered dozens of senior dogs, but let me tell you about Ruffalo—a hunky, blonde, 10-year-old Labrador who was surrendered to us by his owners. He was a guru on how to roll with things, resolve, and absolve because when his former people would come visit him, he'd run over to them gleefully. He harbored no ill feelings toward them. Ruffalo's merciful dog spirit pointed itself at the very people who abandoned him. He helped me see the difference between caution and terror, reflecting and dwelling, how judgment is a cover for fear, but how forgiving takes the wind out of all of it because you can't be afraid of something you love. He showed me that complete and utter forgiveness conserves energy, and with all that excess of energy, he lived chasing balls, eating too many lemons off our lemon trees, and applying the momentum he could have wasted resenting to nurturing the bonds he enjoyed with my family.

Hating and fighting is a waste of time. It's a waste of the gift of life. We can't shame other beings into changing. I wanted to yell at Ruffalo's former owners. I wanted to blame them. I wanted them to feel bad about what they did to Ruffalo. But more than that, I wanted to help this dog. So I followed Ruffalo's lead, and I forgave them instead. It was a choice. Sure, I had to make it many times, but I could do it because when I am willing to step up for an animal, they undoubtedly inspire me every time. That's how I've been able to figure out how to set judgment aside. That's how I've been able to realize that I can't expect everyone to live the way I do. What if it's just a matter of who can care for the dog and get the enormous advantage of learning from that dog? What if everybody has their own journey, and there are various, and they are diverse, and who's to say which one is right and which one is wrong?

Dog love is living a life with dogs woven into it, and that means from time to time hardships may come. Animal rescue is thankless work, yet that doesn't make us faultless, nor give us a pass to be self-righteous when others slip up or meet a roadblock. It's off-putting and does not attract more people into the animal welfare movement. It is possible to "do good" in the "wrong way." I don't know if that cancels out the good, but it certainly fails to create the domino effect of more good, which is ultimately what we need in order to help more animals. We need more people. We need to allow more people to have a place in our circle, to belong, to grow their animal love instead of telling them there's not enough of it. We must hold a *welcome, come in* vibe and extend an open hand. For Ruffalo's former owners, being able to keep in touch with me instead of being condemned gave them the space to tell me why they had to relinquish Ruffalo, which had to do with a family member's health. They weren't heartless. They were in a bind.

With senior dogs, there is no time to waste. The dog's needs takes precedence. I wish we could all keep our dogs forever. I think most people would if they could. But I think that's why senior dogs move me so much: because the road to forgiveness they bring with them is not a long one. I never know how much time they have left. The truth is, none of us know how much time we have left. So why spend it not loving? We can forgive so we can live in love. What else are we here for? Every old dog I meet confirms that it's precisely what we're here to do.

Bonding with Ophelia and Ruffalo.

To me, there is no time as intimate, vulnerable, and sacred as a dog's elderly years. By the time Ruffalo came onto the scene, Ophelia was already a senior too. A fear had begun to grip me about Ophelia's passing. Would I survive it? Would I relapse into my eating disorder? How could I brave the sadness? I constantly felt a squeezing sensation at my throat, a sense that nobody else in the world could understand what was between me and my dog, that nobody else would care enough.

Ophelia's advanced age and Ruffalo's time with us happened during the pandemic, as the world was crashing down. There is nothing like being of service to tether you when life abruptly changes. Fostering gave my family and me a funnel for our worries to go into, a place to channel the panic. We did this thing together, and it was meaningful to do. Sometimes I'd watch Ruffalo shredding lemons throughout the yard and think to myself: *Imagine what a handful he must have been as a puppy!* And I'd wonder if senior dogs are just too tired and weak to be as mischievous as they want to be, could be, or used to be. It made me think about how each of us is worth forgiving and treating with kindness no matter what, because hopefully all of us will grow older and wiser. It's not that it absolves us of our sins or mistakes, but could it grant us a bigger vision, one beyond what we see in somebody today? Ruffalo and his lemons gave me new eyes with which to look at not only him or other dogs but also other people, my family, my kids. To see in them the sweet oldie they would grow into being, and to treat them more compassionately as if they're that now. He inspired forgiveness as a default setting in our home.

Whether the dog we take in has inherently energetic Labrador behaviors like Ruffalo or intense herding instincts or hound dog sniffing tendencies, they are who they are and they are all beautiful. Their inclinations and predispositions can be pardoned as part of them. If a dog has anxiety, I take it as a call for more stimulation and enrichment. If a dog fixates on a walk, I give him a job like Carrier of Stick. If a senior foster dog's hind legs bother him, I feed him in food puzzles so he can "earn" his meals and burn some mental energy so as to require less physical activity. The dogs we take in can be forgiven for what they come with, and in our forgiving them, bring a sense of equilibrium. Mercy has a way of putting things into perspective and proportion.

Ruffalo and Ophelia created a kind of quirky, creaky, kooky Old Age Home energy in our house that saved our lives during lockdown even more than we saved theirs, and the tenderness stirred up in me during this time continues to live on. My dogs continue to churn me into a more generous citizen of the planet long after the COVID pandemic. Since Ruffalo, our home is not without a senior dog or two. Their feeble bodies, white whiskers, and various ailments keep me soft, tolerant, and daring to love life today. They remind me to slow down, and to relish.

Without trying to, and without me even knowing it until after the fact, Ruffalo helped me anticipatorily process the impending loss of my best friend so that when Ophelia's time would come years down the line, I would not fall apart. Instead, I'd know how to make lemonade out of lemons.

> If every senior dog who has been helped by Sherri Franklin got a chance to vote, she'd be president of the USA. Sherri is founder and CEO of Muttville Senior Dog Rescue, dedicated to saving senior dogs, finding them homes, and spreading the word about the value of their lives. San Francisco's favorite rescue, Muttville has saved tens of thousands of oldies and has pioneered ways to make cage-free shelters and thriving hospice programs actually work. Sherri's new campus with its joyful, vibrant vibe was funded by private donors and family foundations. That's how adored Sherri is, including by me. People want to adopt a senior dog because of her and to engage in Muttville's welcoming community. She knows nobody is ever too old to start over or be worthy of cherishing.

Chapter 7 Exercises

The first exercise entails taking a moment to light a candle, breathe deeply, and think about someone who has let you down. Is there a way your dog makes up for it, for them? Is there a way your dog has come into the picture and healed you in the exact wounded spots where somebody has hurt you? Call that person to mind, borrow from your dog's immense reservoir of love, and use your imagination to forgive this person. Take your time. How does your body feel—what sensations arise and where are the sensations—as you envision a situation in which you could talk to them and release some of the hurt or anger? What would forgiveness wear if she were to walk into the room? What might she do or bring with her? How about resentment—what would she wear, bring, or do? If you externalize them and let them speak, what do you hear?

Do it inside of you to live it outside of you. Don't even do it for them, but for you. You don't need that person to do this for yourself. We don't need to wait for someone who will never let us down, because that may never happen. I'd like to think that's why there are dogs, to love us through the let-downs.

The next exercise is to pick something your dog does that you don't favor. Maybe it even borderline drives you crazy. Though you may have been engaging with your dog when the behavior occurred in the past, though you both did the best you could with what you knew at the time, now you're going to ignore that behavior whenever it happens. And you're going to expect an extinction burst, a downright protest from your dog before the behavior extinguishes. Provide positive feedback to your dog (eye contact, encouraging words, touch, play, a treat) whenever they vary their response, which all beings naturally do, and offer you up something you like better. You two are on your way. Show your dog what you want as they demonstrate it and forgive the rest entirely. Always end on a high note with your dog to keep the bond intact.

Keep forgiving them and yourself as you travel onward together.

8

Dog Love Is a Full-Body Experience

From deep in the zone of forgiveness, we're ready to use our whole bodies, unlocked and free, to further bond with our dogs. Canines are supremely sensitive to physical space. They are masters at perceiving even the smallest of physiological and environmental changes, the tiniest of movements, the tightening of a breath.[1] There's a lot out there about canine body language, but what I want to focus on is how your somatic life can improve when you live with a dog because you will get more in touch with your own body, with its intelligence and capacity to send and receive signals.

Bonding with a dog involves tuning in to their body language and also interpreting the clues you pick up on about their bodies in *your* body, noting what your gut says those clues mean. A new language gets constructed between you and a dog: a language that never existed before and cannot be replicated, a language that continuously gets coded in real time just for you two. A dog intuits what your body is saying and you intuit what the dog's is saying, not only through what the bodies do, but through the bodies as they are being. It's as if your fascia tissue chats with their fascia tissue. It's as if the mind extends beyond the head space and permeates throughout. Some unknown part of you understands that your dog is thirsty nanoseconds before they get up for water. Some unknown part of your dog understands that it is nearing five o'clock before you get up to make their meal. Your bodies are talking, bodies that live together in familiarity. Some of it happens during working together, but much of it also happens during the quiet companionship we all love: watching TV together, breathing together, just *being* together.

This symbiosis even happens during the simple joy of cuddling. Cuddling allows the parasympathetic system to take over and calms the body; petting dogs is known to measurably lower blood pressure.[2] I used to keep going past fatigue and burnout. It made me an excellent bulimic, which is not really a badge of honor. But the entire physical self is involved in good dog communication, in good art, and in good love, and that involves rest. My dogs help me rest. Being close to them entails not only looking at their body language and interpreting it by tuning in to my own body, but also knowing that by doing nothing other than lying beside them and enjoying the Cuddle, we are still bonding. From this open, relaxed state, the deepest, stickiest, most rooted aches can be felt, without doing anything or working anything, but rather letting love work on us, letting the body do for us. From this open state, we can heal and our dogs can heal too.

Your body is an entire ecosystem, just as you are also part of a greater ecosystem. You are wired to adapt, to restore, and to thrive. To dislike your own home, your own temple, your own body, is to feel not at home in this world. You can never be home if you're in a hated body. You might feel like a homeless dog, unbelonging, waiting for somebody else to pick you, to house you. But we must house ourselves in the skin we're in, in the bones carrying each of us, in the organs and systems and cells fighting for us, no matter what the package looks like, what we've done well, what we've done poorly, what we have or don't, are or aren't. No matter how much space we take up, we must pick our own selves. When we do, it will be the most natural thing in the world to pick a dog and spread the good fortune of unconditional love because we've cultivated it. We can't wait to run out and share it with others.

We live in a culture that tells us not to love our own bodies, but to instead diet or follow another guru or restrict calories or buy something. We live in a culture that encourages us to look outside, not in. To fix things. To order another product. To dress up. To pretend. To numb out. To stay in the realm of the intellect and ignore the screams stuck in our throat. These tendencies may contribute largely to an economy, but they're a terrible formula for inner peace. Happiness is discovered in listening to our body and responding to what it needs. What lights you up? What makes your body feel good? What are the signs that your body is in harmony and who are you with, what are you doing, when the harmony is happening? These answers are more important than how much money you make, the car you drive, your jeans size, or your number of followers. And if those questions seem hard, there are dogs to help steer us toward the clear signs. By learning to attune to them, we can learn to attune to ourselves. By asking: Is my dog's tail wagging? When is their muzzle slack, in a soft smile? What are they doing when their body goes loose? The signals are evident if we pay attention to what's going on. And then we practice observing and turning those questions onto ourselves. We get to know our entire self better.

"Your body is wise," I bow to my dogs. And so I bow to myself.

Bonding involves nonverbal communication.

Dogs are communicating and seeking communication constantly. Too often they are ignored or overlooked, and the messages they send are not received. Too many dogs are just waiting for someone to notice their bodies emoting and conversing. Dogs don't need more people who come at them with words and a list of things to do and the busy thoughts that run rampant in most human minds, so much so that dogs can't even get through to us when they're sitting right beside us. What dogs do need is more people willing to see them, hear them, and interlace with them. Through their tails and muzzles, ears and torsos, dogs transmit information and warrant being acknowledged and responded to. McConnell and London insist: "The more adept you are at translating the postures and expressions of your dog, the more you'll get to know her, and the better your relationship will be."[3] So it's not about teaching them more of how we talk, but about honoring how *they* talk. It is about getting to know them and their communication signals, both the standard dog ones and their particular individual signs.

More from these trainers on the topic when they exclaim, "It is useful to incorporate space management to communicate with your dogs. Focus on the fact that using your torso rather than your hands is more understandable to your dog. Dogs don't use their paws to control each other, they use their whole body."[4] By simply manipulating physical space, we can convey messages to a dog in the way they convey messages to each other. Deliberately and mindfully knowing when to shift toward them or move away, and recognizing when they do the same, allows us to better communicate. By putting pressure on or taking pressure off a dog we express invasion or welcoming. By shifting the body forward, we tend to stop a dog. Moving back brings them toward us and signals availability. We can use our legs, hips, knees, and core, and even interact with them by guiding them in circles, aka herding them, which often results in a more direct, clear, and quick exchange than all our commands combined.

Dogs respond more quickly to bodies that control their movement and manage the space around them than they do to word-riddled sentences. In the dog training world, we call space management movements "body blocks," and they include maneuvers forward and backward, as well as side-to-side. Dogs can tell how a person occupies the room they are in and what that suggests about them. They notice when access is blocked, and what gaps are left open, therefore are encouraged to move there with less hassle. Using our full frame gently but purposefully and corralling a dog without talking is operating in and adopting dog language, instead of always relying on them to decipher us. Best of all, when we speak more like dogs and less like people, we always have a body on us so we can use this tool whenever we need, without depending on special equipment like certain leashes or collars, gadgets or devices.

McConnell and London put it this way: "Many dogs act like a light bulb has gone off in their minds when they are first exposed to humans using body blocks. Perhaps they feel as though their humans are finally making sense. Of course they can learn to understand humans, just like many of us can learn another language. But oh the joy of traveling in a foreign country and hearing your own language!"[5] I don't know about you, but I can relate to this metaphor and this feeling. I have traveled to places where I could barely understand or be understood, and what a relief it was when somebody finally comprehended me and could translate for me. It made the likelihood of connection so much stronger, and it made me feel safer.

Because canines communicate within the context of whole-bodied language, they motivate us to look and feel and smell, to utilize all senses and involve our entire bodies in order to bond with them. With people, we may just listen or bank on words said. Yet it is good for us to be more fully in touch the way dogs are. To be that dropped in to our own body, that integrated, that expanded in point of view, input and output. Sometimes staying silent helps me use my body more. I have found that through comprehensive involvement and complete engagement of the physical form, I've been able to build more solid relationships with my dogs and with my loved ones, based not only on sound minds but also on resonant bodies.

So dog bonding is understanding the power in backing off, shifting weight, tensing up or relaxing muscles. It is us grasping the natural significance of expressive movements big and small, as well as how we affect the space around us, and what all those changes might imply. The payoff is as much about improving our communication with dogs as it is about the restorative lift it gives us to embody a raw, organic, intrinsic version of self, the type of essential self who is in sync with other organisms and the world at large, who understands that we are sharing space and time, and who is perceptive of their own full body engaged in a full life.

Many cues can be subtle from dogs: the way the nose twitches or the tail swooshes, the way a head turns to the side or the shift in where their eyes focus. In James O'Heare's *The Dog Aggression Workbook*, he advises, "When interpreting communication signals, it is important to look at the whole dog, not just a single part, and to look for clusters of signals, and not just individual signals. The reason for this is that these signals are complex, and they are constantly changing as the dog's motivations change … look for agreement among signals and also look at the environment."[6] So we practice noticing, interpreting, and accumulating information. We make sense of it all somewhere in the summation of elements, not from a single element. We add things up and get the truth in the calculation, in the invisible totaling, in the average of the relationships between body parts, what we know about our dogs, and what we are willing to learn. Everything in them and everything in us participates in the conversation.

We must get to know our dogs. In my very favorite dog book, *On Talking Terms with Dogs: Calming Signals* by Turid Rugaas, the author describes the ways that dogs self-soothe or converse with each other and us to send calming messages of pacification. Approaching with a curved body, squinting their eyes, turning away, and licking their lips or nose are some of the many examples we can learn to read[7] to better understand our dogs. By exhibiting these signals, they indicate their need to deescalate, that they feel nervous or unsure. We can also utilize those signals in return when our dogs might most need a response of peace. Stress-related signals like refusing treats they'd normally eat or showing rounded eyes with large pupils, as well as displacement behaviors like excessive yawning or sniffing in an over-animated way, can tell us even more that a dog is feeling tense or afraid. Understanding our dogs' communication signs helps us identify triggers and associations, which means we can guesstimate future behaviors, which means we have some agency to prevent problems, which means we can give them some agency, which means we can use a whole catalogue of knowledge to support our dogs. We can get proficient in gathering physical clues and become oriented toward seeing solutions, not seeking issues. Through a practice in keen observation, we may even discover what our own bodies might be trying to tell us. Because whether or not we actually check in with or clock our own stress-related signals and displacement behaviors (such as smoking, overeating, scrolling on social media, etc.), if we rehearse caring about our dogs and what they might be telling us, eventually we could be tempted to turn that attentive interest onto ourselves. Dropping into our bodies and not staying stuck only in our thoughts can bring a sense of relief to life.

We combine what we know with the gut feelings we get in our stomachs about what we know. Put these things together, plus the slight or dramatic movements from the dog or in the environment, and you will become the ultimate specialist on your dog. It will be *your* instincts, *your* intuition, the input in *your* muscles and tendons about their muscles and tendons, teaching you to listen to your body and to also listen to theirs. You don't have to be a pet psychic to discern your dog's messages. You just have to be in your body and marvel at how they are always in theirs. You just have to watch and love one another. Sometimes it can all be so obvious. Other times it might be vague, or downright counterintuitive, or baffling. For example, dogs tend to follow in the direction our feet point, so if

8. Dog Love Is a Full-Body Experience   111

your dog accidentally runs out a front door, try turning and running *away* from them, in the direction you want them to go, instead of chasing after them. Chasing usually becomes a fun game and not an effective way to catch a dog. But running away usually turns into the dog chasing you, and thus helps you be able to catch them. Study canine communication signals and body language, but then let it all be specific and unique to your dog, and to what is between your bodies.

• • •

Ophelia loved me even when I was not hearing my own body at all, when I couldn't understand what it wanted. It was as if she could sense that to a degree—perhaps through my sugar level dropping, my fear, or my hormones. And we know dogs can do that work; service dogs do it all the time. Doesn't this mean dogs have the potential to sense what we may not? That their skills are distinct and therefore precious? What did it do to my body for Ophelia to seek out its comfort, snuggle beside me, and let my body know it deserved comfort and warmth?

There are dogs who are overtly, strategically trained to sniff out hormonal imbalances, such as diabetic service dogs and seizure response dogs.[8] Researchers have been exploring the use of specially trained medical detection dogs in diagnosing cancer.[9] But I'd argue this is life with any dog to an extent—that sensing gift they offer over and over again every day. Many of our emotions release hormones along with them, too; they come in a packaged deal.[10] If we are chronically stressed out, our dogs will likely be chronically stressed out.[11] Whether that's because dogs adapt to energy, atmosphere, and pace and/or because many dogs can smell the odor differences that their humans emit when they're stressed compared to when they're calm[12] and they respond to this with greater alertness, possibly every dog has the capacity to offer services that assist their people. Sure, there are dogs who need our assistance with *their* anxiety, but don't they call on us to be a more stable versions of ourselves so they can rehabilitate? Don't these dogs implore us to be well so they can sense our wellness and borrow some?

According to James O'Heare, "When a dog experiences a sudden or acute onset of stress or fear, the body quickly activates its emergency processes. Various chemicals (neurotransmitters and hormones) are released in the body that will prepare the animal physiologically for an emergency. The heart beats faster, and blood flow is guided away from skin and intestines toward the muscles so that they are ready for action…. As a result of these processes, the dog may be unable to access behaviors that rely on inhibition, impulse control, and previously learned coping mechanisms."[13] Think about the tax on the body all of this activity causes. It stands to reason, therefore, that the way we regularly feel produces physiological consequences on the body, and that reoccurring episodes at some point begin to affect behavior. In humans and in dogs, what we feel and its corresponding hormones can become habituated—whether that be negative feelings as a set point and the conflict they bring, or positive emotions and positive hormones as the normal cocktail that makes us who we are. Body awareness, which dogs encourage, helps us decide which we want to be. Once we see how what we feel parallels with how we relate to dogs and how they relate to us, we get to choose optimal feelings and the chemistry that wellness brings to our dogs and ourselves.

I wanted to meet the person Ophelia already saw as worthy of her love, in a body that felt at ease. That want alone pulled me up and out of the dark cave that I'd made for a life. A dog's love can help us listen to what our bodies need and urge us to heed the call. And they do it by making themselves so damn lovable that we learn by doing it for them.

Bonding is a practice in creativity.

When we function as a being who is fully connected to our own body, we operate in the fertile and grounded hub of endless creativity. When we

Clooney less than a week after being rescued from a life of neglect. He savored every meal, sleep, and day with us until he got adopted into an amazing home through Muttville Senior Dog Rescue.

8. Dog Love Is a Full-Body Experience

organize and take action from within all the corners and pockets of our body and not just from the floaty isolated state of thoughts, we get to magnify the breadth of our innovation and our competence. The soul does not think. The brain does. Body awareness infiltrates the meaning-making machine of our minds and turns up the volume on curiosity. This forces us to iterate and reiterate, to explore without being held hostage by habituated ideas or beliefs. Whenever we want to get new behaviors out of our dogs, we can begin by imagining a familiar song playing on repeat, how everybody does the same dance routine. Want new moves? Stop the record player and start over with a new album. Get down the new choreography. Mess up, step on toes, employ grace, twirl, recharge, take up room, stretch, and love what it is to move your body as you create an original waltz to the music. Eventually, through co-creating it with your dog, a new dance routine will be absorbed by you both. What will work? What will be beautiful? What will stick? We don't know. We must approach working together with inquisitiveness and suss it out, trusting that we will stumble upon a cutting edge routine with our friend. Because life with a dog can feel like that, like a party and there's art all around you—art you hear, see, leap to. Art you are.

It's in the movement itself, metaphorically as well as literally, in clawing our way back up after feeling or falling down, that we gain the most. Loving dogs can teach us to view taking a tumble and then moving back toward them as elegant. This is how we step into who we truly are, manifesting an unshakable bond. What I'm trying to get at is this: Using our bodies to relate to our dogs is a doorway into using our bodies to relate to life so that we may be integrated and aligned humans regardless of our circumstances. Unity brings about well-being, and well-being brings about unity. To be a coalesced mind-body-spirit is to be whole. To be built to last. To be uncollapsible. To feel it inside ourselves.

Today, artificial intelligence is looming. Its shadow is growing larger and threatening to take over, but I'd be remiss to leave out the fact that what separates us from AI is everything that makes up who we really are. The bulk is the substance, what flows underneath our skin and bones, and the feelings we get on our skin, in our bones, from doing what we do. We are not robots. We are the buzzing, humming aliveness that is not seen but felt. That is cause for celebration! Because no animals—no living, sentient creature—can ever be replaced by machines if what we value is not the product but the experience. All living beings ingest, digest, and express. That's the journey, and that's the win. Not the production. Not perfection. But the process. Seen this way, humans are not disposable or discardable. Neither are dogs then.

Being is a full-body scenario, it is bliss, and it is the domain of dogs. It is me returning to the animal I am. Lining up the mind with where my body is—not in the future or in the past, but right where my heart beats and feet land—is yet another way to love ourselves. Our dogs out there nudge us to go back again in here, and that cycle will weave more wellness in our lives. Nothing outside of us can fill us up or heal us in the way we are seeking. As a person recovering from an eating disorder, it felt wrong to value what I felt and sensed, what my body was asking for or giving me an inkling about, over what I thought or planned or wanted. It felt wrong at first just to accustom myself to being okay in my body. But nothing was wrong with Ophelia. I could not ignore her. So I could no longer ignore myself.

Bonding with a dog is embodying consent.

One of the most important elements in dog bonding is giving dogs consent over their bodies. According to reports from the Centers for Disease Control and Prevention, injury rates for dog bites are the highest among children ages five to nine.[14] In my experience as a Family Paws Parent Educator who focuses on supporting Double Moms and Double Dads (what I call parents with both kids and dogs), I find that many dog bites happen because kids try to manipulate a dog's body. It is common for kids to model their parents' behavior. But if a child isn't guided by their parents to treat a dog with consent, coupled with the lack of knowledge on how to heed a dog's warning if they dislike something, this puts kids in a risky situation. We must do a better job of protecting our kids by teaching them what compliance means, modeling appropriate behavior with dogs for them to mimic, and preparing children to communicate with and understand dogs.

Dogs have their own bodies, just like we do. They belong to themselves. Their bodies are not for us to snuggle or move or hug or push or tickle or do whatever we want to them whenever we want, despite how cute they are. In order to live in a world where our children's bodies are respected, I believe we must educate them to offer the same to animals, to practice this sort of compassion and kindness day in and day out in their own homes. To get it by being it.

Even if running up to your sleeping dog to dress him up in clothes would never lead to a bite in your house, I've seen many dog bites occur because the way a child handles their own dog at home is expected and assumed when that child is taken out of the home. This can lead to major trouble. Even if you are lucky enough to have a dog that tolerates your kid pulling on his feet or riding him like a horse, kids often go to a friend's house or elsewhere not understanding that this other dog does not know them or may not tolerate the same treatment. The worst part is that usually the dog is punished for defending themselves or for expressing fear. It's the dog who pays the price. But another being's body is not ours to handle. Maneuvering a dog's body should not be normalized, not only for the dog but also for the safety of children and what it implies for their own bodies. For consent to be nonnegotiable for humans, we show that by giving it to animals.

Teaching children to call a dog over to them instead of going over to the dog is one of the single most significant ways we can decrease dog bites. This gives a dog consent, demonstrates consent as a significant thing for kids, and allows a dog body autonomy, the right to say yes or no. This pays off big for safety and for bonding potential, so children get the chance to enjoy the same kind of transcendental love with an animal that we want to benefit from too. If a dog comes toward us, they want to be touched. If your hand is petting a dog and the dog's body tightens, they do not want to be touched any longer. If your hand lingers hovering above them, and the dog presses into you or meets your hand, then they want more contact. The point is, dogs are not stupid and they know how to ask for petting if they seek it. They also know how to ask for space and need to be allowed to ask for it. We must stop forcing ourselves on dogs and enforcing a demand that their bodies exist for our needs.

A dog's body should answer to their own needs. Giving a dog the right to choose, giving him the option to take up space and increase his distance, will always help him and always help the relationships around him. Calling a dog over will be more bonding than going over to that dog and hoisting ourselves into their space. But what about when a dog does not consent, people ask me? What about when I need a dog to do something or stop doing something? I recommend in these cases to think about implementing an incompatible behavior, which is a term used to describe an approach for decreasing problem behaviors by reinforcing a different activity that your dog can't practice at the same time as the problem behavior.[15] For example, I've walked reactive foster dogs with a dog backpack strapped onto them, and a can of beans stuffed in each side of the pack so it weighed them down. They didn't go bonkers and lunge at the sight of another dog on a walk because carrying the backpack was incompatible with bucking. Whenever a new dog comes into my home, I don't know how sensitive they are to touch, and I don't know how much they like to be handled. I want to respect their body, avoid negative habits between us, and enjoy moving in tandem. So calling them over for touch is the standard protocol, instead of me reaching for them.

Incompatible behaviors are not only a great tool to have when you wish to alter your dog's behavior; they are also mighty useful when it comes to ourselves, and a solid outside-in tool to help us enhance our own wellness. Karen Pryor says, "Training incompatible behavior is quite useful in modifying your own behavior, especially when dealing with emotional states such as grief, anxiety, and loneliness. Some behaviors are totally incompatible with self-pity: dancing, choral singing, or any highly kinetic motor activity, even running."[16] We don't always have to convince or push ourselves out of something. We can choose to engage in behavior that's contrary to the one we're performing or to the mood we're in. We can clash with discordant states by performing joyful actions.

As a person who had learned not to be in her body, whose own body was at war with itself, one of the greatest and most indirect advantages of having dogs has been the newfound relationship I've developed with my body, born out of the sheer desire to be close to dogs. I trust myself to pick up on a dog's signals, to translate those signals into the language the dog and I have built together. And it is specifically because I trust my own body that I can trust a dog whenever they communicate the need for space from me.

Bonding with Ophelia and Clooney.

Then there was Clooney, a Boxer mix who I spotted sunbathing in a random front yard, on a random street in Los Angeles when the highway was too congested and I exited to take a slew of backroads. He was so skinny, so flea-infested, eyes sealed shut with so much guck, that I immediately pulled over. Before I even knew what I was doing, I called out to his people. I explained how sick he obviously was, how badly he needed to see a vet, and though I don't think his guardians knew better, neglecting an animal on accident instead of on purpose doesn't absolve a person of the cruelty. Every living being wants a chance at a real life.

What nobody knew at this time, other than Ophelia, was that weeks before stumbling upon Clooney, I had relapsed. There was something about having to pick up Clooney's wrecked body and deposit him into my car, about having to feel the full effect of his brittle bones, the physical desperation of his muscles needing more sustenance. There was something about wiping his eyes, applying medicine, staring into his crushed gaze, packed with years of waiting and holding it together and hoping and hunger and survival. There was something about involving my own body in order to rescue him, to bond with him, and to heal him that helped restore something in me. Over the time we shared together, Clooney filled out, grew strong, and renewed before my very eyes. He showed me just how much there is to appreciate about the body's ability to regenerate and seek equanimity.

Ophelia would snooze near him on her cat-like perch on the top of the couch, sort of hovering over him as he slept deep, as I hovered over her. My husband asked me during this time, if we were lost at sea and I had only one life jacket left, would I give it to him or to Ophelia? I told my husband the truth: I'd give up my jacket so they'd both live. (Note: He'd recently seen Ophelia and I bathe in the tub together so he wasn't terribly surprised by my answer.) I was already certain by then that I wouldn't know what to do without Ophy's love, that I wouldn't know how to be.

A dog like Clooney probably waited 10 years to begin enjoying the kind of love Ophelia and I shared her entire life. But at least he got it. I'm so grateful he got it at all. His brindle coat gleamed and shined from healthy food. He got adopted into an amazing home and lived happily ever after, sleeping under a heated blanket. I never drove by his former house again.

I have never made myself throw up again either.

Beth Bellanti is the Program Director for Vodka For Dog People at Tito's Handmade Vodka. This is not an endorsement for alcohol. This is an endorsement to get yourself the kind of friend who identifies as a dog person and who then supports other dog people with a generous spirit, putting her body on the line. Beth doesn't do things the way everybody else does things—she's too busy following her heart and trusting her gut for that. She has rescued and rehomed dozens of animals without any formal support and without taking any credit for it. She doesn't care about that—she cares about getting a dog with severe hip pain a golf cart so the dog can still feel the wind. She cares about smiling and partnering and living each moment like it's the best one there is, fully awake and aware to the connection between everyone and everything.

Chapter 8 Exercises

This chapter ends with a dance party. Jam out with your dog! I recommend the Grease or Footloose soundtrack, but whatever music you like to blast works. Lose yourself, use your entire body, and share the experience with your dog. See what they do and how they react to the energy of you moving freely, joyfully. Dance parties are an exceptional way to elevate your energy and mood, bond with your dog and have some fun. Get out of your limited head and back into your full, fabulous body.

In addition, so that you may rely on your dog's specific body language, sketch your own dog's posture during certain situations at home—as you cook and there's food around versus while you watch television. In the backyard versus at a café. When friends come over to your home versus when you're alone together. How do they move, and what on them tells you what they might be feeling, what they might want or be sensitive to or capable of in any given scenario? Are any calming signals on display?

Pay particular attention to the way their eyes appear—stretched and whale-eyed, scanning you from the corners, or soft and smiling? Is their stare hard and fixed or are they able to look elsewhere? Are their ears forward and erect or back, like they're wearing a headband? Is their muzzle hanging open in a slack pant, or taut? Is their body tight or relaxed? Are they showing their belly, or stiff and leaning forward as if preparing to pounce? How about their tail—is it positioned high or low, tucked underneath them or waving and moving? Take stock of your dog's features, his level of muscle tension, his breathing. Create an illustrative reference of your dog's physical state in different settings. You don't have to be an artist, it's just about getting in touch with the emotional and mental correlations you sense based on what your dog's body is telling your body, once you pause to notice. This helps you love your dog as they grow older, so you can track when they might be in pain or what may change as they age.

Your dog has already memorized your signs and messages. It's only fair that we get to know theirs. This dictionary is just for you two, for the language between you.

9

Dog Love Is Planning for the Unpredictable

Our bodies are totally engrossed in bonding, up to our elbows! We're listening and helping our dogs rise to their highest potential. Can we go now? Not so fast. We know things change. Things always change. So what about when the dog "misbehaves" again, when they regress, will we be able to stay bonded without labeling them as wrong or catastrophizing? Things are rarely an ascent up to the top and then plateau, a life of coasting, baby. Nah, life tends to move in spirals up and down despite how much we wish for happily ever after to be a fixed point.

Feeling disappointed in a relapse is normal. But staying there isn't, because prolonged disappointment intensifies stuckness. It squanders energy circling the drain. I am not advocating for complacency when things shift with your dog, and I'm also not advocating that we should pretend it isn't frustrating if our dogs backslide, or speed past our feelings. But I am suggesting again that we plan for slipups so that we can tolerate lapses from the ones we love, and that we find outlets to metabolize our emotions. Because imagining a dog who will never change will invariably make us mad. It's unfeasible, unreasonable, and unsustainable.

Despite setting my dogs up to succeed within the systems and structures I implement, I still expect accidents. If a new rescue dog comes into my house, for example, I plan for pee on the carpet, even though I do what I need to do in order to potty train them. Continuing on in this example, I'm either pleasantly surprised when there is no pee, or I'm ready with a spray and a towel so I can clean it up, but either way, I'm not angry. There is nothing to need to forgive later, for I have prepared for this. And regardless of what the behavior is that might irk me, I build in the reality that it will likely happen, or something else will at some point happen to concern me or challenge me with my dog. McConnell and London articulate: "If (when?) you catch her having an accident in the house, don't yell or rub her nose in it. That will at best confuse her, and more likely alarm her so that the lesson she learns is either 'Never urinate or defecate in front of a person,' or 'I need to be careful. This person is a little crazy.'"[1] Consider the dog's perspective. Just because you spent too much on a rug, doesn't mean they understand that. They are doing a natural thing by going to the bathroom. It's your job to teach them where. Furthermore, your dog may be perfect today, but won't likely stay there forever, just like I likely won't weigh the exact same number of pounds every day for the rest of my whole life. None of us can exist as if balancing on top of a needle, holding our breath to never rock the boat. (Yeah, okay, that was mixing metaphors.)

At the end of the day, I can either strengthen the connection with my dog or I can spew out my feelings, but I can't do both at the same time. Dogs don't learn while we're having a meltdown or in the throes of dissatisfaction. Dogs don't learn when we criticize them or punish them for being real, complex individuals. News alert: We don't learn that way either, as real and complex individuals too. We must also plan for our own transitions. We must make room for things to be different from what they were, from what they are. Otherwise, we risk feeling helpless and not even trying. Emotional shutdowns can happen to dogs as well as to people.

Anticipating alterations from and with our dogs makes things less intense when they occur. Building in not the possibility but the inescapability of changes signifies that we want our dogs to benefit as much from our togetherness as we want ourselves to benefit. That we understand that as time marches on, they will adjust and so must we. Both people and dogs deserve to get what they need, whether a phase of their life together is going swimmingly or not jiving at all. That is the nature of a long-term relationship—you grow together, riding the ups and the downs, love each other when it's easy and when it's not. Expansion is often followed by contraction. Valleys are part of a landscape filled with peaks.

Mentally organizing ourselves to view disruption as normal makes the (stained) rug being pulled out from under us much more palatable. It helps us not hate the dog. It builds up our own tolerance level, sort of like the equivalent of doing bicep curls but for our spirit.

"We will walk through whatever comes," I assure my dogs. And so I assure myself.

Bonding is an awareness of fight or flight.

Surprises will happen, and the unpredictable will come. Dogs usually respond based on the associations they've made, so when something unfamiliar is presented, fear is common as there is no association to an unknown entity.[2] Any time a dog is afraid or stressed, they have four main ways to deal with it: fight, flight, freeze, or fidget.[3] They don't get to journal or call a therapist. The truth is, every animal has these reactions in their repertoire, but often one takes precedence over the others, kind of like a default setting.

In his *Dog Aggression Workbook*, O'Heare shares that when a dog feels notable fear or stress, "This sets the stage for fight-or-flight behaviors such as escape or avoidance. The threshold for aggressive behaviors is lowered when dogs are under stress."[4] Once dogs enter that physically altering zone, it's a less cognitive and more reactive state of being. He goes on further to explain how emotions correlate with a dog's reflexes: "Fear involves the release of various neurotransmitters in the brain and hormones into the bloodstream. This creates things like narrowed tunnel vision and churning stomach sensations, and these reactions motivate the dog to act; they trigger the fight-or-flight mechanism."[5] Fear is real, and happens in the body as well as the mind.

There are dogs who, when facing an unknown person or situation, might freeze up or fret, unable to settle, ranging from totally crashing to hyperactivity. There are dogs who hide or get skittish, or prepare to dart at the first opportunity. Then there are dogs whose default is to bark or lunge, to enlarge a display of aggression. Some utilize a combination of responses. What's interesting to me is that these reactions come from the same *feeling*—a desire to protect themselves against something new or strange or scary—meaning that often the feelings that drive a fight response drive a flight response too. So why do we tolerate one over the other? Why do we coo when we see a dog at the shelter cowering and shivering or lying still, but reject the dog lunging and jumping at the kennel door? Both of those dogs are terrified and unsure.

It makes me wonder about our relationship to anger, to expressing rage. It makes me wonder about the difference between fury and avoidance, and how we can make room for both as normal responses, albeit within safe ranges. It makes me wonder about the difference between dogs who have lived on the street versus owner-surrendered dogs at the shelter, one always on the run, searching for somebody, and the other stuck and pent up, eager not to be forgotten. Fight and flight are acts of kinetic desperation. They are opposite ends of the same spectrum. Fawning can also be a natural appeasement gesture that falls under the fidgeting category. It involves a dog rolling on her back or being overly friendly or submissive[6] and can also be a fear reaction.

When a dog is pushed beyond discomfort and pushed beyond their first response tendency, it has the other responses available to them. This means every dog has the potential to fight. Whether a dog just got adopted or experienced a life change at home, such as a house move, the arrival of a new baby, adapting to a caregiver's new work schedule, or the inclusion of an additional family pet, to name some of the most common examples, they will only have these built-in ways to deal with and express themselves during the transition. They will not be able to *tell* you why it's upsetting them. You will have to plan for a change to potentially upset them and then watch their behavior to help them along the way.

Why am I highlighting all of this? Because we are the ones who make most of the life-changing decisions that affect our dogs. We're also the ones with countless tools and approaches to get ourselves ready to handle the many variations on life that impact us. Our dogs will be as prepared for the changes as we allow them to be, as we reinforce them to be. It is on us to expose them to new sights, sounds, smells, people, places, routines, and situations. It's on us to help them acclimate and give them time. It's on us to also assume that as they change, their health will too, and we will be responsible for supporting them. I recommend gradual, consistent experiences before throwing a dog into the deep end to sink or swim amid huge lifestyle shifts. I suggest this because it helps them adjust, yes, but it also helps our sanity remain intact because small bursts of exposure are usually more manageable. Otherwise, we're sort of gambling on how a dog might react to being immersed in a new reality, and how those reactions might bear upon us. Why not get ahead of it at least somewhat and be part of a dog's transition, for their sake as well as for our own?

Flooding a dog with newness can impede their ability to use their cognitive mind and make proper decisions, because staying at an alarmed level of danger assessment keeps them stuck in adrenaline-pumping loops of fight or flight.[7] Instead, by settling their nerves and providing them with enough exposure so that they learn to feel safe, we allow them to make better choices. By employing ongoing patience and foresight, you can offer gradual desensitization that will support the bond between you.

I got a sense of how survival instinct impedes cognition when I drove a dog named Mandy home from the animal shelter. In her state of extreme panic, combined with my extreme exasperation about how intense her panic was, she jumped out of my cracked-to-let-the-breeze-in car window. I leapt out of the driver's seat to chase her, and my car continued down the street. On its own. Without anybody, namely me, to drive it. A man on the corner fortunately caught Mandy. And I chased my car. Thankfully, nobody was hurt. But the thud of my heart took over my entire being as Mandy's fear and my fear became one and the consuming same. It took days for the adrenaline to dissipate from my system. And I got a taste for what it must feel like to be locked in a kennel with stress-induced cortisol piling up, day after day, and then suddenly life alters and you're going home with Lord-only-knows-who.

9. Dog Love Is Planning for the Unpredictable

Whenever I take in a new foster dog, I expect there to be hurdles and speedbumps. I am ready for the dog to be in a state of fight or flight, having just met me and not knowing who I am or what is expected of them in this new place. I understand that there have been various ruptures to what they recognize and are familiar with—their former home or the streets, as well as however long they spent in a chaotic shelter environment—and that they should be handled with patience, preparation, and compassion. There is no right formula as to how many days this will take, although some rely on the 3 × 3 rule; but by holding it in my awareness and conceding to the myriad of ways change impacts a living being that we cannot always account for ahead of time, I remain committed to building the dog's resilience and my own. It is a testament to my and their hardiness that we can make it through changes together, and live beyond instinctual survival—that we can show up one day at a time and keep relearning how to live in harmony.

Bonding is shaping.

When big changes happen to a dog, they'd benefit from being given time to adjust and adapt to new circumstances. At the same time, keeping things basic and developing routines as a foundation can help them during transitions, so the dogs can rest in what they can count on. How do we toggle this duality of consistency yet openness, how do we straddle the line? I like shaping.

Shaping is learning through successive approximations. "It is like going up rungs on a ladder. This gradual raising of the standard until, sooner or later, you are reinforcing your original target behavior is called shaping,"[8] explains dog trainer Jean Donaldson. It affirms that behavior is built in small increments, not large chunks. It entails observing, rewarding what a dog is doing that is closest to what you want them to do, although usually not yet exactly what you want. It is slow and at times dull, but when life events affect dogs, we can *gradually* increase movement toward the behaviors we want from them. We can *gradually* accustom them one small step at a time toward any ultimate goals because behavior is always variable. The trick is to capture alterations towards the goal by pairing responses we like from dogs with positive feedback from us, otherwise known as positive reinforcement. It can be surprising how different dogs offer different behaviors. But regardless, cheering a dog on to make choices is the backbone of the shaping process.

"If you stop relying on control of misbehavior and start shaping good behavior with clear-cut conditioned signals for reinforcement, your dog will respect you in a new way; to your dog you will be making sense, at last,"[9] Karen Pryor states. Communicating through shaping involves self-illumination. It's about knowing what you want and how to best go about getting what you want. Self-illumination requires self-introspection, time in quiet, time attending to yourself. Shaping toward a desired behavior works as a way to inspire your dog to do what you want her to do without sacrificing your connection. McConnell and London suggest: "In this form of operant conditioning, you reinforce her for doing any part of the behavior you'd like her to perform."[10] So you get to be excited that she got to step two and almost sat but didn't quite sit yet! You get to celebrate the closest thing she's doing! It's not compromising what you want. Intimidation is not the way to encourage a dog to meet their potential. You don't have to just wait to praise her when she sits obediently because you said the command, missing out on the dozens of connective moments along the way. There is all this love to build between you as you get there.

After Mandy busted out of my car and we finally got home, she took space for herself and very slowly settled in. It took weeks of nurturing her cognitive mind to help her out of her shutdown mode so that she could make it to the other side of fight or flight and finally show her full personality. I simply, slowly, looked for what she did that I could root for. With Mandy, giving her a predictable schedule made room for the unpredictable activities and behaviors she began to offer over time. To start, I relied on free shaping,[11] which means I did not use any deliberate prompts or attempt to manipulate the environment to lure her into doing anything. I simply watched what she did, what she organically offered, and reinforced what I wanted her to do more of. This flow allowed for her best self to come forward through a series of estimated behaviors. I marked the tiny steps along the way, but most importantly to me, this facilitated our bond. It's how she learned to sit, go to her bed, wait by the door, and many more behaviors.

Then our shaping grew more targeted. We loved to play a Post-It note game. I would hold a Post-It out on the palm of my hand and wait until her curiosity won out and she'd come over to touch it with her nose. When she did, I was ready with a treat to reward her. Once the game became touching the small square of paper on my palm for a treat, we shaped further as I moved the Post-It around, prompting her toward items she could touch other than my hand. Mandy would boop her nose on the Post-It on the wall or a door, and then I'd reward her. Then I started to shape specifically at the refrigerator by luring her over to it, eventually hanging a piece of cloth on the handle of the fridge. She'd boop the Post-It on the fridge, I'd reward, and there was the cloth. One day, she pulled it, and opened the fridge for me! She earned a jackpot of treats for that variation of behavior! And what an excellent sous-chef Mandy turned out to be. And what a boost to her self-esteem[12] it was to learn new things in a positive light, to have a job, and to believe that in trusting what was already inside of her, she could change and grow.

Bonding is a lifestyle.

Updating routines is exponentially harder for us people than it is for our dogs. Dogs often adapt to new sequences more quickly than we do, probably because they don't burden every moment with ruminations about the past and projections about the future. We're the ones who have to break the habits of jumping to conclusions and making assumptions. In order to give our dogs the sense that change is okay, I recommend doing daily drills for approximately 10 minutes where you and your dog intentionally work on something that's nonhabitual, whatever that may be. Whether that's gearing them up for an impending change or targeting a behavior, I believe it means more to our wellness to incorporate modifications in bite-sized bits. The absorption of information as a normal part of living will stick if it feels good, rather than turning it into an obligated task to work on intensely once a week for an hour and a half. The name of the game is associating change with possibility, with lightness, so we may feel good about altering our own habits too, and develop an aptitude for weaving in noninvasive, viable, steady practice.

I urge you to set aside a little time daily to bond with your dog within the confines of predicted unpredictability. We never know what we will get, especially when we're shaping with them. Bonding is a lifestyle choice, like eating well. It's not a diet or a one-month plan, but a new pattern. By setting aside time regularly for the love between you and your dog to take center stage, little bits of inclusion will keep your dog ready and flexible and able to bounce back from whatever comes, just as you will be. You don't have to work with your dog for hours a day to be close to them. Just invite short bursts of connection and use your imagination. I'd like to think this is why their love is so significant—it serves as a constant when life changes around us. All we have to do is let the bond be a paperweight, anchoring us so we don't blow away.

• • •

We have become a species that goes away from ourselves regularly. We check our phones, our emails, our social media accounts, our pantry, our neighbor's house size, our own thigh size. We turn on the TV, the news, the video game. We move away from what is, not only from what is present but from what is real. We get lost in our heads, in our egos, in our distractions, and in virtual living, but the frightening thing is that our heads, our egos, our distractions and virtual reality are all meant to, designed to, make us want more awayness. They make us want something else, something shape-shifting and endlessly elusive. If we are away from ourselves we can never bond with another being fully because we're not even really there.

The act of going away, the very act of going into head, ego, distraction, unreality, is an act of robbing ourselves of the resilience we need to practice as life changes. We can't leave ourselves and what is happening IRL and also be adaptable, capable of recovery and snapping back. Unfortunately, as a result then, when changes come, we rage on, wail louder, try to conquer something or buy something or laugh at something, to go further and longer away, for we can't stomach how inexperienced we are at being present in the midst of all we do not control. Why don't we see it's the act of leaving that keeps us imprisoned? It's the going away that makes us miss the opportunity to be met. The awayness causes us pain because it comes from wanting and waiting in a line that never moves. Worse than that, it's the fact that we keep ourselves in that line that hurts most. If we are awake, we step out of that line. Bonding with a dog is not leaving what is, and not leaving the dog, but rather it is a way to leave that line. Because if you want to have a good relationship with a dog, you can't go away. It is a voluntary connection predicated on the idea that when we adopt this dog, it's because we do indeed want that connection. Having a dog around inspires us to say goodbye to ego, to head noise, to distraction, and to technology in order to be fully in the room where we can obtain the downloads, fill up, and actually feel the buzzing of life moving through us because here we are, moving with it where it moves.

Dogs are not burdened by technology, their mood is not affected by what they read on Twitter, they are not coveting their neighbor's car (although they may want another dog's bone), and they do not live mired in the fake news of their minds or the TV. Dogs do not prioritize the daydream state, the past or future; they stay—and when we spend time with them, they require us to stay. In fact, dogs stay whether they have a good life or a bad one. They stay whether they are tethered to a chain or snoring on a plush couch. I'd argue that they access love and give love and are love because of this staying. They stay despite all the changes that swirl around them. We should follow their lead and join them. Their way of being is more in tune with our original nature than ours currently is. We need dogs to revert to what we were made for. A staying being is like the rooted tree. It must blow with the wind, it must sway in order not to break, it rides out a storm. It encounters the rain and bends its body, it goes on.

Bonding with Ophelia and Mandy.

When I help a dog, I can usually tell if they've known punishment. The cumulative fallout from their lives—when they were coerced, where punishment defeated its own goals—is visible in their body language. Mandy would wince if I raised my hand to comb my own hair out of my face. I paid attention and tried to use those clues to tailor the best responses I could for her. Whether I rescue a 12-year-old dog or an eight-week-old puppy, I still cannot predict the full extent of the experiences that have shaped or will shape them, what's coming, or how they will respond to what's coming. But I'd already made mistakes with Ophelia. I'd already yelled at her and apologized 47 times in a row in a stupor of guilt. I'd already insisted and willed, and then realized I love her too much for any of that noise. By the time Mandy came onto the scene, it was not an option on the menu for how I deal with dogs. If lifting my arm startled her, as best I could around her, I would not lift my arm, or I'd be mindful to do it slowly, uttering soft words.

When we force dogs, we reflect our own resistance. When we use coercion, what we're really doing is teaching dogs to avoid us, to opt out of life, to do things behind our back, or to push back. When we succumb to frustration and punish our dogs, we forget that coercion does not produce energy conducive to learning. We still speed when the police aren't in sight, don't we? I'm not suggesting that punishment caused all the problems in the world (although one could argue it has), but when we use force, we break the bond and annihilate any influence we might have on the friendship we could enjoy instead. As James O'Heare puts it, "There are basically three types of homes in which your dog can live: a home in which the humans use force and intimidation to get the dog to be obedient; a home in which your dog has all the social control and gets what he wants whenever he wants it; or a peaceful, harmonious household in which you are a wise, benevolent leader. You get to choose. Just remember, your dog can't."[13]

That's the truth. Dogs are at the mercy of people who make the choice to bully and intimidate them or to influence them with love. I handled Mandy's tender wincing, her penchant for running away, and her uncertainty about humans by understanding how that could be her outlook, giving her full permission to be where she was and to surprise me when she wanted to. I gave her as much of a reliable schedule as I could and offered a container of security by leaning on a routine that set her up to succeed. And Mandy in turn taught me. Thanks to her, I learned that when anxiety is around, we can listen to it and treat it like it has something valuable to say about warnings, about our intuition. We can be tender with ourselves when we're anxious and not push the panic away, maybe even consider letting it stay too, letting it fuel us in ways we hadn't considered it might. We can even begin to understand that when there is anxiety, it's easier to assign our displeasure onto another being, like a dog, and harp on them rather than free float with the general unease of living in a mysterious world. But by consciously inhaling and exhaling, we can regulate our own nervous systems despite unknowns. When we're thinking about our breathing, we're not thinking about everything else, and the stopping of all other worries allows us to recalibrate—because it's not about knowing things will be all right and that we can live through it, it's about feeling that in the body. We get to train ourselves to trust in our ability to face what comes and recover, just like we want our dogs to be able to do.

Though there are plenty of valid reasons to be nervous and our emotions should always be processed, though I'd never propose otherwise, we don't get to take out those feelings *on* our dogs. Bonding requires self-regulation. Not surprisingly, controlling our dogs does not champion self-regulation, as that is an opposing force to its own interest. With dogs, we can either use our voice, body, and energy to modify their behavior because we believe *both of us* deserve to feel safe, or we can use our voice, body, and energy to relieve ourselves of overlooked emotions that desperately demand only *we* feel safe. Our dogs offer us a chance to notice the rise of feelings inside, honor our emotions, and also consider what we want a result to be. What do I want my dog to learn or experience here? What do I want for them, and for myself, and for what is between us? In the moment where we teeter on the edge of rowdiness, if we start to pay attention to the full scope of what we feel and take care of our own needs, we can move forward without being moved by life as if we're pawns on a chessboard. We're not. We are in charge of ourselves. When changes are looming, we get stressed too, and our emotions heighten too. Through building ample pauses, we can protect our dog bonds from getting eclipsed by kneejerk explosions from us that will inevitably impact our connection. We can create a space between what we feel and how we act. That space is resilience, and resilience builds more of that space.

The past does not indicate the future. What is is what's happening now, and not necessarily what we're thinking about. With Ophelia, we moved from Laredo to Boston, to Los Angeles, and back to Austin. In the homes we shared, we raised babies, redecorated, confronted challenges, changed and grew and stayed bonded, together through all of it, whether we were frazzled by life or not. She and I were works in progress and that was a fine thing to be. Because of the relationship we had, Ophelia and I were able to face whatever happened, even though we didn't know how to do everything that came our way and couldn't possibly predict it or ace it all. We didn't know how we would respond to it all. But we knew we loved one another.

Even today, when I sit outside in the dark before sunrise at five in the morning with my dogs, I sense like I believe my dogs sense. Like I know Ophelia did. I sense what may be coming, what may be there, and what may not. It's all happening in the unfurling surprises of vitality, and my brain catches up. There is an immense freedom to it, to my mind being behind my body, to my thoughts trailing after what I take in and feel, with nothing to distract

9. Dog Love Is Planning for the Unpredictable

Mandy was unsure, panicky, and on high alert when she was in a Los Angeles shelter, but eventually learned to trust, rest, and thrive.

me, for the blackness is all around and I must sense from tip to toe, with my nerves, with all of me, what it's like to be inside of not knowing, and fully reside in that not knowing. It can add to our wellness to experience sitting in unknowing and stay there, noticing anxiety coming online to tell us all sorts of stories, some founded in reality, some just the brain running rampant trying to make meaning of it, but almost none of it is within our control. It's how an adopted dog must feel going to a home.

And we breathe through it. And we trust. Whatever unfolds, whatever does not, all we have to do for dogs and for ourselves is love through it by facing substantial uncertainty.

> Heroes make an impact but not for the glory. Just visit a feral cat colony to understand that somebody chooses to dole out nourishment and love in the middle of a dark night for animals they may never touch. Tom Kiesche is among these advocates in the dog world, bringing focused communication and steady relief to complicated dogs across California shelters that most would not imagine interacting with. He insists on structure, he speaks up for those unjustly treated, he lavishes dogs with his time and completely gives them his heart. He offers shelter pets stability and comfort while they're on Earth, regardless of what outcome may befall them. Many people say, "That's so sad, somebody should do something!" Few realize they are that someone, and they can do it. Tom does.

Chapter 9 Exercises

For your first assignment, take a field trip and pack a journal. I want you to visit a dog park *without* your dog. (I'm mostly not a fan of dog parks. They are rife with people who don't pay attention to their dogs or know the signs that forecast an advancing altercation on the horizon. If you do go to a park with your dog, as long as your dog is spayed/neutered and enjoys it, I urge you to consider going during off hours when there are often fewer people and dogs at the park.) For this activity, just watch dogs interact. Notice the communication and cooperation present during canine play—one dog is on top, then the other, they chase, roll, take a break, flop and switch around. Notice how unpredictable it is, how wild abandon vibrates with unknowns and with enthusiasm. Watch how one dog or many give messages with their bodies, how they look away, shake out, sniff, or move, following their own path as things develop moment to moment. See surprises lead to splendor.

Grab the journal and think about your dog growing, how you are growing alongside him. Think about what is changing. How could you help your dog acclimate to these changes? Letting go of the frequency of the past allows us to facilitate a new future full of possibilities. Jotting down our thoughts helps us process feelings so they don't get stuck. Writing allows us to remove some of the cognitive bias we tend to taint our memories with when we just remember. Continue to reflect on your dog but also glance at the dogs in the park as you hang out under the sky. See what connections arise. What comes out on the page could be data that might help illuminate patterns and cut through emotions to offer insight. I have found that it is in nature and in the presence of other dogs in the midst of their thrilling spontaneity that I can most pour my heart out.

Next, shape a human to do something you want them to do with only the help of a clicker. What I mean by that is, have in mind a simple task you want someone to do, such as hit the light switch or fluff a pillow. Do not directly tell them what you want of them, just have them come into the room and reinforce them with a click whenever they get closer to the task you've identified. If it's hitting the light switch, you would click as they walk closer to the light switch, indicating to them to keep going in that direction. Shaping can sort of feel like a game of "Hot or Cold," and involves patience as you wait for the person to offer you more behaviors. Anything that takes them away from the desired outcome (away from the pillows you want fluffed) would be met with no click, no reinforcement. In this way they learn to assess movements toward what you want until eventually the person will do the behavior you envisioned. You can react with a big, celebratory reinforcement of clicks (and claps!). Notice how unpredictable the guesses were along the way.

Notice whether you believed that they would inevitably get there, how you trusted. Then swap and experience what it's like to be that person, to keep exploring and offering and trying. Feel in your body what it's like to meet another's unknown goal. Feel the gratitude that comes up when you're permitted to try, when trial-and-error is baked into the process, and therefore the other person is prepared for you to get it wrong until you get it right.

We teach dogs words, forgetting that talking is not native to them, their style of communication or understanding of the world. This exercise will give you a sense of how your dog lives. With that empathy in mind, you can begin to shape a new behavior in your dog, reinforcing any successive approximations towards what you want in small increments, letting yourself be amused by what the dog offers along the way. Above all, believe that your dog will get it in time. Believe in them. Believe in yourself. Believe that the love between you can outlast whatever life throws your way.

10

Dog Love Is Daily Ego Adjustments

We're consistently prepared to shape for the unexpected. Now, let's respect the dog in our dogs. Many of us want to be seen as having a perfect, pretty pup with no issues. Yet every dog has strengths and weaknesses, just like every person does. So what if the area your dog needs to work on, they need to work on with you? What if the dog we adopted encompasses the exact dosage of difficulty that our transformation calls for? What if they bring with them the exact brand of love that's required for us to evolve? What if that must be the case, for why else would you be so infuriatingly triggered by your dog's behavior?

People can get very caught up in the superficial façade of having a dog and what that dog might say about them. When we look at animals as things, when they are acquired to fulfill our own interests, we are unconsciously or deliberately using them. But breed doesn't matter for many reasons, not least because dogs are not things and thus they will never fit the ideal fantasy about what they can do for our lives or our status. They are wildcards, each and every one of them. To boot, status seeking is, in and of itself, a lost cause because in the wanting of it we are moved further away from it. So if breed does not matter, what does? The bond.

Bonding is irrelevant to who we believe we have to be in the world, in our family, or at a job. Bonding is releasing what our dogs appear like *out there* so we do not miss the best part of them, which is what dogs do to us *in here*. What dogs gift us circumvents pedigree, papers, and presentation. It has nothing to do with the right fur color or weight. In this chapter, I share the indescribable unshackling that comes from renouncing external ideals that are arbitrarily decided as markers for goodness.

What makes us want what we want? Are we addicted to wanting? Could it be that our very own wants limit us, limit what could be possible, limit the unconditional love available to us, and all we have to do to heal is merely set those wants down? Could it be that the wants are getting in the way of what is best for us? Could it be that we have bought into the lie that outsourcing our well-being is the only option—to want and get X instead of to find, cultivate, and give to ourselves as we are *now*? To bond with a dog is to see beyond stereotypes, looks, "good girl/good boy" paradigms, and the belief that what is now is wrong. It is to see beyond ego. We must tweak our ego regularly, becoming our own egoic chiropractors, cracking and adjusting the knots, breaking free of the persistent desire to go after the stuff we think will fill us up so we can instead access what really counts and what we really need, which is to love and be loved. Why wait for love? We don't have to. Dog love is always available.

If how a dog appears signifies so much to us, it may say more about our own issues with appearances and validation-seeking than it does about the dog. But that does not stop with a perfect, expensive breed. If how a dog acts represents you, then so does what you wear, what you drive, what you weigh, where you live, and so on—the slippery slope of that is unending. It is an outlook of superficiality that costs not only you but the natural world. Just walk into any animal shelter and you will see that our hangups are paid for by the animals themselves. Our egos cannot be fed so that they become bigger than who we really are. The magical electricity, the consciousness, the aliveness that moves us—none of that requires approval or applause. It just is. And because it is, it is worthy. It is in us, and in animals.

Advocacy, at its finest, is a soul-centric endeavor, and like the soul in its truest form, it goes beyond. Advocacy should not be bordered by what is convenient and what is not, what is "us" and what is "them." What I'm getting at is: There is no other. Human liberation cannot exclude animal liberation. We cannot leave out the many species of sentient beings, including canine, and think it won't impact us and our planet. Everything is energy much more than it is matter (a fact). One day we will look back in horror at the ways we've exploited animals, including dogs. Just as it was once acceptable to mistreat women or kids or other marginalized groups, I am optimistic that one day animal use and abuse will be seen for the disgrace it is.

Sure, I too want things to be easier. I want my dogs to behave. I want people to think I'm an amazing dog mom, woman, professional, writer, person. I want to be awesome. I want to be successful. I want to be important. That's very human of me, all those wants, and I can even love my human. But that's not where I end. It is my job to step around my individuality and its long list of wants in order to access the collective pulse of shared beingness, to be the Me that loves my human, and all creatures. To be the me that wants, and expand into the me that is. Because who is that?

How we live and whatever we do, we affect one another. Dogs, animals, nature—everything is part of a greater picture that is inextricably

Coy side shot of beautiful Ophy in the moment (photograph by Casey Chapman Ross).

connected. So I am worthy because I am. My dog is worthy because he is. No matter what we look like, our size, our age, our purebredness or muttness or DNA results. It's a marvel every time a dog in my home chooses not to hurt me, with those sharp teeth. It's a marvel every time I stop forcing my agenda on an animal's life, with that sharp ego. The responsibility of a pet parent is to be marvelous with a marvelous animal beside us.

"You are enough because you are here," I chant to my dogs. And so I chant it to myself.

Bonding is authentic community.

I have gone to many feminist gatherings where short ribs are served. I've attended humane society fundraisers where the main course is turkey. And I always wonder why and how human beings can be so compartmentalized, so dishonest with ourselves. If we digest another being's despair, taste a life that did not want to die, do we not then metabolize that fear? Or at the very least, don't we then metabolize the ability to disregard it? If we can turn away once, if we practice switching off and deactivating our compassion, it means we know where that switch is. It means we know how. It

10. Dog Love Is Daily Ego Adjustments

means we can avert empathy again because we have the ability, the muscle is in place. If we then habituate this muscle's use, turn off our hearts every time we eat a meal, well, then that muscle is not atrophied at all. It's strong, and our aptitude for switching ourselves off grows stronger. We are only a decision away from being able to apply what we do to animals to other humans.

The truth is that an animal's heartbeat sounds and thumps as loudly as mine does. It is no less valuable just because the meatsuit that houses that heart is made of dog and mine falls under the class of *Homo sapiens*. The eventual domino effect of dog love then is recognizing the intrinsic worth and sovereignty of every breathing being. It can be revolutionary to see animals as enough on their own. It can be revolutionary to see ourselves that way. We are so disconnected from others, the world, and ourselves until an animal happens to us. Dogs are the gateway drug to acknowledging the innate value in every living creature. It can seem way easier to care about dogs who live with us versus some random chicken at a factory we've never seen before. After all, we clean our dog's poop. We might even touch their poop on accident. We must *really* love another living being if it's their poop we're handling! But just like it doesn't actually make a difference if the poop comes from a body that cost five thousand dollars or a shelter dog you're fostering for free, it doesn't really matter if it's a dog or a chicken who pooped. Pooping is an activity performed by living beings. I can't believe I'm making a point about love by talking about poop, but here we are.

Having sympathy for one group of animals and not the other occurs because we've been programmed that way, because society moved us into a stream that normalizes eating one and not another. It is convenient, perhaps tasty, and conditioned behavior. But just like we can counter condition our dogs, we can counter condition ourselves. The many of us who are dog people and animal lovers, we are the prime leaders in this space. We are the first line of defense, the ones who can widen the breadth of kindness and make it cool and popular and possible.

Look, I will admit to you: I'm not a perfect vegan. I don't think that's the point. I think the point is that I am truthful with myself about pain and about love. I think the point is that we open our arms in the animal welfare movement, not tell people they don't belong if they don't do it perfectly, but instead embrace people for choosing to grow their love for animals one day at a time as they walk their own path at their own pace. I think the point is that we try. Every time I try again, I value the connection between me and my dogs, me and a chicken I will never meet, me and me when I look in the mirror, me and you. I care about that more than I care about what society at large thinks of me or doing it the way everybody else is doing it, especially when that way of doing it isn't best for us or our bodies. It's not about being vegan for approval. It's about not hurting others.

At the end of the day, I don't think we can have a sincere discussion about loving animals without relinquishing our concern over what other people might say about us, whether they be meat eaters or other vegans. Similarly, the sacredness of bonding with a dog is contingent upon letting go of other people's opinions, what they think of our dogs and what they think of us because those are our dogs. It is on us pet parents to value connection over aesthetics, the internal over the external, the way we feel and the way our dogs feel over the way others perceive us or the conclusions they draw about us. Because actually what we do may highlight or not highlight what *they* do.

If, for example, your dog charges the backyard fence and howls when other people walk past, could we allow the dog to bark, especially if it's not in the early morning or middle of the night? Barking is a normal dog behavior. Can we let dogs do dog things without minding so much what people think about our dogs or us as they do dog things? Why do other people's thoughts penetrate our own? Why do they cause us to think certain things about ourselves? Why do we give others that right, that authority, that real estate in our minds? Allowing dogs to be dogs (without excusing any harm) takes the heat out of many exchanges and leaves an opening for something else between us and our pets, something new, something more loving. But it can't happen without cherishing the dog and the bond more than whoever is walking by. It can be one of the most profound beacons of wellness a dog gives us, to care less what other people feel about us than we do about the relationships we enjoy. To ask ourselves, *Could this be okay?* What if I don't say or do anything, and just be here?

When we stop farming out our sense of self, or attributing our worth to what others think of us, our lives change. Because when we let go of caring about other people's opinions, we begin to prioritize what *we* think, what *we* feel, and then we can assess what the ones we love truly need from us. We begin to weed out the people in our lives who require us to put them first because that benefits them, and we begin to naturally sync up with people who put themselves first. I am not encouraging you to stop caring about others or to be unkind. But it is not selfish to give precedence to yourself or to spotlight how you feel. As the 12 Steps promote: We cannot give what we don't have. Love yourself so that you can love your dog and animals and people. Love yourself because they cannot love you for you. Letting others determine who you are and who you should be simply doesn't work. And if you need a cheerleader to remind you of this, to empower you to prioritize you, look no further than a dog who is devoted to you.

Meeting others who feel the way we might feel about animals is one of the many rewards dogs give us. Those who understand interconnectedness not just in terms of advocacy but also in terms of liberation, those who do not demand we do it perfectly but rather that we do it humanly and keep going, they stand for what is sustainable and real. Dogs help us find our people, don't they? On walks, at the park, at the shelter, at protests, at vegan restaurants. We build friendships around an elevated view of animals and they prove how connected we truly are. Animals are a great equalizer. Our rescue dogs help us create community, the kind of community we may have been searching for, and definitely the kind that will help shape a more compassionate future for all.

Bonding is discernment.

We need to help animals. But we need to help people in order to help animals. We need to even help people who don't care about animals the way we do. There must be space for everybody wherever they're at, wherever they fall on the spectrum of animal love. We must rely on diplomacy and open heartedness to reach more people because in the end, it's the animals who pay most for human defects of character, including martyrdom and exclusivity. There is nothing wrong with being off-putting, offensive, or defensive if we choose to be, but we must recognize that these traits may not inspire others to hear us, or change how they feel about rescue dogs, or motivate them to join animal welfare causes. We can't reach the "other side" of any aisle if we're not listening or speaking to the other side as our equal. We don't have to agree with them. But once we think we are even a dot better, we shut our hearts and our minds to incorporating another's experience. And if we don't understand an experience, how could we possibly evaluate it?

If we believe in dog love, we have to invest in humans coming around to it little by little, over time on their own time, even if they haven't come around to it at all yet. If we believe in animal welfare, we have to welcome more people into the club so that they can identify with its attributes, so that they can add to the movement even if what they add is different from what we would add. Especially because what they would add is different from what we would add. By making room for them, they may be encouraged to care more. What I'm getting at is this: Inclusivity helps animals. It also helps people—the ones being invited as well as us, the ones expanding our perspectives so that we may cast a wider net of compassion. I wonder if the part of us that ignites when someone treats their dog in a way we don't approve of responds out of fear. Fear in the familiarity, in the recognition that it could be us who act that way, a fear we want to distance ourselves from. We want to be better. But what if we're not? What if we look for all the ways we are the same? How many more animals could we help?

How much better would we feel, daring to be optimistic, daring to see the good in others, and thus ourselves?

• • •

After volunteering at the animal shelter for a few years, my specialty became taking the "Red List dogs" out for a walk. This referred to the dogs who were on the euthanasia list. For reasons I cannot explain, it did not deter me that I knew what was going to happen to them the next day. I could leash them up, bring snacks, and sit under a tree with each dog and just love them. Let them know before they got put to sleep, not through my words but through my active, attentive presence, that they mattered. I don't know why I was able to surrender and pour into them, knowing they were going to die. And yet, I got way more out of it than they did, for I found that facing their last day with them was nothing short of holy. I could stop making it about me. I could make the end a bit more tolerable for them. I could let a moment be a lifetime.

We have no control over who lives or dies at the animal shelter. I believe the animals feel this as a world of terrifying hurt. They hang onto any shred of hope they can, which just might be your face walking by. We should be thoughtful about how we use that face. Sometimes, I think we have to use it to be strong for them, to be honest about what kind of life they'd get outside of the shelter, and to hold space for what's coming, for what might be best for them even if we hate it. In an animal shelter, there are dogs with complex aggression issues or highly sensitive triggers. In my experience, that is the minority. And the truth is, there may be just as many challenging dogs at breeders or puppy mills, the same percentage of tougher-to-go-home cases, but we would never know. Businesses unify around the bottom line, the dollar, and don't share that kind of data. The other truth is that thousands of adaptable, high-threshold dogs who could fit into various environments and families are waiting at animal shelters. I wish to live in a world where each and every living creature gets the resources and time they need to recover and rehabilitate, where we can actually save them all. Because the sad fact is that most "hard dogs" or "long timers" would and do rehabilitate and recover in a home that offers them consistent love, understanding, structure, and patience. But I must accept that most people—especially those who aren't as dog obsessed as I am—don't want to do what is required to bond with those dogs or tailor their lives around them to get them there.

I say this as somebody who rescues the difficult dogs for my own family. I don't regret that. I love them. Giving up on them might feel like an injustice to me, yet it also feels like an injustice to me to generalize the world and expect everybody to be just like me. I cannot condemn people

10. Dog Love Is Daily Ego Adjustments

because they live differently or have requirements other than the ones I have. I cannot judge the circumstances that determine another person's reality, however dissimilar from mine, but which is just as valid. We need to respect other people's bandwidths and embody a spirit of collaboration if we want to make the save-them-all dream come true one day. Because to make it come true, we need more people. Could we love dogs so much that we pivot, adapt, and do what is necessary to embrace *more* people?

This may be a good time to remind you that you don't have to agree with everything I say in this book. Take what you want and leave the rest. Humans will disappoint you, including me. Nobody can pass the unachievable litmus test of somehow being perfect for everyone. My point is that if we make animal rescue impossible, then it will be less possible. It hurts our cause and it hurts the category that is rescue dogs. The animals pay the ultimate price for that. It should be a pleasure to rescue! Because it is! We can make the experience of rescue pleasurable too, and I think if we do, more people will choose to rescue.

None of what I am saying is fair, but it nonetheless *is*. None of it is objective either, which is why I believe we must entertain and accept more opinions and perspectives, not less, and definitely not just our own. Whether a dog ends up lucky enough to find the right forever home or doesn't get the opportunity to make it out alive, whatever a dog's path, assignment, or destiny, I try to do my part, which is whatever it takes to make that dog feel that they have value now, while they are breathing, however it will go for them in the end. I don't get to decide all the endings. But I can make the living moments count.

Dogs today are constantly bombarded with imbalanced energy from too many people, too many cars, too many buildings, from other dogs and other animals, from their own family members who are often so fixated on screens that they're entirely checked out. As dog trainer Sue Sternberg explains, this world is harder than ever for a dog to be in—less room to roam, less freedom to explore, less choices to make, less need to forage, less movement, less of the natural world. Screw the Tempur-Pedic bed or the booties for snow, dogs aren't living the way they were designed to live. So when adopting a dog with issues such as severe resource guarding, aggression, or separation anxiety, all of which come in subjective degrees, I hope people consider seeking outside professional help. It's worth it to try. It can get better! But for the most part, the modern world puts constant strain on dogs. We're asking them to put up with a lot and remain okay. Some can do it. But some can't.

Ultimately, *we cannot take care of this dog the way this dog needs to be taken care of,* is a legitimate reason an adoption doesn't stick. Being incompatible is not a crime. Labeling a dog might be, though, for it makes them seen as "bad" and can rob them of the opportunity to find a better fit.[1] Labeling a dog comes from labeling people. It's the same pool of accusation. If we blame people, they blame the dog. If we blame people, we push them away from rescue. If we blame people, more dogs suffer, languishing in kennels for too long, to the point where being put down is mercy. I'm not saying we should give people a pass for returning a dog because they don't like the patch of grass the dog peed on or because the dog's fur doesn't match the couch or because a dog is not perfect four days after he comes home. But there are dogs whose parameters are so limited, who need five acres of farmland to patrol in order to be all right or an adopter who can commit to making no errors or else it could get dangerous. The other extreme is shaming people for concluding that it won't work after they've tried. There has to be a healthy middle ground that does not give people reasons to run away from rescue dogs and those who advocate for them, but instead keeps them returning to the shelter. We are all flawed and fallible, including you, including me.

Citing irreconcilable differences is responsible pet guardianship, to know when the pairing won't work. That can be a loving act, especially if an adopter has given the dog some time to adjust. It may not make rescuers happy, and it may not result in a long, happy life for the dog. That's one of the saddest facts I struggle to swallow. But if you do what is not good for you because you're prioritizing what's best for the dog, for the sake of the dog, in the end that's not good for the dog either, because dogs don't need the unhealthy energy of pet parents who overextend themselves and disregard their own well-being. These are the hard revelations of not a black and white world, but the in-between gray of real life. It is a blessing to live in that gray. For me, a naturally hardwired black and white person, it's dogs who grant me the wellness of what is in between extremes. Gray is shifting, always shifting, and it keeps me on my toes.

The ego brags about absolutism and exactness. The human in us does not want to change or be in mystery or hold duality. But your soul, your consciousness, the vastness flowing under all those disorganized thoughts, that's the place from where we can cherish dogs, the world, each other and ourselves. That part of us—the Real Us—is nonbinary. It is messy and contradictory, always changing, progressing, and evolving in order to stay in the middle because that's where more beings can be folded in under the tent of love to stay dry and warm. From there you can decide if a dog is your forever dog or if you are incompatible, not one of you right and the other wrong, but both deserving. Maybe you can make sure the dog gets the right fit, which will make you an integral part of the dog's story even if it's not a tale about the two of you. Beyond ego is a land of possibility.

10. Dog Love Is Daily Ego Adjustments

Bonding involves the whole family, including children.

When I was a child, my dogs were there when *I* wanted to play with them. In my mind, they revolved around me because that's what was shown to me. As an adult who has and will again roll out of a moving car like a 007 Bond girl to help a stray dog I've never seen before, let's just say the pendulum has swung. I am bombarded with proof of how we shove dogs into tangential corners and force them to orbit our world, then we get overwhelmed that they orbit our world. We've standardized this and taught it to our children, and the term for it is speciesism—treating members of one species as morally superior or more important than members of another species. It is a form of prejudice, as philosopher Peter Singer put it: "To give preference to the life of a being simply because that being is a member of our species would put us in the same position as racists who give preference to those who are members of their race."[2] Dogs—and all animals—are meant to explore, enjoy, experience, love and be loved, not as a decoration for or an addendum to our lives, not when it suits us only or is useful for us, and not as extended family, but as their own creatures who exist.

If you have kids around, have them frequently play with your dog. Thread the dog into your kids' lives, not just when the kids are bored, but as a regular occurrence to model that dogs are family members. You can start with Hide and Seek, having your children hide somewhere easy to let the dog find them. The kids can gradually make hiding harder once the dog understands the game. And what a big, celebratory reaction your dog will get when she finds your children! There's a bonus here of having your dog practice tracking your kids' scent,[3] which I endorse because I like a family dog to keep tabs on where the children are. Encourage your kids to throw a ball or Frisbee with the dog in the yard and get into your kids' bones the notion that dogs aren't houseplants. They need to be stimulated, appreciated, and engaged with. (Make sure to teach your dog "drop it" and remind the kids to immediately reward a "drop it" by throwing that ball again!) Sometimes we actually need to orbit around our dogs, to center them and revolve around them for all the hours upon hours that they do so for us.

• • •

Although I am a dog fanatic, I have loved dogs who have unintentionally represented for me a human relationship I didn't feel good about. The dog did not volunteer to be such a representative. My brain crossed those wires and decided that yes, yes, this dog stood for the rescue group I fostered for that took advantage of me. Or yes, yes, this dog stood for that friend who ghosted me unless she needed something from me that was canine-related.

A dog can stand in for a husband who is always at work, a husband who loves that dog, and then the dog becomes a symbol for our resentment. People I care about have grown to hate a dog they used to love because their mother-in-law moved into their house and she liked the dog! Moms can suddenly harden to their dogs because they now have children to take care of, and all the responsibilities fall on their shoulders, and they're (justifiably) pissed off about that. The dog becomes one thing too many. I am not judging any of these people; I can relate. But what we project onto a dog (or onto other people) speaks volumes about us, yet very little about the one projected upon. So we need to be honest about the connotations we apply to dogs so we can tease out our demands, our ideas, and our feelings. We need to unpack and uncouple what a dog represents and recognize them as separate entities who have nothing to do with the disappointments or dead ends in our own lives.

My point is: My feelings, your feelings, as valid as they are, they're not a dog's fault. We can choose new meanings and consciously improve what a dog symbolizes. They can be a daily outlet for us to take a walk alone, or that one loving family member who always notices us and our every move.

Dogs are not an outlet for our whims or grievances, for what we wish for or the needs we don't get met. That's not what any living being is here to be, especially not a being as loyal as a dog. The story we might unconsciously put onto a dog can affect our connection with that dog and can affect the quality of their life. Confronting this helps us stop scapegoating our dogs and facilitates bonding. Letting dogs be seen independently from us is a gift for them and for us because it prompts us to be honest and straightforward where we need to, facing off with whom we need to.

I figured out that the kind of mother I wanted to be was the kind who had compassion, who showed her kids how to be of service, and who could shake things off. A mom with a soft, open heart and a bountiful capacity for awareness. Not a mom who secretly harbored resentment about what angered her. Not a mom who felt like a burdened, spinning top and who could not catch her breath so she took that out on the dog. The best way I could do this was to be it, and invite my kids to join me. I continuously ask myself: What would the world look like if more children knew the truth about animals from the start instead of coming to it later in the game? Wouldn't they be able to love with more ease if they didn't have to undo so much? What would it look like if more people practiced patience and tenderness with animals in order to have more patience and tenderness with children? Dogs can help us learn how to give people space and time and understanding. They can help us slow down. They can help us listen. They can help us honor where someone else is as we work *with* them, not against them. Every time I see my dogs as a way to be better at loving, I lay patterns in my brain for the kind of parent I want to be and the kind of modeling I want to offer my kids. My dogs and foster dogs have given me 10,000 hours to get good at doling out love so I can do it for the people in my life too. But the dogs deserve it no less than the humans do.

I am beyond proud of my kids who show up at school bragging about a new senior foster dog we've taken in. I am proud of the ways they help me, whether it be by drawing welcome home pictures for the dog, or getting their crates comfy, clean, and cozy, or helping me walk and feed the dog. Are there extra difficulties that come up, as a mother who is committed to animals? Sure, sometimes. Do I get flustered and stressed? Sure. My husband and kids are not "animal people" or vegans. I know they should not have to pay for my tendency to overcommit myself to animals. It is good for me to be tasked with loving others who think and eat differently than I do, and who keep me rediscovering the gray, keep me balancing family and purpose. It causes me to learn again and again how to hold multiple truths. How to surrender my addictive tendencies. How to be well. How to stay open and available.

Though my family is supportive of me, sometimes they say no to a dog I want to bring into our house. And I respect their voice, their boundaries, and their choice, even though they might not align with mine. It's an obstacle. It's an opportunity. It is a continual mixing of input, of ingredients. My family doesn't have to be me in order to be loved by me. We're not clones, and they take nothing away from me by adding what is theirs. Know who taught me that? A stinky old Pitbull we adopted on Mother's Day.

Bonding with Ophelia and Frito.

I'd worked with dozens of fantastic Pitties at animal shelters, but had never adopted one in our home to be ours, until we fell in love with Frito—a big, old Pitbull who was so kind he broke my heart. He could have lived with a baby bunny. Adopting him was one of the best things I've ever done. Although he looked like a real live Shrek, he was a most beautiful boy. Perhaps no dog bears the weight of what others think of them more than the Pitbull. They are not allowed to have a bad day, a bad mood, or make a single mistake. Even when they defend themselves they have to defend it. But Frito dared me to stop worrying about being "that person" in the neighborhood walking "that dog," to bypass the critical inner voice

The senior Pitbull who converted me into a senior Pitbull lover. Frito was our first big boy, and every senior Pittie we adopt reconnects us to his goodness.

that insisted I fit in or get a leg up. I felt like more me than ever before when I was with him.

Frito taught me about embodiment. About what we plan to do and why we're doing it. About how when you intend toward something, you're already on your way. He clarified my purpose to love animals, to make compromises because of that love, and to make concessions with living while still loving living, which in essence came from no longer abandoning myself or my values. This is slow, quiet, intuitive, responsive work with no manual and no formula. Nobody sees it. It's you with you.

Pitbulls motivate us to advocate for justice because we can't have a fair world while ignoring the plight of animals at the same time. We place unreasonable standards upon Pitbulls, and too many people numb their empathy to them because of their size and strength—size and strength

10. Dog Love Is Daily Ego Adjustments

which bear zero reflection on the good-naturedness they are inherently born with, size and strength that they did not ask for and that they have no idea can be used for nefarious reasons. Only when a human trains a dog what to do with that size and strength would a dog practice misusing it. The terrifying one in that scenario is the human.

Ophelia and Frito got a kick out of each other and coexisted nicely. We moved to Texas with both of them, driving for three days with all of our stuff and two senior dogs folded up like origami amidst it all. Frito was already near the end of his life when he came to us, having been a stray for years, with evidence he bore as scars and scabs across his body. Then he was a tester dog at the shelter, which means he was so good with other dogs that they used him to see how other dogs would do. I actually think Frito's wartiness and stinkiness were a lift to Ophelia's self-confidence as she was aging too, as she was beginning to feel less like my baby and more like a mom to me. For the chance to make peace with giving another being peace as an act of supreme love, I appreciate senior dogs the most. But for the chance to unpack how oppression anywhere is oppression everywhere, I love Pitbulls most. People warned me Frito "could turn," commented on his jaw size, and recoiled in his presence. But not once did he give them the justification.

Seven months after he came to us, he passed away. We can't imagine our home without a senior Pittie in it now because of him, because he took us to the next level of giving to those most in need. You can give money to a rescue group, donate old towels to the animal shelter, send well wishes, or spend your time there, and all of it is necessary and respected. But whether as a family or alone, whenever you can, consider putting your body on the line and sharing some of the gifts you have to offer. Contribute to the wellness of the most vulnerable, at-risk dogs by taking them into your house. Animal shelters are full of Pitbulls. Have you ever asked yourself why that might be? Not because anything is innately wrong with them, but because they tend to be the least cared for, least spayed and neutered, and quickest to be disregarded. So when you can, love a Pitbull and get to know them. Confront your prejudice along with the human desire to hedge, hem, and haw. Nine out of ten Pitties never make it out of the shelter, the majority of which would make for great pets. But they die because they are what they are.

Dogs can be made by bad people or by good people. Dogs who are seen as "bad" before they're even known will have every negative reaction or flaw highlighted by cognitive bias, which is what we call systematic errors in human thinking based on personal perceptions, judgements, memories, or beliefs.[4] That is to say, those dogs never stood a chance. They did not begin at the same starting line as other dogs. They were not regarded with as much leeway. They were not given the same allowances to feel or express the full scope of emotions. For many of these dogs, this is because they were labeled as Pitbulls, not because of how they behaved. Pitbulls are not somehow uniquely worse than other dogs. If you want to live in a world where we don't make blanket statements about groups of people, we can't do it with dog breeds either.

Frito was three times Ophelia's size and strength. And yet he did not dominate her. Community, collectivism, pack mentality—these are inclusive canine modes. *I get my identity within the context of us* is fluid and flexible. It has nothing at all to do with breed, age, aesthetics, or anything outside of compatibility, needs matching up, personalities with a symmetric inclination to each do their part and let others do their part. Dogs don't have cognitive biases with each other. That is a distinctly human problem. I hope this can motivate people involved with dogs to strive to recognize and overcome their own intolerances. Dogs are the true radical activists. They can teach us what revolutionary love really is, and how when we apply it, we don't see othering as possible. We are too busy seeing reasons to bond.

> What Rebecca Corry lacks in size, she makes up for in might. There is nobody as tenacious, passionate, or committed to helping Pitbulls and Pitbull-type dogs as Rebecca. She also happens to be awfully funny, like she'll give you a stomachache because you won't be able to stop laughing. Rebecca straddles the line between fire and inferno. She is not embarrassed to harness flames, to ignite a blaze, if it's in the name of animals. She won't burn the house down, but she will singe away stereotypes, call out wrongdoing, and touch hearts through the power of comedy. Her nonprofit Stand Up For Pits inspires and activates massive change. Rebecca is in the ring till the end so the inherently good can win.

CHAPTER 10 EXERCISES

This exercise asks you to plan out the words you will use to advocate for your dog. Frito taught me that allyship is in what we do and say. For social expectations to mean less than our loved ones, we must prepare how we'll respond in order to protect our bond in the world. So go ahead and write it out. What will you say when someone comments on your dog's strength or his size, his looks, or his breed? What will you do when someone shudders or grimaces or crosses the street to avoid your dog? You do not have to antagonize or instigate fights. You do not have to care so much what they think. But if and when necessary, you get to stand up for

10. Dog Love Is Daily Ego Adjustments

yourself and for your dog. Reflecting ahead of time on what we might need from an encounter, or how we want it to go when other people meet our dog, can help us understand our own wishes and craft responses according to what we're searching for. If we want calm, no incident, chill walks, how can we do our part to ensure they happen to the best of our ability? If we want our dogs to be positive representatives for their breed or mascots for how wonderful pet adoption could be, how will we behave and how have we worked with our dog so they behave a certain way? As we say in the 12 Step rooms, we can "Focus on our side of the street." That is its own form of activism.

Second, reciprocity fosters bonding. If you have a family, consider drafting a contract that states what everybody's role will be in taking care of the dog. And by taking care, I don't just mean of their basic needs, but also of their emotional and mental requirements. Have everybody sign the document and leave it up somewhere central so all parties can refer back to it. You could also create a "Pup Bucks" currency, where every time your kid does something for the family dog, they get a "Pup Buck." Ten Pup Bucks might get them a candy at the store. You get the idea—come up with a reward system that positively reinforces them to think about the dog and be responsible for the dog's well-being. This is a way to teach accountability, and encourage self-starters who may come up with new ways to engage the family dog. If you don't have kids, you might still want to create Pup Bucks for yourself!

11

Dog Love Is Healthy Boundaries

With our egos a little quieter, we might be able to discover how parenting someone human, canine, or otherwise is reparenting ourselves. It's trying to do things better than we might have had them done for us. When there's a dog in your home, you will likely gain some insight into your own functions and dysfunctions because anytime we take care of somebody who depends on us, we get to take a closer look at ourselves and at what we may have inherited or concluded from being parented. This is not a book about blaming parents, nor is it a book about having human kids. This is a book about how connecting with a dog can transform us, largely because—as the dog parents out there might attest—loving pets calls forth in us a longing to establish a happy home for them. And in that pursuit, we bump up against ourselves.

Wanting better for somebody we love can morph into controlling, which enables neediness or being needed. Dogs help people face the roots of codependency because dogs are overly dependent upon humans and will force us to implement boundaries for the sake of our sanity. Sometimes we figure out how to draw lines because the lines are missing. I used to dote on Ophelia constantly. I hesitated to go to a party, to dinner, on tour for my solo show, because what if Ophelia needed me? What if someone broke in and I wasn't there to protect her? I felt overly responsible for everything in her life. It was a long road of being scared to put myself first while being angry that I put myself last. It was a long time doing that because that is what I knew how to do. But what I had going for me as a codependent person with an Ophelia was that I loved her *so much* that I followed her lead. And Ophelia was self-possessed. She was cool. She didn't need me the way I needed her. She didn't want me to need her the way I needed her. What was best for her was for me to know when to back off. My codependency could not penetrate her greatness! It did not stick because *she* didn't allow it. What had been such a big part of me shifted

11. Dog Love Is Healthy Boundaries

with Ophelia, because of Ophelia. I didn't have a healthy sense of self in relation to others before her. Ironically, the reason I discovered one was because I didn't want to tarnish my relationship with her. I didn't want to smother the love we shared. Her love may have been my nourishment, but she showed me how to nourish myself.

Though it is normal to want something back from our connection with dogs, the opposite of codependency isn't independence, where getting our needs met happens 100 percent outside of them and animals can't possibly add to our existence or be significant. Interdependence is the goal, which occurs when both parties healthily depend on each other. In an interdependent connection, two beings are involved in each other's lives without sacrificing themselves completely. On the outside, it might seem like having a pet is a one-sided dynamic when it comes to the actual labor. While it's true that dogs can't provide shelter and food, they offer us a companionship that's tougher to detect, but still requires great effort from them. Emotional support animals exist for a reason. Interdependence implies equal giving. I won't get into a debate about whether or not animals are "equal" to us (I think they are) because regardless of where you stand on that, they have feelings and needs, and their feelings and needs matter. So do yours.

Dogs don't like us due to our opinions, bank accounts, what we wear, or what music we listen to; they like us because of how we treat them. Going into an animal shelter and taking in the harsh smells and earsplitting barks and desperate eyes from behind kennel bars is all you ever have to do to be gifted with unconditional friendship from someone eager to receive you. It may be about the validation rescuing a dog gives you at the beginning, but as you bond with your dog, it will become about the competence it gives you, the feeling you get for being part of a good thing for no other reason than it's a good thing to be part of. And you will look at yourself and respect the reflection staring back at you in the mirror. This swell of love is a feeling you create in yourself on your own, not relying on anybody or anything else for it, and that will mean something. By being in a relationship with a dog where the dog does not *need* you, and you don't *need* the dog, and rather you both *choose* to love each other whether you're in the same room or apart, you can begin to break the chains of codependency.

"What's best for you won't cost you my love," I affirm my dogs. And so I affirm myself.

Bonding with dogs is boundaries.

We realize that if we want to do right by our pets, if we want well-balanced dogs, we must create boundaries because boundaries *are* love. London and McConnell prove this point when they say, "Be a calm and confident leader, projecting a sense of benevolent power. You can do that by setting boundaries for your dogs without intimidating them, and by loving them without spoiling them."[1] They go on to describe, "Giving your dog what they want all the time does not necessarily make them happy. What they want in the short term is not always what is best for them in the long term, so love your dogs enough to resist giving in to them every time they look at you longingly."[2] Caving in or being too lenient tends to be a sign that we want to be liked, to be validated. But that's not a dog's role. Liking and validating ourselves is our own duty. By putting it on the dog, we fail to grant them balance and wellness. Overindulgence contributes to creating self-centered, neurotic, strong-willed, or clingy dogs.

If you don't know how to set boundaries or how to approve of your own self, there is something to acting as if. As if you are a benevolent leader. As if you love yourself. How would that dog parent, that person, act today? As if it—because acting as if can move from pretend to real over time. Saying yes to our dogs all the time can produce dogs who act like tyrannical opportunists. When dogs don't use their own skills, they don't get the opportunity to feel a lift in self-esteem or to appreciate us, things that in turn motivate us to appreciate them. It's not a favor to ask for nothing from them. We often coo over our dogs for doing nothing other than … being alive. (They're so cute!) But what's the incentive for our affection? If we don't want to have to resort to threats and bribes in order to be heard, I'm not suggesting that we withhold our love, but that we dole it out appropriately. Perhaps we keep *yes* as something special, which means we also need to know how to say *no*. *No* can be kind. *No* can be an invitation to try something else because it's safe to be clever and a new behavior may result in praise. *No* can be a request for curiosity because our dogs trust that we don't punish in this house. *No* does not have to be a power move. Our pets give us a blank slate on which to reconstruct the idea of family and create our own, so if *no* has never been an assuring message from someone who loves you, it can be now. Our dogs give us a chance to practice a sympathetic *no* along with a *yes* that retains value.

Bonding with dogs forces us to recognize that saying yes to them all the time and not knowing how to say no is a way to dodge our own discomfort while preventing them from building their own tolerance. We see the fallout of that when the dog's inclinations skyrocket, whether toward anxiety (Someone new is coming over!!) or aggression (*Someone new is coming over#$*?*) or withdrawal (someone new is coming over…). They will take advantage of us, nudge our hands with their snouts demanding to be petted, go into a frenzy when we're apart, or follow us everywhere, even to the bathroom. Those are just a few common examples I've experienced

11. Dog Love Is Healthy Boundaries

Eric being amazing to Ophelia and Feebe.

with dogs who lack boundaries in their lives. We cannot rob our dogs of the ability to cope, to learn patience and self-soothing, not if we want well-adjusted pets. Not if we want to be well-adjusted people. This might require curbing some of our own behaviors so that our dogs don't develop an overdependency on us.

Implementing boundaries gets dogs right in the mind because boundaries turn out to be pretty significant for mental health, theirs and ours. Boundaries make life more sustainable. We become benevolent leaders by stepping into the type of love where there is an *us* but also a *me* and a *you*. Or as writer and poet Kahlil Gibran put it so beautifully, "Let there be spaces in your togetherness."[3] That space is not only a testament to love, it *is* love.

• • •

I love my dogs and foster dogs a lot. Like a lot *lot*. I love how I never have to sell myself out for a dog's affection or perform to earn their approval. I just have to be decent and show up. Yet codependency is a subtle merging, and without awareness of it, it can overshadow love itself. Even being guarded by a dog can unhealthily, confusingly become flattering when we are unaware of codependency. However, what makes a good leader, dog trainer, or pet parent is someone who is aware. Someone who can regulate their own feelings and handle their own needs. Defining ourselves apart from our dogs affords dogs a sense of equilibrium, and nurtures it in ourselves too, striking the sort of dynamic where we both get to express ourselves because we know that feelings are meant to move. Emotions pass if we allow them to. We don't have to squash each other's autonomy to feel safe. We don't have to get absorbed by the one we love. When we are provided with a nonjudgmental space to fully feel in the presence of another, we are afforded with co-regulation, something dogs just might do better than any person out there. Co-regulation builds trust inside of us.

If a dog is upset or bears a sad backstory and it feels like their hurt has jumped off their body and merged into your body, untangling from their stress and story may be your work to do. Shelter dogs, stray dogs, neglected dogs, dare I say all dogs, they don't need our pity. They need our stability. They need a sense of security. Codependency may be an impossible paradigm for dogs to break out of on their own. We must do it with them, for them, as well as for ourselves. We create the container for a shared wellness.

Shelter dogs are often dysregulated by the unnatural realities of the shelter itself. It's too much to ask them to regulate us. They need help regulating themselves so they can get out of the shelter and get on with a good life. When we overly depend on dogs or excuse them or coddle them, we tend to implement less boundaries and exacerbate more intense behaviors from them. We must ask ourselves if we are hiding behind a dog's behavior or the litany of issues a dog presents in order to get out of showing up where we don't want to show up or changing where we don't want to change. We must ask ourselves if we expect dogs to emotionally tend to us, or if we're tending to ourselves and each other mutually, in synchronicity, healthily. If we don't have boundaries with dogs, we probably don't have boundaries with people. Letting ourselves be taken advantage of signals our insignificance. We may even use a dog and their challenges as an excuse to say no to people because we don't know how else to say no, how to be significant to ourselves. When we dodge acting upon a sense of self-worth, we don't improve what is being avoided. We don't improve something in us, for us. We don't improve something for our dogs.

We must ask ourselves if the magnitude of a dog's adoration feels good to us. If a dog you barely know is overly affectionate with you, that can be a sign of insecurity or imbalance.[4] It may seem sweet in the moment, but rest assured that if there isn't an earned bond built on shared joy, then the dog might be unable to read cues or regulate their excitement, or may even be treating you like their property. None of this is something you want to encourage. Resource guarding can be especially challenging because it is the tendency to protect a possession—food, a bone, a bed, an area, the

11. Dog Love Is Healthy Boundaries

dog's own body or a person—as if this thing is solely theirs, and as if it is being threatened even when it's not.[5] A dog's response when they resource guard can range from mild (scarfing food) to dangerous (biting without warning). The aggression can be directed at other dogs or humans. All creatures resource guard to some extent, including people; we guard our homes, our children. Resource guarding is *not* a hallmark of a rotten dog. There is a level of normalcy to defending what we love, and competitiveness is natural. As James O'Heare puts it: "Object guarding is easy to understand. Using aggressive behaviors in order to avoid having a valued object removed is common, and adaptive."[6] It's a behavior learned through experiences that works to protect a coveted asset.

However, when the behaviors get extreme or excessive or worsen, resource guarding can become risky. The reality is that it's often a management issue. We cannot "cure" it. We cannot make it disappear. But we can teach a dog that scarcity is an illusion, that there is more than enough. We can resolve it not through forcing lessons, but through changing contingencies and bonding with established boundaries. This may improve a resource guarding dog's tendencies and curb the heightened levels of instability or insecurity that drive it. And we get to hold the energy of abundance. We get to let go of a scarcity mindset.

In order to implement boundaries, though, we have to first become aware of ourselves, of our dogs, and of where we lack demarcations, not so we can feel guilty but so we can adapt. Every dog and person benefits from their own unique set of parameters, which should be based on how long the two of you have been together and whether you're ready to make some concessions. The questions become: Can we let dogs be who they are, be where they're at, with their distinctive thresholds, triggers, level of sociability, and sensitivities which might evolve? Can we let ourselves be who we are too? Can we kindly yet firmly implement boundaries based on what's best for everybody now, instead of needing anybody to be different, or to be all right in order for us to feel all right? Do we need our dogs to need us to be all right? Asking these questions is bonding. Restrictions are not a bad thing. Setting up systems that support care for ourselves and others at the same time, that let us and our dogs feel good simultaneously, does not make us love the dogs any less. We're not better pet lovers if we are victims or martyrs. But being in balance likely makes us better pet parents. Balance requires us to be able to stomach their discomfort instead of taking it on for them, to respond with a *no* when it's warranted, and to hold our boundaries if they're ultimately in the dog's best interest and also our own.

Before I basically dog poop all over codependency, I want to point out that codependency can produce some good qualities too: The ability to care deeply, to tune into what another needs and to offer it, by god, to provide it. Empathy is brilliant. I never want to lose that part of me, and I'd never promote that anybody care less. I'd also be remiss to leave out that there are people who are codependent but it doesn't bother them and so in their case it may not be an issue. Yet for those of us who knowingly or unknowingly need dogs to need us in order to get that hit of okayness from being needed, we may benefit from considering that it actually does not help the dog, as hard as it might be to own that fact.

Bonding creates secure attachment.

We are superstars to our animals. For those of us who've felt broken and ignored, it's dogs who give us the chance to feel truly celebrated. It's dogs who give us the chance to be in the type of relationships we may have always dreamed of. It's dogs we can sink into if we've felt unseen or unsafe. And it's dogs who highlight the insecure attachments that may have dictated our lives.

Attachment theory is a psychological term first coined by psychoanalyst John Bowlby, and refers to the idea that infants instinctively need to develop a close relationship with at least one primary caregiver.[7] We know it doesn't have to be the mother and that the results from attachment or lack thereof during infancy aren't a fixed fate. Yet according to this theory, the behaviors babies exhibit when they are separated from a caregiver, like crying, screaming, and clinging, and the reactions babies meet in response to those behaviors, become established patterns which shape, form, and maintain future relationships into adulthood.

People generally fall into one of these categories: Securely attached infants act distressed when they are separated, but search for comfort and easily adjust when their caregiver returns. The anxious-resistant attachment style describes those who are highly distressed when parting and seem angry, almost as if they're trying to punish their parents upon return. Those who are classified as avoidant react with minimal stress when parents leave as well as when they come back. And lastly, though not part of Bowlby's original list, the disorganized-disoriented lot describes children whose responses are unpredictable.

Unsurprisingly, infants who receive ample and consistent amounts of support and love supposedly grow up to behave like more secure people than those who experience inconsistency or negligence. I am not a therapist and this is a more complex, noteworthy, and debatable theory than what I am summarizing and oversimplifying here. But what's important to me is that many people have felt like they didn't belong in their families of origin or their neighborhoods or their friendship circles. For those of

11. Dog Love Is Healthy Boundaries

us who have felt like outcasts, it is often dogs who give us an opportunity to securely attach, whether or not we got that feeling as babies, whether or not that even matters. Each of us loves the way we love and needs to be loved the way we need to be loved. Sometimes those things don't match up with who we're born into or with the people we meet in life. But we get to pick our dogs, and form a bond step by step. And through bonding, we can create an interdependent, healthy love with someone at last.

Carrying the emotions of others, trying to please somebody, trying to save everybody, fearing that love could be taken away from us—codependency doesn't mean we don't feel the chain around our necks or know that this way of living is not good for us. It means that somewhere inside of us we believe we can't do a damn thing about it. Codependency is a cycle of need. The sense of reward or identity we get from relying on or being relied upon motivates us to put others before ourselves. Codependency can show up as control-seeking, intense fear of abandonment, the misbelief that love is earned, and various other toxic presentations, in our relationships with dogs just as it does in relationships with people.[8] I can't speak much to codependency on a human-to-human level, although there are great books out there that can. But I can speak to what this looks like with pets, and how to release these patterns for a dog's sake as well as for our own. Because what hurts deeply is to come to dogs with codependency and dilute the love, when instead we can heal some of our codependency along with dogs, thanks to dogs.

Case in point: Whenever I reached out to connect with Ophelia, she was there to reciprocate. But she never pushed me to forget myself, never shoved her guilt onto me, never tried to hold on tighter when I walked out the door, never manipulated me. She accepted my coming and going, was fine when I wasn't there and rejoiced with composure when I returned. We could have been together or apart, but the love remained. Sometimes I didn't even care if I was left out of an event, if I was close to my friends, if I had any. Because I had Ophelia. I had Ophelia, and she was everything, and everybody else was missing out on what an Ophelia could mean. This got me through a lot, even though it kept me hovering on the edges of codependency.

Learning how to love without codependency was not something I set out to do, wanted to do, or even thought about doing. It's Ophelia who made it happen, who gave me the chance to see how adjusting is a marker of resilience, how transforming myself to grow with her was a gorgeous thing, but how bending past the border of my well-being was not okay, not even if I did it for her. She drew boundaries against me! She needed time and space away from me! Avoidance disguised as need disguised as fear was not a way to live. She wanted more for herself and for me. Secure attachment is not just snuggling on the couch, although that might be part of the repertoire for recovering from unhealthy relationships. Secure attachment involves trust and gentleness and *willingness*. Willingness to contribute to a dog's life and let them contribute to ours, but to do so while surrendering the inclination to be defined solely by them or train them to constantly need us. Willingness

Seventeen-year-old Ophelia a few days before she died. Pink sweater, soulful eyes ... now I know what my heart would look like outside of my body.

is the seed of love. Willingness stems from security. Security is born out of willingness. If we're willing, the bonding process will feel synchronistic. Can there be willingness without reflection? Can there be secure attachment without reflection? Can there be willingness without sacrifice? Can there be contrary action without sacrifice? Perhaps the hardships we face with a dog generate the sacrifices, and living through the discomfort those sacrifices bring propels the willingness.

The duty we have to dogs for how their love improves the landscape of our souls, is that we humans—with our big, brimming lives, who get to have careers and go to the grocery store and see family and friends and do Pilates and go to bars and museums—we must remember that our dogs only have us and what we provide for them. So, what do we provide for them? Do we provide them with opportunities to feel who they are without our influence? Not ignored and bored and neglected, but alive and well without our input? Do we let them have fun separate from us, without habituating them to seek us? Do we encourage them to be balanced—stimulated as well as rested, learning as well as processing?

If we are codependent, our dogs probably will be too.

Bonding with dogs is detachment, too.

Regardless of the nature of our traumas, big or small, regardless of whether we go to therapy, do breathwork, or make art to deal with our wounds, the benefits of adopting a dog are substantial. Our inner and outer worlds collide under the umbrella of dog love because when we experience what it is to care for another being and be cared for by another being, emotional flexibility flourishes, empathy and confidence surge. The feeling of fitting in with someone is valid, and it builds new pathways in our brain, thanks in part to the release of oxytocin.[9] We coexist with a dog, share experiences, speak to each other, and hear each other without relying on words.

As we act like decent people (especially when nobody is looking) to make our dogs happy, it becomes hard to feel crappy about ourselves. Life can be pretty spectacular when you have a dog in it, when you're being adored, when that adoration transports you closer to adoring yourself for how you act toward this dog. For the people like me who want to plan what's coming, who want guarantees, when we bond with a dog we recognize that we can be less afraid of the unknown. Though we may have been scared before, we found our dog, which means we can't predict life and some of it might turn out to be tough, but plenty of it will be amazing.

It can be difficult to loosen the grip on certainty, on the deck of cards we've been given, even if we're unhappy, even if it's a mirage that we're holding onto these cards in the first place. But the idea of a reshuffle can be petrifying. Reshuffling means knowing less, doesn't it? Will the new hand deliver what we want? Will it take away something? Will we be taken care of? By going through the bonding process, we will be able to answer with this: We met our dog, we reshuffled, and we came out better because of it. Bonding could be one of the best decisions we ever make, precisely because we couldn't predict how it would go. Therefore, though our dogs might trigger us, exasperate us, and push us to the brink, they also help us detach from how it has to be or how things have to go. They show us that there can be expansion on the other side of circumstances, no matter how strenuous or sorrowful or uncertain.

Besides, rescue dogs get their decks shuffled and sometimes reshuffled repeatedly, yet keep playing their hand. We can learn from being in relationships with them that braving life and love is a mark of wisdom. Now, I'm not keen on guilting or pressuring people to keep a stiff upper lip and tough it out with a dog even if they're suffering. But I would suggest bonding no matter what, courageously leaning into and not running away from complicated feelings. Sadly, sometimes a dog and a family are not a good fit. I cannot refute that, as much as I dislike it. But if animal shelters functioned as places for pets to come when it truly wasn't a match, I don't think we would be euthanizing thousands of dogs a month. Only humans have the capacity to dig down deep inside ourselves and discern when we are giving up, and when what we have to offer the dog and what the dog has to offer us do not align. Either way, less dogs need to be bred if we take the time to assess honestly, if we value life over profit. If we want a culture that prioritizes people over profit, we have to *be that culture*, each of us, and not just demand it as a nice talking point from politicians. I know of no better way to start than by extending this theory into practice for animals, for dogs.

Whether a dog is the right match or needs to be rehomed, whether things have to be tightly supervised and managed for a dog to live in our house or we find ourselves traveling with a dog across the country with ease, every rescue dog can give us the opportunity to healthily attach to them yet also to healthily detach from how everything plays out. And they do both simultaneously. What a glorious affront to our relentless struggle for control! Shifting our relationship to control and the way we think about control is one of the Big Jobs we have. Dogs are my model as to how. Because we don't control dogs or what happens to them or even to ourselves. But we *do* control the decision to enjoy dogs and our own lives, nonetheless. As we detach from trying to manipulate and maneuver, we stop trying to control people, places, and animals. We stop trying to force things to go the way we

11. Dog Love Is Healthy Boundaries

want and having tantrums when they don't. We get to securely attach while detaching from results. We get to meet life as it unfolds. We get to go with the flow, get to roll with things, and get to love and be loved the way we were designed to. This is how we stumble into secure attachment as we bond with a dog for however long we get the pleasure of their company.

I say all of this as if I hit some switch and it was easy for me ever since. But not even Ophelia's love could block the resurgence of my inclinations to fix, manage, and conduct others once JillieBean, a Cattle Dog–Australian Shepherd mix foster dog with separation anxiety and darting eyes, scurried through our doors. Unless I tolerated JillieBean's distress, unpacked my own control issues, and treated her as an individual with specific needs, we were fated to be in a jail of our own making. JillieBean's chance to get adopted hinged upon me facing my codependency in a deeper way. What Ophelia had taught me about love was put to the test.

JillieBean and me working on tuning into wellness, together.

Bonding with Ophelia and JillieBean.

When JillieBean came into my life, I was not conscious of the fact that I over-sympathized with her shelter story. I was not aware that I'd enable her neediness or that I would get hooked on being needed by her. I was on a path for "She was a wonderful woman who lived for dogs" to be said at my funeral, which would be totally fine if it was all I wanted, but not okay if it was an unconscious habit for me to give at the expense of myself. It was not okay if this was just another addiction having its way with me.

JillieBean would herd my children and husband away to block them from me. She'd howl when I would leave the room even just to pee. She associated the relief of anxiety with me and only me, and would have a barking–panting–shaking fit when we were separated for more than ten minutes. I fretted about her being unhappy and about the neighbors hating me because of the noise, so I made myself an overly available Band-Aid for her anguish. It took a while for me to see that JillieBean had to detox from needing me and I had to detox from preventing her distress (aka being flattered by her needing me). I had to tolerate her unhappiness and dislike of me, as well as the neighbor's, but mostly my own. The alternative would have been that I could never leave JillieBean's side. Not only would this have reinforced both of our anxieties, it would've made her adoption, along with my wellness, impossible. No shame to anybody who may relate to this. I feel for you if you're trapped in this prison.

It is human to become consumed with another's well-being instead of living in response to your own. It has become normalized to meld with another until you don't know where you end and someone else begins. But luckily, dogs shine a light on that, often by acting like punks. Matching JillieBean's keyed-up mood with my own keyed-up mood exacerbated her nervousness. One morning, Ophelia stared me down and in the quiet of a new day it dawned on me that JillieBean didn't need me to run home to make sure she was okay or cancel plans to keep her from freaking out. She needed what I needed: neutrality and serenity. What Ophelia's love gave me every morning.

Furthermore, it wasn't JillieBean's job to give me what I really craved, which was my own sense of center and my own sense of alignment, not only by being of service to others or doing anything outside of me, but by taking care of myself. We all have an internal purpose to love ourselves. I had to do right by JillieBean, by the rescue group I was fostering for, by my family, and by me, the one who had to treat herself so well that she could then dole that rightness feeling out to others. I had to relinquish how JillieBean's clinginess served me, how her being delirious gave me the justified reason I'd been looking for to say no to other people as if it wasn't

11. Dog Love Is Healthy Boundaries

good enough just to say it for myself, how when JillieBean controlled others' access to me, I felt secretly complimented, even if her eyes were crazy as she did it. The price I paid for her and me to have a healthy relationship was the pain of those realizations, how I'd been hiding my fears and insecurities underneath her dependency. It was easier for me to fill myself up with others than with myself. But now I needed to cultivate the willingness to be with myself again.

Ophelia had been the beginning of my excavation, pointing me to my strength and my own inner sanctuary so that years later I could be here, preparing JillieBean for a life that was real, that included all the shades and emotions that we all come to Earth to experience. It was horrendous and exhilarating to draw boundaries, meet JillieBean where she was on her unique journey, and allow for more time separate from her, not less.

It was Kongs, bully sticks, and food puzzles in the crate so that solo time was fun for her, because enrichment proved as essential for her as was time away from me. It was a lot of letting her just be without my involvement or catering. It was me focusing on myself and not "using" a dog to circumvent whatever I didn't want to think, say, do, or feel by obsessing over a dog. All those ways I felt inadequate had to be faced. All those low-self-esteem thoughts had to be acknowledged. I had to be with what was present instead of distracting myself with a new foster dog, and not get so busy with that new foster, not myopically focus on the dog so that I could hear how hesitant I was to change or to dare or to upset others in order to honor myself. I had to feel myself.

Love that is marked by healthy activities challenges codependency. It allows us and our dependents to earn valuable things, find solutions, and discover relief within themselves, not by relying on us. Of course I totally wanted to love JillieBean to pieces, for her to sleep in bed with me, Netflix on the couch with me, to treat her exactly like my Ophelia. But she was not Ophelia and could not handle Ophelia's life. I didn't even know if that life would ever be best for her. JillieBean's anxiety forced me to ask myself time and time again: *Is this for her or is it for me?* I had to let things be "unequal" without turning that into "unfair." Karen B. London and Patricia B. McConnell put it as such: "It may seem counterintuitive, but one way to create a harmonious pack is to give up on the idea of equality."[10] Because if everyone gets preferred access, nobody does. If the various thresholds and personalities aren't considered when offering privileges and setting up structures, then we are not taking our dogs into account. We're assuming they're all the same and would all benefit from the same—which is both untrue and risky. It requires them to figure out an order for themselves. It means we're dodging honesty for our own comfort.

I trusted that boundaries would work for JillieBean and began to look for that evidence. Her behavior followed. We followed each other, as she began to really decompress. We found the right life *for her* day by day. Dog love is an active and animate force. With space apart from JillieBean, I felt into the discomfort of not knowing who I was when I wasn't interpreting others' thoughts of me or making somebody else's opinions a personal reflection of me. I had to figure out who I was when I was not "the dog lady." Time and time again, dog love has offered me the specific touchpoints I've needed in order to address my own healing. I am thankful to Ophelia and all my fosters for that, but also to therapists, hypnotherapists, healers, and 12 Step meetings so I could unpack why fixating on others was a drug to me. Preoccupation had felt safe, as did clinging and over-attaching, worrying about them not having to deal with me. And so my medicine was to craft my own identity, to focus on my side of the street, to find a sense of reward through healthy behaviors, and to embrace all of myself.

Within two weeks JillieBean had untethered from me, her mind was more tranquil, and she was a different dog, despite the resistance that had been in both of us initially. That is the thing I appreciate most about taking in shelter dogs: No matter how much I know, I always learn something new from each one of them. Even though dogs teach us so much, it's the humans who have the mental ability to recognize what's going on and to envision the progress that can be made for dogs' greater well-being and our own. This makes us responsible for the dynamic and its changes. This is what transforms us into people who are well—that we must answer the call.

Life with a dog will entail the pulling in close and the space between times together. We will have lives separate from our pets, and how they react to that will reveal a lot, mostly because we will be the ones reinforcing those reactions. So animals inadvertently guide us to a co-regulating, restorative type of love, a lifestyle that is counteractive to being codependent, a *this is good for you and this is good for me* feeling that yields more peace. Because of JillieBean, I came face to face with my desire to lose myself in others. I inspected it, dissected it, and ultimately unraveled its grip (for now). Because of her, I am at least not blindly placing these same habits squarely on the shoulders of my children. Together, JillieBean and I assembled interdependence into something sturdy.

If it takes months of boundary-setting and bonding for you and a dog to hit your stride, it's not the result at the end of the months that makes it all worthwhile. It's those months that transmute you. It's moment-to-moment work, the hundreds of interactions you walk through in a day. The prize is the cumulation of time and togetherness, like when

11. Dog Love Is Healthy Boundaries

every member of an orchestra plays their instrument and they practice and sweat and toil and then—bam!—they make music. It's not just a song, it's all the rehearsals and sessions coming out together, at once, in harmony, in symphony.

If a person is sleepwalking through their existence while everyone around them cheers them on to stay asleep and exploits them for choosing others over themselves, then I hope that person will rescue a dog so they can be loved into wakeful balance. What would the world look like if we were all taught to care with inner stability? What would the world look like if we did not confuse need with love? What would the world look like if we were encouraged to maintain a sense of compassion for others as well as a feeling of sticking with ourselves? What would the world look like if we weren't tricked into thinking making others happy was all we needed for us to be happy? Staying connected to our feelings healthfully shows our dependents how to manage their own. It requires us to allow trying things, falling, learning, failing, and processing, and it requires our loved ones to figure out the same. We cannot do it for them. We must lay down the notion of anybody being taking advantage of, including ourselves. It begins in ourselves.

JillieBean found an incredible forever home. Ophelia and I sent her off feeling good about how ready she was. Ironically, dogs are the most reliable creatures to depend on as they help us mitigate our codependent ways. It might be a lifelong exploration for me, but I'm humbled that there will always be another rescue dog to travel with and that Ophelia will forever be the foundation of my recovery. People ask me constantly: How do you pick such good dogs? I think it can be boiled down to this: I love them, and they help me love me.

Thus, every dog I pick is good.

> It takes a unique brain to come up with names like Sweatpants, GinnFizz, and Slick Rick for rescue dogs. Someone not terribly earnest, who can see into a dog's eyes all the way down to the specifics of their soul. Hillary Rosen is smart and strategic and funny. She shares apples with her dogs. Her organization, A Purposeful Rescue, takes in the seniors, the hurt, the sick, the magical unicorns as she calls them who nobody else picks from all the rest. Then Hillary endows them with oddly perfect names and attracts top-notch fosters and adopters, so it's just a high caliber of care all the way through. What I appreciate most about Hillary is her humble grit, the devout sincerity with which she relates to dogs and fiercely treasures them.

Chapter 11 Exercises

We can't trust our dogs if we don't trust ourselves or if we become so overpowered with guilt whenever we assert ourselves that we'd rather not speak up. Take a moment to consider the ways you may not be honoring your own boundaries. How is the story you're telling yourself serving you (even if it actually holds you back)? Are you willing to let go? Are you willing to explore new meanings you could make? Are you willing to respect your needs and be in relationship with yourself? What would it take? What would have to be set down? What would fill the empty space left behind from surrendering codependent patterns? What would you think about if you weren't thinking of others? Where do you really want to say no? When is a full-body yes alive in you?

Second, bring to mind a situation that aggravates your dog's anxiety. Once you identify it, consider how you might be able to contribute differently to it. For example, if your dog's physical activity were increased before the panic-provoking situation started, would it help? If you offered a mentally stimulating activity to her, such as a lick mat smeared with wet food, would it decrease a dependence on you for relief? (Lick mats are textured silicone mats that invite licking, which is a calming activity for dogs.) Could you desensitize the clues about separating from the dog? With JillieBean, I'd carry my car keys around sporadically and go through the motions of leaving when I was staying. I followed the suggestion laid out by McConnell and London: "Make your 'departure cues' the sign that good things are coming: The trick here is to link the beginning parts of leaving with the toy or the food so that he LOVES it when you pick up your keys."[11]

Shift the scenario and cut the chords that cause you to internalize your dog's feelings. Too much empathy can drain you, drown you, take you down. Love your dog enough to let them feel. Let yourself feel. These are distinct energies. Hopefully, physical and mental activities or a desensitization of clues to your impending absence will allow your dog to have a different experience away from you. Gradually increase the time you're apart. Let it be okay to be apart, just as it is okay to come back together. Both are normal, healthy parts of living and loving.

12

Dog Love Is Saying Goodbye

We won't become both the drug pusher and the drug itself—we don't encourage love addiction in our dogs or ourselves. Love is the outline of our lives. It's as if love is a black Sharpie marker that holds the full picture, delineates the other colors, providing a container for contrast. It is art, and it leads to more art. It does not suffocate beauty.

Despite the fact that we heal dogs and they in turn heal us, canines don't exist for us. Even if we invented domesticated dogs, even if they add so much joy, that's not why they're *alive*. You know where this is going, since we touched upon it in Chapter 10. When a dog is more than a tangential decoration or a purchase symbolic of status, when a dog is not a toy for kids and does not need to perform on command, then a dog is not a thing but a *someone*. It's scary to love everyone like this, with no controls put on it. It means loss is constant and that we're exceptionally vulnerable. I get it if you're mad at me now. Nonetheless, if we look at our dogs as whole, then their lives and the way they relate to the world is significant and should affect us, should be important to us. Animals are unique personalities with individual needs, wants, and opinions, each and every one of them. This does not mean exactly that they are the same as us, but that they deserve happiness as much as we do. That we regard them to be valuable, sentient, irreplaceable beings, strands of the weave that make life a tapestry worth living in.

I was raised Jewish, but consider myself an interspiritualist these days—someone who embraces the shared aspects across a variety of spiritual paths and believes not as much in one religion so much as in one love. I relate to many different faiths and the mystical. I respect the diversity of beliefs. Above all, I uphold the union among all living beings. That being said, there is a word I cherish that's fairly important in Judaism. It is part of a Passover song, the holiday that commemorates when the Jewish people were liberated from slavery in Egypt. The song is called "Dayenu," and we repeat that word over and over again as we sing it. The word translates into: "It would have been enough." As in, *if God had done this for*

Ophelia and me—both of us became both of us (photograph by Casey Chapman Ross).

us ... it would have been enough. But then God did this! Which would have been enough. But then God did this! And on and on it goes. You get the gist. I'm going out on a limb to say that dog love is the walking embodiment of Dayenu. Dogs bypass the line, go right up to the front door of you, don't knock, don't wipe their feet, just barge in with wagging tails and wildness and hope. Their love represents *this could be enough*.

This could be enough, Ophelia said to me in the kindest way I've ever known.

This could be enough, leave everything that isn't love!

This could be enough, life is happening everywhere right now and you get to be part of it!

You don't have to be born into any religion to hear it. You don't have to subscribe to religion or to a certain God. Just listen. Dogs are telling us all the time:

You are enough.
We are enough.
This love is enough.

I believed Ophelia. I believed her so much, and I did not know how I would feel enough without her beside me. There would not be enough anymore without her love in my life.

Dogs want comfort at the end, but they don't seem afraid to die.[1] For us, there can be so much anticipatory fear, so much grief in our never-readiness to say goodbye. Yet even though we are aware that a dog's lifespan is shorter than ours going in, we show up for it anyway. Loss is built into the relationship, and still we love fully, knowing we will have to tackle the devastation that comes when that full love goes away. The entire fucking point of bonding is so that we know how to handle leaving. It's the worst. It's life. It's better with a dog in it.

"You can let go now," I told Ophelia. And so I told myself.

Bonding is being allowed to mourn.

There is often a need to grieve our dogs before they die. With every dog who has lived in our home, I've had to tease out what I expected from the dog, along with my ideals about life with this dog, and fully, truly grieve those expectations. I have had to accept each animal as an individual so that I could fall in love with the reality of them. All of my dogs chose to "be good" and uphold the relationship they had with me and my family through the suggestions and tips, mindsets, and exercises I've laid out in the previous chapters. The core reason I was able to uphold the relationship I had with them, though, was because I'd admitted who I wanted them to be and renounced that fantasy in exchange for who they actually were. What I ended up with was never what I'd envisioned because dogs are real. In allowing myself to mourn my ideas about them and our life together, I could love them. But first, I had to feel all the way through the loss of what I wanted, cooked up in my mind, hoped for, maybe even had before, and wouldn't be getting with this dog, so that I could enjoy what I would be getting with this dog.

Bereavement—not only due to death, but as a part of life—can be an impetus for clarity, for change, and for helping us feel differently about others and ourselves. It can inspire us to identify our values, make choices that align with those values, and catch ourselves whenever we act in contrast to those values. How we handle dying and all the mini deaths that are endings throughout our lives, even if they do not involve the loss of life, can generate deep meaning alongside an aching heart. Grief can result in a great rewriting that is vital to great healing.

I wouldn't have been able to come home to myself without all the dogs who have come before to teach me all of these lessons. And they wouldn't have had the space to impact me if not for Ophelia, the one who altered me, drew me, and painted me so I could live. During her final months, I scurried and scoured in desperate attempts to make sure I wouldn't relapse after she died. I tried to plan ahead, to create cushioning for myself and my sure-to-come fall. I am not able to tell you yet that it's better to have loved and lost her than never to have loved at all because I'd rather Ophelia be here with me. But I am able to tell you that I did not relapse. And I'd argue that the main explanation for why I didn't was because I genuinely mourned. That mourning renewed my spiritual tethers.

Losing a pet is true grief, whether the rest of the world validates it or not. Grief entails not just sadness, but anger, and sudden change, and severing separation, the many ripples of fallout, and so much more. It merits attention. The rest of the world might say dumb shit like "But it's just a dog" or "You can get another one." But you and I know better. You and I understand. We've experienced or will experience the avalanche that is their final chapter. With senior dogs, how their health deteriorates and we run after the snowball of problems for as long as we can until it gets too big and goes too fast, and we can't divert it or delay it or even catch up to it anymore. Alleviating or avoiding the impending conclusion becomes impossible.

As humans, we try to prepare for death, but there is no prepare, there is only acknowledging that love comes with pain, like when you laugh so hard you cry or cry so hard you laugh. A grief like jumping into a pool after a hot tub and back to the pool. Hot and cold, erratic fits of laughter at the memories of them and the silly things they did, and then the breath-stealing longing for them, wishing for them to undie—the feelings come whenever they want to. They have their way with us. When I first started writing this book, Ophelia was still alive. She would sleep on me so I could only type with one hand. Her kidneys were failing, her back legs shook, her hips dragged, she hardly ate, and I would have to battle the urge to force-feed her every day. She subsisted on raw goat milk and the subcutaneous fluids which I administered nightly and which cost a fortune. She was 17 years old. But she was here. It was grueling, it demanded all of me, my entire participation, and I'd do it again. In fact, I miss it. I miss loving her with all that I am. I miss realizing what I am made of.

Yet as frightened as I was of losing my sacred love, every time I was able to recognize it and put aside my fear and sorrow so that I could still enjoy the time we had together in the present, I acted out of extreme love for Ophelia, and out of extreme love for myself. I prioritized what we had over the burden of trying to control what I could not, or to know what I could not know. (When will she go? How? Will I be there? What more can I do?) One breath at a time, I tried to tune in to her one breath at a time. Ophelia snoring now. Ophy's wet nose now. Her body in croissant position now. The depth in her eyes, the regalness, her diva-ness, her availability, what a comedic genius, what presence to her presence, the gravitas, the buffet of emotions and insights! To be enveloped by her love. With a dog, I don't always know when it's the right time, but I believe when we start asking if it's the right time, it's a sign we're nearing the time. If you're asking, it's not now. But that wondering, that clutching of sadness, means an answer is coming.... *Now. Now's the time.*

You'll stop asking. And you'll know. They'll tell you.

• • •

By my nature, I tend to withdraw and withhold. I have a penchant for constriction, for squeezing the tourniquet. But during Ophelia's last months, I began to ask myself why. Why do I need to control? What is left behind in control's wake when I release? A good friend of mine who is a fantastic veterinarian (Hi, Dr. Mike!) told me he'd rather help a dog transition a week too early than a day too late. But I wouldn't sacrifice one minute of time with Ophelia. I could not let the snowball out of my sight. There were times my kids would tell me that they were jealous of me and Ophelia, jealous of our love. My husband would try to comfort me, but I didn't want to feel better, I wanted to feel whatever was there in the moment with her, because it meant being close to her, that her and I were together. It was me and Ophelia till the very end.

After she had a seizure one night while I held her in my arms, Ophy let me know it was time. It felt like hands opening from the tightest grip.

I think we fear the knowing, that the feeling of knowing might kill us. But we can't stop them from dying. Not even me, not even Ophelia. There is no such thing as love without the threat of loss. The grief was heavy, but it showed me how strong I'd become because I could bear it. There has to be room for this part; we have to make room in one another's lives for mourning. For the holiness of mourning. It can't be silly or weird or immature to love an animal and to grieve over their death, not if we want empty shelters, not if we want loved animals who thrive in homes, not if we want peace in this world, not if we want to carry forth love and peace inside of us.

Disenfranchised grief is a term coined by counselor and grief expert Dr. Kenneth J. Doka, used to describe a mourning that isn't commonly recognized, such as when somebody loses a job, gets divorced, has a miscarriage, or says goodbye to a pet.[2] Many of us are still too afraid of grief, of succumbing to it in all its fullness. We might feel too attached until grief happens to us. But sometimes the only thing that can help us live through the rupture of death is not getting what we want but getting support instead. Grief is to be supported, witnessed, handled with care, including when it's over a dog. Especially when it's about a dog. That was somebody's best friend, that was somebody's family, but more than that, that was somebody's constant reflection of self.

Because there is so much talk about fostering dogs in this book, I want to also take a moment to validate the sadness around a dog going from your home into another home. Fostering a dog who gets adopted is an amazing model for loss. It is practice for death. There is a real despondence around having a dog with you and then suddenly not with you. The somatic turmoil in knowing in advance that they won't be around one day, not to mention the shattering gloom over the fear that the dog might feel abandoned by you once they go, may bring up a fear of abandonment in you. The truth is that *this* is the hardest part of fostering. Not bringing them into your house, and all the changes you have to make—the transitions and the training and the adjusting because *holy moly, there's now this new being in my home and I have to manage more relationships and how can such a small body change the whole vibe?* No, that is a piece of cake compared to letting them leave. Because that part—if you're bonding, if you're experiencing the magic of dog love—there's nothing to do for it or about it. It's just sitting in a bathtub of big emotions without any doing. It's breaking and mending going on in your heart, and you being with you as you witness each crack, each repair.

Pet mourning overall, whether due to the reality of a dog not being what you wanted, a death, a foster getting adopted into another home,

12. Dog Love Is Saying Goodbye

or something else entirely, tends to fall under the disenfranchised grief umbrella because society's attitude and empathy about dying rarely extend to animals. "The implication of the concept of disenfranchisement is that the general discourse exerts power over what is regarded as acceptable, normal, and true," professors Lorraine Hedtke and John Winslade write. "Wherever the dividing line falls, some will lie outside of it."[3] So we might cry and worry when a dog goes away, and other people will likely not get that and may not be sympathetic toward it. It may feel like our mourning means less, like we should be embarrassed over the pain we feel, like disempowerment makes sense because how dare we think our anguish over an animal counts. But none of that is valid.

There is no circle of acceptable heartache as if everybody else might fall outside of it if it's different. You may be left with unresolvable questions when a foster goes into their adopted home, just as I am every single time: "Will the dog be loved now? Will they be loved right? Will they be safe? Are they okay?" And you may be forced to confess to your Higher Power and to yourself that you have no sway, that you cannot manage everything that happens to these dogs you care about. And you may likely hate that as much as I do, and twist up against it. And you may have to learn to just be with all of this. And by being with all of this, you will be truly grieving. But you could also be on your way to becoming the most healed, the most well, and most self-loving you you have ever been, because sometimes that is what grief can do.

No matter how long a dog is with me, two weeks or sixteen years, if I am doing the relationship right, this is the unavoidable part. The hurting cannot be mitigated or watered down. It is evidence of the love we're willing to take in and the love we are willing to give back. It speaks to our capacity for growth and our willingness to tolerate all that comes with growing. It is why I often say that recovering addicts are the gems of this world: We know how to bury someone we loved—our old selves. We do not cover up the mourning even though it might be a long funeral. We show up not knowing who will emerge in us afterward. We do it anyway. We have to.

Mourning is a process, it's not a box to check. It's personal and creative and layered, and it happens in relation to others. There must be room for all kinds of, cultures of, shades of, and contexts of grief, from all kinds of sources. "Through all of this, we have held to a belief that the best way through the pain of grief is not to follow a prefabricated model but to craft one's own responses,"[4] Hedtke and Winslade explain.

What if we cope with death in dribs and drabs? What if there is no set time to grieve, and there are no proper grievable parameters? What if we don't "treat" grief because it's a process, not an illness? What if it's important to think about, talk about, write about, and share about what you miss when you think of the one you lost because the memory mixes into the love, and it will serve as a sort of parachute of wellness for the next time you're falling? What if the ones who die become part of the meaning of love itself, and redefine the word, redefine all words? What if it's not about getting over a loss or following a formula, but about curiously exploring the continuation of the relationship somehow, someway, even after they are gone? What if the reward for enduring and for riding the waves of love is a sense that the one you miss in fact never goes away?

Bonding is waiting until you are ready.

Our dogs seem to come from somewhere above. I am certain that the dog you picked, the one you felt that thing with which brought you to them, the dog with those very challenges that produced friction inside you, this exact dog was with you not only because you could face what came up with them, but because you *had to* face what came up with them. Does that sound woo-woo or like too much work? Maybe I am woo-woo and maybe it is a lot of work, but maybe it is also wonderful because the very area where we have to dig down deep is where we find out what we're made of. If you're reading that thinking *No way*, that's fine, but I'd like to invite you to consider for a moment that your dog is part of your destiny. Matched just for you.

Your dog is a spiritual teacher who can reveal to you as much as you reveal to them. Who cares if it's true or

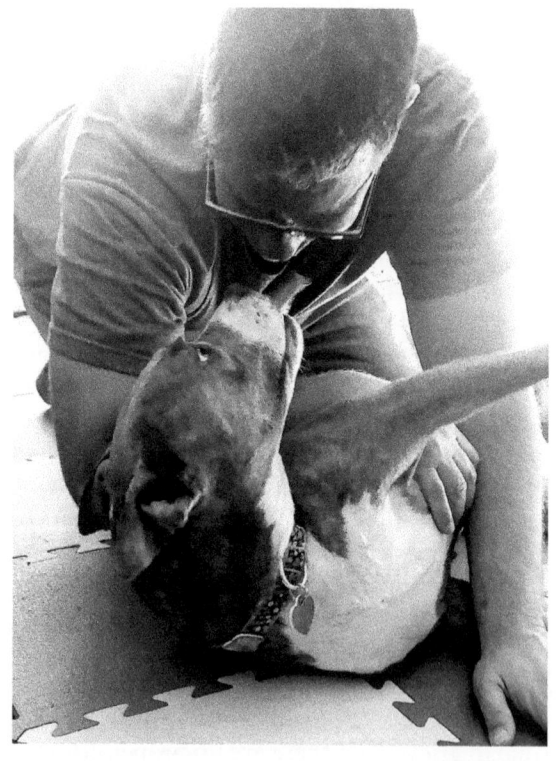

Eric loving up a new foster dog.

12. Dog Love Is Saying Goodbye

untrue, when it could be equally either? The question really is then: Which belief makes you feel better? The dog you have could be the dog that was sent to you, meant to come to you, with their exact triggers because they exactly trigger you. How else can you explain that what triggers you came with that dog right to you? Couldn't they be extensions of Spirit?

It's the most human thing in the world to resist inconveniences even if they come with high-quality love. We people would rather hedge our bets, make it cushy for us, even justify why we don't need that kind of love. Some part of us may even be ahead of us, protecting us, suspecting how we could not survive the love going away. But it's the most canine thing in the world to *not* resist love, to just give it all purely and freely and absolutely. Dog love is the most generous force in the world. It has the power to brainwash us into letting them in, taking them in, and then before we know it, we're sobbing because the dog is dying and we wonder, will we die too? Will this best part of us, the part they've brought forth and made manifest, will it go with them? How can I stay this fantastic after the dog is gone, without them as the touchstone for my fantasticness? Is it strong enough to last without them? Am I strong enough?

It is. You are.

Somehow they die when they know it is possible for us not to lose ourselves, the self they've watched us become, the awesome self they've helped us step into. And then eventually you will feel the space for a new dog to come in exactly as they are, who they are, and the timing will work out. We adopt another dog when we're ready, which is an individual process that merits all the space it requires, all the time it desires. We will miss the dog who has died but here's the thing: We won't need the lessons the dog who passed brought with them, for we won't be the person we were when that dog came into our life anymore. We'll be this new version of us who already knows what they taught us.

So we will need another kind of dog, we will need to start over. We will open our hearts to other dogs and we will want to compare them to the beloved who died, and that's natural. Only we are new now, which means we need new things, we need something else from these tender, completely loving souls in furry bodies. And it will be uncharted ground again, a mysterious path forward again, not one of reflection and contemplation after the fact when you already know it all works out wonderfully, but reflection and contemplation at the beginning, a dedication to making it wonderful along the way, which is a hell of a lot more work that insists on a hell of a lot more effort in order to generate a hell of a lot more progress.

You will continue to miss the one who died. You will continue to miss the you that you were when the one who died was alive. And that missing is essential, it is a crucial burning, it is them coming back to life, however briefly. It is you healing more because you are choosing to stay with the love they gave you as you weep because it was taken away. You want to go back but the love pushes you forward. It is the cycle of life and death happening at the same time, both held in love and made out of love. You and a new rescue dog will begin this new phase of your journey together from this richer, wiser place. Your devotion will persist as you prepare to welcome another level of you.

Bonding with the dog who now lives inside of you.

There is a fading, a dimming, a whispering that happens towards the end of a dog's life that is as potent as life can get because of its proximity to death. The dog is still with you, but you're just watching, waiting, not knowing when the end will come, sensing that you're getting close to it because each day it seems like they are a little less there. During this time, you will feel how much it's not attention in and of itself that is an act of love, but presence directed through attention, how giving somebody a sense of agency that you are there to fully witness is the most meaningful offering. I let Ophelia decide when it was her time, and I listened as deeply as I could to how she wished for it to happen.

Ophelia's death was beautiful. Her death was brutal. Her death swallowed me whole. I'm still lonely without her even when I am with friends and family. How could I not be when she was the one who got me the most? It's as if she and I were on an island no one else could reach. The love felt like it was always just ours, just us. But had I not been Ophelia'ed, I'd be in a pantry or over a toilet bowl instead of with family and friends in the first place.

Through my grief process, I realized that Ophelia's love extends well beyond her body. It's as if before she passed, she successfully set up a channel in my brain. The Ophelia Channel. I hear it when I hang out with myself. And so once again, Ophelia brought me to me. Our island remains because she is now part of what makes me *me*. I feel her again when I love myself.

Dogs are an extension of self. The kind words we say and kind things we do for our dogs, we are saying and doing for ourselves. The loving relationship you really want is with you, and your dog takes you there. You will arrive there, to you, and you'll have your dog to thank for it. You will look in the mirror and see the person that stunning soul-dog adored and adorned. This is not only for some people or some dogs. It's for anyone who chooses to bond with a dog. And I don't want you to miss out.

Because I continue to have my bond with Ophelia, I can share love with others. Dogs are how I get to practice having the relationships I want,

12. Dog Love Is Saying Goodbye

the kind where I don't abandon myself. Dogs are spiritual fellows, teachers, playmates, fitness trainers, soft companions, adventure buddies, and healers, all in one. They are a way in. Some people choose yoga or crystals, but for me it's dog bonding. Maybe it is for you too. And then, if you are blessed enough to love a dog to the very end of their life, their death becomes another gift. Because although our beloveds do not live as long as we do, in the most courageous last act of dying, dogs force us to let go, leaving behind a you who is able to go on and be more intimate in your relationships because they were yours. Maybe that's how dog love can save not only you, but the world: They surrender us to surrender.

And so I invite you to surrender into loving animals as wholly as you can, just give that love away. Much more of it will come back to you. How am I sure? Because on the other side of Ophelia's passing, I take care of other dogs and love them in her name. I am fighting for every Ophelia out there, giving them all I've got, giving it to the people who love the dogs, giving it to you ... and I am satiated, I am satisfied, I am settled. *Dayenu*.

> David Meyer and Abbie Moore are two of the most influential people in my life by doing nothing but being themselves. They are both dedicated to animals in a lofty way, through everything they each do professionally and personally. Abbie and David are wise and witty, and never back down from an opportunity to be heroic. I worked for David and Abbie at Adopt-a-Pet.com, and they taught me that it's not for-profit or nonprofit, it's not environmental sustainability or consumption, it's not either-or. It's and-both. It's using our intelligence, pushing ourselves, and living in accordance with heart-led and brain-fueled values. Abbie and David envision a world where animals are revered, not used to bolster systems that have been designed to benefit humans. They are brave and bold in vision, and enhance my own.

CHAPTER 12 EXERCISES

The final exercise of this book entails thinking about a dog's departure. If you are lucky enough to have a senior dog, then sooner rather than later, this will apply to you. If your dog is not that old yet, or not sick, you may have plenty of time. If your foster dog is getting adopted or your old dog has already passed, this assignment still applies. I'd like for you to request letters from your loved ones (and your dog's loved ones) in which they share and describe what your dog signifies to them. A kind word or two, a line from a poem, a funny story about your dog ... it will mean a lot to you, and I believe it means a lot to the dog. Just gather a collection of love letters about your dog. Keep them on hand should you want to read them to him before a surgery or treatment, when the time comes to say goodbye or you simply yearn to remember them because they've already passed.

It has been my personal experience that having these notes to lean on can help you express what you may not be able to say in the moment. Having these letters to go back to may make your dog feel alive to you again in the way you long for. These letters also give people who matter to you and your dog the opportunity to pause and reflect on how special your dog truly is or was, to honor how you feel about them as significant. It will allow the love you and your dog feel between the two of you to spread out and become part of the wider web of love you share with your community.

This book's first exercise was for you to write your dog a letter, but here at the end, I'd like for you to be held as you hold your dog. I'd like for you to read other people's letters and grasp the preciousness of your dog beyond you. To have the tightest circle of love imaginable embracing you, which you and your dog can sink into when you need it. After a lifetime or just a few months, however long you shared life with your dog, every morning and every night, laughs and arguments and sleeping heart-to-heart, they will remain one of the best things that has ever happened to you. By being able to ask for support when your dog is slipping from this world, or after the fact, by being able to ask for help when it was your dog who had helped and supported you. I hope you will feel some okayness. These letters could serve as a way to help you say goodbye to Great Love or craft the narrative you need about letting go.

Then the second exercise is another collection, this time, gather a dozen or so rocks. Try to find some with weight, size, and heft. On each rock's surface, write down an attribute that your beloved pet presented or embodied in your time together, something specific about them you might or will miss. When you need that thing close, carry the rock with you. On days when the grief is particularly intense, carry all the rocks in a bag, and let people feel it, let people feel the weight of your loss. *This is what I am holding today*, these rocks will impart for you. It's not that you're trying to speed up the grieving process or elicit sympathy. It's that you are trying to externalize, own, and feel the full impression of saying goodbye. When you are ready, you can set those rocks down, all at once or one at a time. Perhaps you can leave them some place peaceful where they will bask in the glow of sunlight and be caressed in the dark by moonlight. My hope for you is that you will be able to feel your dog's spirit in every breeze.

Dog love goes from being here to being everywhere.

Epilogue

There are many different kinds of dog parents, and I am not here to say which one is better or worse. But this book is for the kind of dog parents who understand that dogs come with experiences and that they're shaped by those experiences, yet who still hope that the new experiences they can offer will benefit their dogs. The sort of humans who see their dogs as part of the family, who can tell when their dog seems a little bit off, who feel for their pets without becoming addicted to needing their pets, and who take care of them as a privilege, not as an obligation. There are many different kinds of people who rescue dogs, too. Different personas who find themselves drawn to animal rescue because they love animals, or because they feel like they don't belong with people, or because they're working out their own traumas. But if we become addicted to helping animals in terrible situations in order to get what we need, then we will need animals to be in terrible situations in order to feel what we have been looking for.

Instead, my wish for both dog adopters and dog rescuers is the same: that we may be well and bring that wellness to the dogs we love, continuing on our wellness journey with well dogs through bonding. That we may nurture the love between us as individuals who are both separate from one another, choosing life together. If we come to saving animals, rescuing animals, or loving animals because of heartbreak only, with our broken hearts and open wounds, mascara stains and sinking stomachs, heads shaking no, no, that couldn't have just happened to me, no, this can't be my life, then the love we get back from these dogs, and only their love, may heal us and whole us. This is a logical reason to seek out connection with an animal, and a significant call to fill ourselves. But it is not the complete picture. It should not be where we begin and also where we end.

At some point, we must deal with our own hurt, in large part thanks to the animals we adopt, and because of the animals we help, yet I believe we must also overcome that hurt *for* the animals. We must stop playing out our compulsions and cravings with them, we must release our grasp on stress and sadness, and we must welcome in a level of searing honesty because our dogs deserve to become more than what we need them to be for us. They deserve to be their full selves too, to be seen for who they are, to exist onto themselves. They deserve to be met with the energy of balanced individuals so that they can access their own balance. We can be a team, a great team, who enjoys life together.

I say this for adopters and rescuers, animal welfare staff and volunteers. I say this for fosters, animal advocates, and dog lovers. I say this for any of us who are mortal. I say this knowing it may be obnoxious to hear it, but it is nonetheless true: Dogs are not made for us to have cozy companions inside the places we are stuck. Dogs are not here so that we have company inside our limiting beliefs and our lowest points. Dogs are not punching bags for our fear, anger, hurt, or incompetence. The danger in thinking they are is that at some point or another, in order to feel better or attain our own well-being or because we finally got what we think we wanted, we will end up having to leave them. And we can't do that. We can't use them or else we will abandon them. If we all go, who will be left?

I know this may be confusing, as this entire book has been about making a selfish case for pet adoption! Although I have written here about how we can adopt dogs to enhance our own wellness and how we bond with dogs and love them in order to do so, it is in giving wellness to them that we most end up enhancing our own. Even with our fear, anger, hurt, and fallibility, we deserve love, and they deserve love. It is our duty to commit to our own wellness for our sake but also for our dogs' sake. It is our duty to love them for the entirety of their lives. They are precious beings who change with us, journey with us, and who remind us that we are precious beings too. Staying with them is staying with ourselves. The level of capacity we have for ourselves will be the level we have for others, including our dogs. And so, in adoring them, in wanting more for them, we are inspired to create more for ourselves.

My dogs see everything I do that nobody else sees. Animals on four legs with giant teeth live in my home. They learn my human routines, my customs, my tone of voice, and I learn theirs. And never, not once, after all the dogs I've cared for, even the ones who have driven me bananas, never have I regretted it. I have never, not once, ended up coming to any conclusion other than that I'm falling in love with them. Ophelia was the first, and thus the forever. How she waltzed into my life and rearranged it, evicted me from what I had known to give me the courage to do the riskiest thing a person can do: Relinquish the known identity for a better one. I was Katya, the girl with the eating disorder. I was Katya, the one who felt not enough. I was Katya, who disliked Katya. That Katya was not working for me. And Ophelia helped me let that person go. She helped me kill her. She helped me entomb that me. I did not know what identity waited for me on the other side, if I would like it, if the other people in my life would like it, or if I would be okay. But I had Ophelia. I had her to go through it with, and because I had her, I had faith in whatever came and in my ability to withstand it, to welcome it, to discover it.

Ophelia gave me the courage to become the unknown me because I knew she loved all of me's—the one dying, the one without a shape, and the ones to come. She had faith in me, she was the faith in me, and already loved the identity of me who did not yet exist. That's how divine a dog can be. So I stepped into that me and received there Ophelia's warm weight pressed against my chest at night; Ophelia licking the corners of my eyes in the morning; Ophelia in my arms as I held her like a baby and made up songs about her tiny teeth and tiny tucked-in feet; Ophelia my living proof that there was a power greater than me who is pretty wonderful because that power brought Ophelia into my life; Ophelia who I chased around with cups of water when she was too old to walk for a drink; Ophelia who crunched on ice cubes delicately like a queen would; Ophelia who wrapped me in a million moments of comfort.

But from an expanded vantage point, I was able to see more of who Ophelia was. To give her the credit that she was not alive only to add to my life, but to be her own. A dog who liked to eat snow. A dog who liked to chase fresh apples picked from trees as if they were balls, and when she'd bring an apple back, she would take a bite, let the juice drip down her fur before dropping the fruit in my palm for another toss. She was the dog who liked to howl as an enticement for play, even if it was at an insufferable decibel level, and she did not appreciate being tickled on the butt, and she preferred to poop in the ivy where she could be hidden, thank you very much, she was a lady who demanded privacy. She low key judged everybody, and she was regal in her grandiosity, and she was hilarious, and she was my family.

Had I not seen the full Ophelia before me, I would have missed out on spotting the full me in the new me, which came only after the total collapse of the Jenga tower that I'd built as the old me, because yes, it is like taking that piece from the bottom, and it is scary as hell to change. Less so when you have a dog in your life who you're bonding with, who is loving you, who you love. Yes, I still treated Ophelia "like a dog" because her needs as a dog were wired into what she was. But I also treated her like more than a dog. Like my closest friend. Like a sovereign being. Like an extension of my Higher Power. Like my Great Love.

I have so much skin in the game to convince you to adopt a dog and to care about helping animals. I won't lie to you about that, I won't pretend or be coy. But as I've harped on for almost 200 pages, it's not only for the good of the dogs. It is indeed beneficial for the animals if you adopt, obviously, so they do not wither and decline or atrophy in an unnatural enclosure which they are not capable of escaping. It can't be all right to put beings to sleep due to the crime of not having a mailing address. But I hope I've made a case by now for why it is also so good for you.

As for the broader thinkers, the collective-minded out there, allow me to add one more layer: Adopting a dog is also a gift for the community. To start with, please consider the other human beings who work or help out at animal shelters. Include them in your awareness. People who spend time at animal shelters are forced to endure more pain than they should witness and more stress than they ever desired. We dump a colossal responsibility on them and take advantage of their soft, open hearts, when in reality, the homeless pets problem is not meant for a few, but for everybody to bear.

An animal shelter is a microcosm of the country it resides in. It's what is happening in that country, that state, on a smaller scale—there are all its strengths and challenges on display. Go to any shelter in the United States and that is America. An animal shelter is a petri dish of every municipal and government issue at play, unfolding before your eyes. Furthermore, animal shelters are community spaces. You pay for them with your tax dollars. You support them. You are of them, and they of you, whether you go there or like this fact or know it or not. Of course I understand why people don't want to go to an animal shelter. They can be depressing, dirty, overwhelming, loud, even downright frightening sometimes. And yet, we need more people to visit animal shelters in order for them to improve. It's not that the shelter needs to level up so that then the public will come, it's the other way around. You showing up will help them upgrade. You showing up and caring about the people there as well as the animals there, you understanding that you are part of this space is what will make it brighter, better, lighter, more effective at its mission and more functional. We can boost a shelter's atmosphere through our presence.

Shelter workers and rescuers are part of a system that takes advantage of them. What is inside of these people that makes them stick around and take it and why we exploit that is a subject for another book. But mull over what that says about the rest of us. It does not have to be like this, accepted and compartmentalized and conditioned. If the only chance at wellness that people who work for animals have requires them leaving the field, then animals will be doomed. How can things ever change with the constant turnover and dissatisfaction? It's too dangerous to ignore or belittle the retention problems, substance abuse problems, compassion fatigue, and suicide rates among animal people, who happen to be my favorite people. It's also too dangerous to keep operating as if these people and these animals don't need our support, or as if denial works, or as if guilt does.

We can change things from the outside in as well as from the inside out, and I believe we must. I believe it matters not just for "the animal world" but for the whole world because shelters are emblematic of the world. Animal shelters demonstrate how much we care about one another, our willingness to help each other, to listen, learn, and love. To be our best selves, healthy, balanced, well and unified under the spiritual guidance of rescue animals.

I am not suggesting we need to rescue the animal rescuers as well as the animals themselves (although there is an argument to be made for that). I am suggesting that we need to rescue the system by being part of it, constructively criticizing it, sure, but also participating in its reform, and advancing it by getting involved. We are one of many, part of a greater network, part of a relay race for goodness. If we can see animal shelters this way, it might elevate the way we save lives—dogs, humans, and all animals. And when things get hard and devastating and the answers seem further away than ever before, we can stop running the race and be with our breath. Our breath, the core of wellness. Our breath, the friend all this time sustaining you, doing for you, breathing you without you worrying about it or needing to pay attention to it or even thank it. By simply noticing your breath, you acknowledge all it does, you acknowledge its love, its aliveness, its nowness and your connection to all that is.

And you know who else is breathing and noticing and in that same moment with you? Dogs. Sometimes we must go forward. Sometimes we must stand still. Your dog and your breath have so much in common. They coincide in the present, both offering you love, not answers, but love. When we're chasing answers we can miss out on the love. But love means more than any answers we will ever find. And love is always available to us. We don't need to earn it or achieve it or deserve it. It's ours.

So I hope you will walk with me. Or run with me. Or pause with me. Sit and look at the view with me, and just be. Take my hand and join me on this path of More by caring about dogs as a way to care more about yourself. Let's heal ourselves, part by part, and keep healing, keep spiraling up and down, side to side, diagonally too, because well-being is not linear. It is progress, it is energy, our energy, being turned on so that we can step inside the ride to move with the thing that is moving us. The force moving us that brought us here. The force moving us that brings us to our dogs. Dogs are already part of this momentum, and I think it's why we want them around, because our souls know it's where we are meant to live, it's how we wish to be, it's who we really are. The cost of this is not a cost at all, for bonding with dogs and taking care of them is the assignment, the test, the why. The invisible often carries the insight.

I've heard in the 12 Step rooms that we "Brush our hair to get clean teeth." And the meaning of this saying is we do all this step work in recovery, but how exactly does writing down answers to questions with a sponsor or going to meetings help us stop being addicted to a specific behavior or substance? How does it work, when nothing else did before? I think it's because the steps create a place for devotion to show and shine. They demonstrate to a Higher Power that we're available for miracles to come in whenever they are sent to us, however they bump into us, because we realize that we can't force them to happen, and we have become all right with that. Imperfectly, sometimes patiently, sometimes impatiently, all right with that. We let the work work on us, we let the breath breathe us, and in that vein, bonding with a dog is the same.

As we do all of these things to bond, love comes into the spaces in between those moments, comes into the current underneath those activities, and we feel better with and because of this dog than we did without this dog. It doesn't have to make sense. It doesn't have to be scientific. It doesn't have to be what you wanted. It doesn't even have to ultimately be your process or journey. But it's here for you if you like it.

I don't know a cuter packaging that stumbles us onto the doorway of love. I don't always know what to say or do or even what to write, but I know dogs. And because of that, the prayers of my heart and the contemplations of my mind and the rhythm of my body ends up forming into whatever it is I needed to share. I am led to songs and stories and letters that guide me in the world, that offer a soundtrack of love playing throughout my days. So dogs are never "just dogs," not to me. Cultivating their love nourishes all the loves in my life. That is to say, they are my love teachers as well as my love students. They are the watering can that pours forth the love, but also the seeds that grow the love and bloom it. Anything that can be that much, that many, can be all the things, is nothing short of sacred.

I learned to get comfortable staring up into the sky with goosebumps and questions, with no answers and lots of feelings as I meditate on the mystical nature of dog-living. I hope to sense you there, under the stars holding many unknowns. I hope to chat with you on a walk in the park with our dog packs, or to be of service together while volunteering at a shelter. I hope to hop on a Zoom or exchange emails. And if I won't meet you, won't know you, I'll still wish for you to find yourself sitting beside the exquisite friendship of a dog, or to keep in mind that bonding with a dog would be for the benefit of the dog *as well as* for you. May it keep you returning to the idea of adopting, faithful in the treasures that would await each time you did. If we let that be possible, one day there could be empty kennels.

Every day there is a more serene, more well version of you to discover simply because you are here. It is miracle enough to be alive, but I think it's even better to share that alive with a rescue dog. As you stroll forth together, may the world wink at you, the flowers stamp their sweetness in the air, the birds tweet their sermons from high up on the treetops, and the earthworms work under your feet. May you feel a part of all of it. Because you are. And whenever the doubt returns, for you are human and so it will, may you glance down at the dog beside you and remember that you are love. You always were. You always will be. You may have brought a dog home, but the dog brought you home to this.

And then … go help more dogs. Volunteer at your local animal shelter, visit homeless pets and the people who work for them, fundraise, hold a donation drive, visit a sanctuary, go vegan, adopt, foster, bond. Love like their lives depend on it. Love like your life does too.

Chapter Notes

Preface

1. Marlene Cimons, "Your Dog Can Make You Feel Better, and Here's Why," *Washingtonpost.com*, September 2016, https://www.washingtonpost.com/national/health-science/your-dog-can-make-you-feel-better-and-heres-why/2016/09/19/fde4aeec-6a2a-11e6-8225-fbb8a6fc65bc_story.html.

2. Lauren Silva, "Breathwork: What Is It and How Does It Work?," *Forbes.com*, March 2023 (updated January 12, 2024), https://www.forbes.com/health/mind/breathwork.

Chapter 1

1. Patricia B. McConnell, *The Other End of the Leash: Why We Do What We Do Around Dogs* (New York: Ballantine Books, 2002), 9–10.

2. Leslie McDevitt, *Control Unleashed: Creating a Focused and Confident Dog* (South Hadley, MA: Clear Run Productions, 2007), 63.

3. Deepak Chopra, "The Important Role of Noticing." *Medium.com*, September 14, 2020, https://deepakchopra.medium.com/the-important-role-of-noticing-b755ee8084e7.

4. Leslie McDevitt, *Control Unleashed: Creating a Focused and Confident Dog* (South Hadley, MA: Clear Run Productions, 2007), 62.

5. Leslie McDevitt, *Control Unleashed: Creating a Focused and Confident Dog* (South Hadley, MA: Clear Run Productions, 2007), 71.

6. James O'Heare, *The Dog Aggression Workbook: A Positive Reinforcement-Based Guide to Understanding, Assessing & Changing Aggressive Behavior in Your Dog* (Ottawa, Canada: DogPsych Publishing, 2007), 93.

7. Patricia B. McConnell, *The Other End of the Leash: Why We Do What We Do Around Dogs* (New York: Ballantine Books, 2002), 9.

Chapter 2

1. Paul Klein, "What's Different, and What's Not, About Training Deaf Dogs," *DeafDogsRock.com* (accessed August 6, 2024), https://deafdogsrock.com/whats-different-and-whats-not-about-training-deaf-dogs.

2. Crystal Hoshaw, "What Is Mindfulness? A Simple Practice for Greater Well-Being," *Healthline.com*, March 29, 2022, https://www.healthline.com/health/mind-body/-what-is-mindfulness.

3. Sue Sternberg, *Assessing Aggression Thresholds in Dogs: Using the Assess-A-Pet Protocol to Better Understand Aggression* (Wenatchee, WA: Dogwise Publishing, 2016), 95–99.

4. Leslie McDevitt, *Control Unleashed: Creating a Focused and Confident Dog* (South Hadley, MA: Clear Run Productions, 2007), 44.

5. Saul McLeod, "Operant Conditioning: What It Is, How It Works, and Examples," *SimplyPsychology.org*, updated February 2, 2024, https://www.simplypsychology.org/-operant-conditioning.html.

6. Adrienne Farricelli, "The Four Quadrants of Dog Training (With Examples)," *PetHelpful.com*, updated May 19, 2024, https://pethelpful.com/dogs/The-Four-Quadrants-of-Dog-Training.

7. Murray Sidman, *Coercion and Its Fallout,* revised edition (United States: Authors Cooperative, Inc., Publishers, 2001), 238–239.
8. Annie Wright, "How Does Someone Become a Family's 'Identified Patient'?," *PsychologyToday.com,* February 8, 2022, https://www.psychologytoday.com/us/blog/making-the-whole-beautiful/202202/how-does-someone-become-familys-identified-patient.
9. Leslie McDevitt, *Control Unleashed: Creating a Focused and Confident Dog* (South Hadley, MA: Clear Run Productions, 2007), 36.

Chapter 3

1. "Classical Conditioning: How Dogs Learn by Association," *PupfordAcademy.com,* January 23, 2023, https://pupford.com/classical-conditioning-dogs.
2. Mardi Richmond, "Classical Conditioning—How Your Dog Learns by Association," *WholeDogJournal.com,* May 4, 2001, https://www.whole-dog-journal.com/training/classical-conditioning-how-your-dog-learns-by-association.
3. Kendra Cherry, "Pavlov's Dogs and the Discovery of Classical Conditioning," *VeryWellMind.com,* updated on November 20, 2022, https://www.verywellmind.com/pavlovs-dogs-2794989.
4. Kendra Cherry, "The Unconditioned Stimulus in Classical Conditioning," *VeryWellMind.com,* updated on November 20, 2023, https://www.verywellmind.com/what-is-an-unconditioned-stimulus-2796006.
5. James O'Heare, *The Dog Aggression Workbook: A Positive Reinforcement-Based Guide to Understanding, Assessing & Changing Aggressive Behavior in Your Dog* (Ottawa, Canada: DogPsych Publishing, 2007), 38–39.
6. Patricia B. McConnell and Karen B. London, *Love Has No Age Limit: Welcoming an Adopted Dog into Your Home* (Black Earth, WI: McConnell Publishing, Ltd., 2011), 79.
7. Patricia B. McConnell and Karen B. London, *Love Has No Age Limit: Welcoming an Adopted Dog into Your Home* (Black Earth, WI: McConnell Publishing, Ltd., 2011), 67.

Chapter 4

1. David Robson, "Catastrophising: How Toxic Thinking Leads You Down Dark Paths," *BBC.com,* July 26, 2022, https://www.bbc.com/worklife/article/20220725-catastrophising-how-toxic-thinking-can-lead-down-dark-path.
2. Patricia B. McConnell and Karen B. London, *Love Has No Age Limit: Welcoming an Adopted Dog into Your Home* (Black Earth, WI: McConnell Publishing, Ltd., 2011), 47.
3. Karen Pryor, *Getting Started: Clicker Training for Dogs* (Waltham, MA: Sunshine Books, Inc., 2005), 14.
4. Karen Pryor, *Getting Started: Clicker Training for Dogs* (Waltham, MA: Sunshine Books, Inc., 2005), 18.
5. Karen Pryor, *Getting Started: Clicker Training for Dogs* (Waltham, MA: Sunshine Books, Inc., 2005), 81.
6. Leslie McDevitt, *Control Unleashed: Creating a Focused and Confident Dog* (South Hadley, MA: Clear Run Productions, 2007), 36.
7. Saul Mcleod, "Operant Conditioning: What It is, How It Works, and Examples," *SimplyPsychology.org,* updated February 2, 2024, https://www.simplypsychology.org/operant-conditioning.html.
8. Murray Sidman, *Coercion and Its Fallout,* revised edition (United States: Authors Cooperative Inc. Publishers, 2001), 221.
9. Murray Sidman, *Coercion and Its Fallout,* revised edition (United States: Authors Cooperative Inc. Publishers, 2001), 238-239.
10. Murray Sidman, *Coercion and Its Fallout,* revised edition (United States: Authors Cooperative Inc. Publishers, 2001), 209-210.
11. Murray Sidman, *Coercion and Its Fallout,* revised edition (United States: Authors Cooperative Inc. Publishers, 2001), 79-81, 221.
12. Murray Sidman, *Coercion and Its Fallout,* revised edition (United States: Authors Cooperative Inc. Publishers, 2001), 77.
13. Adrienne Farricelli, "How to Use the Premack Principle in Dog Training," *PetHelpful.com,* updated March 11, 2023, https://pethelpful.com/dogs/How-to-Use-the-Premack-Principle-to-Train-Your-Dog.

14. Leslie McDevitt, *Control Unleashed: Creating a Focused and Confident Dog* (South Hadley, MA: Clear Run Productions, 2007), 51–52.

15. Leslie McDevitt, *Control Unleashed: Creating a Focused and Confident Dog* (South Hadley, MA: Clear Run Productions, 2007), 152.

Chapter 5

1. Kristin Wong, "How to Add More Play to Your Grown-Up Life, Even Now," *NewYorkTimes.com*, August 14, 2020, https://www.nytimes.com/2020/08/14/smarter-living/adults-play-work-life-balance.html.

2. Saya Des Marais, "The Importance of Play for Adults," *PsychCentral.com*, updated November 10, 2022, https://psychcentral.com/blog/the-importance-of-play-for-adults#benefits.

3. Patricia McConnell, "What's the Key to Polite Dog Play?," *PatriciaMcConnell.com*, May 1, 2023, https://www.patriciamcconnell.com/theotherendoftheleash/whats-the-key-to-polite-dog-play.

4. Cesar Millan, ""Ears... In that Order." But what does he mean exactly? #cesarsway Dogs see the world differently from the way we do. We communicate using our ears first, then our eyes, and lastly our nose. Dogs begin with the nose, then the eyes, and lastly the ears. Allowing a dog to experience our scent before we engage it in eye contact or speak to it is one way to establish trust early on." Facebook post, December 17, 2013, 12:10 p.m., https://www.facebook.com/cesar.millan/photos/youve-probably-heard-cesar-say-nose-eyes-ears-in-that-order-but-what-does-he-mea/10152161012904954/#.

5. Dr. Elizabeth Racine, "13 Fun Facts About Your Dog's Sense of Smell," *CareCredit.com*, March 27, 2023, https://www.carecredit.com/well-u/pet-care/how-well-can-your-dog-smell/#:~:text=Scientists%20report%20that%20a%20dog's,more%20acute%20than%20a%20human's.&text=One-%20of%20the%20reasons%20a,a%20dog%20has%20about%2050.

6. Ryan Llera and Lynn Buzhardt, "How Dogs Use Smell to Perceive the World," *VCAHospitals.com*, https://vcahospitals.com/know-your-pet/how-dogs-use-smell-to-perceive-the-world.

7. Patricia B. McConnell, *The Other End of the Leash: Why We Do What We Do Around Dogs* (New York: Ballantine Books, 2002), 72.

8. Molly McDonough, "The Connections Between Smell, Memory, and Health," *Harvard Medicine, The Magazine of Harvard Medical School*, Spring 2024, https://magazine.hms.harvard.edu/articles/connections-between-smell-memory-and-health.

9. Patricia B. McConnell, *The Other End of the Leash: Why We Do What We Do Around Dogs* (New York: Ballantine Books, 2002), 46.

10. "Dog Nose Work: Scent Training Sport for Dogs," *BestFriends.org*, https://resources.bestfriends.org/article/dog-nose-work-scent-training-sport-dogs.

11. Christen Brownlee, "Mapping Aroma: Smells Light Up Distinct Brain Parts," *ScienceNews.org*, May 25, 2005, https://www.sciencenews.org/article/mapping-aroma-smells-light-distinct-brain-parts.

12. Patricia B. McConnell and Karen B. London, *Love Has No Age Limit: Welcoming an Adopted Dog into Your Home* (Black Earth, WI: McConnell Publishing, Ltd., 2011), 31.

13. Patricia B. McConnell and Karen B. London, *Love Has No Age Limit: Welcoming an Adopted Dog into Your Home* (Black Earth, WI: McConnell Publishing, Ltd., 2011), 24.

14. Adrienne Farricelli, "8 Exercises for Training a Dog's Impulse Control and Frustration Tolerance," *PetHelpful.com*, updated March 6, 2023, https://pethelpful.com/dogs/Understanding-Dog-Frustration-Tolerance.

15. Leslie McDevitt, *Control Unleashed: Creating a Focused and Confident Dog* (South Hadley, MA: Clear Run Productions, 2007), 62

16. Leslie McDevitt, *Control Unleashed: Creating a Focused and Confident Dog* (South Hadley, MA: Clear Run Productions, 2007), 159.

17. Patricia B. McConnell, *The Other End of the Leash: Why We Do What We Do Around Dogs* (New York: Ballantine Books, 2002), 78.

18. Mary Grace Descouroue, "What Excessive Screen Time Does to the Adult

Brain," *Stanford Lifestyle Medicine*, May 30, 2024, https://longevity.stanford.edu/lifestyle/2024/05/30/what-excessive-screen-time-does-to-the-adult-brain/#:~:text=The%20study%20shows%20that%20in,%2Dmaking%20and%20problem%2Dsolving.

19. Patricia B. McConnell and Karen B. London, *Love Has No Age Limit: Welcoming an Adopted Dog into Your Home* (Black Earth, WI: McConnell Publishing, Ltd., 2011), 51.

20. "About Animal Testing," *Humane Society International*, https://www.hsi.org/news-resources/about/#.

21. Jean Donaldson, *The Culture Clash: A revolutionary new way of understanding the relationship between humans and domestic dogs* (Berkeley, CA: James & Kenneth Publishers, 1996), 49.

22. James O'Heare, *The Dog Aggression Workbook: A Positive Reinforcement-Based Guide to Understanding, Assessing & Changing Aggressive Behavior in Your Dog* (Ottawa, Canada: DogPsych Publishing, 2007), 128.

Chapter 6

1. Patricia B. McConnell and Karen B. London, *Love Has No Age Limit: Welcoming an Adopted Dog into Your Home* (Black Earth, WI: McConnell Publishing, Ltd., 2011), 55–56.

2. Patricia B. McConnell, *The Other End of the Leash: Why We Do What We Do Around Dogs* (New York: Ballantine Books, 2002), 148.

3. Patricia B. McConnell, *The Other End of the Leash: Why We Do What We Do Around Dogs* (New York: Ballantine Books, 2002), 150.

4. Patricia B. McConnell, *The Other End of the Leash: Why We Do What We Do Around Dogs* (New York: Ballantine Books, 2002), 149.

5. Leslie McDevitt, *Control Unleashed: Creating a Focused and Confident Dog* (South Hadley, MA: Clear Run Productions, 2007), 73.

6. Adrienne Farricelli, "Understanding Dog Behavior Chains," *PetHelpful.com*, updated March 26, 2023, https://pethelpful.com/dogs/Understanding-Dog-Behavior-Chains.

7. Ruby Leslie, "Intentions + Negative Emotions and Associations = A Poisoned Cue," *Welfare for Animals*, July 5, 2021, https://www.welfare4animals.org/blog/intentions-negative-emotions-and-associations-a-poisoned-cue.

8. Leslie McDevitt, *Control Unleashed: Creating a Focused and Confident Dog* (South Hadley, MA: Clear Run Productions, 2007), 26.

9. Melissa Alexander, "'NRMs' No Reward Markers," *Karen Pryor Clicker Training*, July 1, 2003, https://www.clickertraining.com/node/179.

10. Leslie McDevitt, *Control Unleashed: Creating a Focused and Confident Dog* (South Hadley, MA: Clear Run Productions, 2007), 26.

Chapter 7

1. Karen B. London, "After a Fight, Do Dogs Forgive?," *The Wildest*, July 23, 2021, https://www.thewildest.com/dog-behavior/after-fight-do-dogs-forgive.

2. Turid Rugaas, *On Talking Terms with Dogs: Calming Signals*, 2nd edition (Wenatchee, WA: Dogwise Publishing, 2006), 2.

3. Joseph Stromberg, "Why Scientists Believe Dogs Are Smarter Than We Give Them Credit For," *Vox.com*, updated January 22, 2016, https://www.vox.com/2015/4/7/8360143/dogs-intelligence-science.

4. "Smarter Than You Think: Renowned Canine Researcher Puts Dogs' Intelligence on Par with 2-Year-Old Human," American Psychological Association press release, 2009, https://www.apa.org/news/press/releases/2009/08/dogs-think#:~:text=According%20to%20several%20behavioral%20measures,of%20these%20differences%2C%20Coren%20says.

5. Leslie McDevitt, *Control Unleashed: Creating a Focused and Confident Dog* (South Hadley, MA: Clear Run Productions, 2007), 153.

6. Patricia B. McConnell and Karen B. London, *Love Has No Age Limit: Welcoming an Adopted Dog into Your Home* (Black Earth, WI: McConnell Publishing, Ltd., 2011), 35.

7. Patricia B. McConnell and Karen B.

London, *Love Has No Age Limit: Welcoming an Adopted Dog into Your Home* (Black Earth, WI: McConnell Publishing, Ltd., 2011), 35.
    8. Patricia B. McConnell and Karen B. London, *Love Has No Age Limit: Welcoming an Adopted Dog into Your Home* (Black Earth, WI: McConnell Publishing, Ltd., 2011), 31.
    9. Patricia B. McConnell and Karen B. London, *Love Has No Age Limit: Welcoming an Adopted Dog into Your Home* (Black Earth, WI: McConnell Publishing, Ltd., 2011), 31.
    10. Karen Pryor, *Don't Shoot the Dog! The New Art of Teaching and Training*, revised edition (New York, NY: Bantam Books, 1999), 108-109.
    11. Karen Pryor, *Don't Shoot the Dog! The New Art of Teaching and Training*, revised edition (New York, NY: Bantam Books, 1999), 44.
    12. Kendra Cherry, "How Extinction Is Defined in Psychology," *VeryWellMind.com*, updated on November 15, 2023, https://www.verywellmind.com/what-is-extinction-2795176.

Chapter 8

    1. Pat Miller, "How Dogs Interpret Your Body Language," *WholeDogJournal.com*, updated January 16, 2018, https://www.whole-dog-journal.com/lifestyle/human-focus/how-dogs-interpret-your-body-language.
    2. Roshina Jowaheer, "How Petting a Dog Can Lower Your Blood Pressure by 10%," *CountryLiving.com*, September 28, 2018, https://www.countryliving.com/uk/wellbeing/a23503266/petting-dog-lowers-blood-pressure.
    3. Patricia B. McConnell and Karen B. London, *Love Has No Age Limit: Welcoming an Adopted Dog into Your Home* (Black Earth, WI: McConnell Publishing, Ltd., 2011), 35.
    4. Karen B. London and Patricia B. McConnell, *Feeling Outnumbered? How to Manage and Enjoy Your Multi-Dog Household* (Black Earth, WI: Dog's Best Friend, Ltd, 2001), 12.
    5. Karen B. London and Patricia B. McConnell, *Feeling Outnumbered? How to Manage and Enjoy Your Multi-Dog Household* (Black Earth, WI: Dog's Best Friend, Ltd, 2001), 13-14.
    6. James O'Heare, *The Dog Aggression Workbook: A Positive Reinforcement-Based Guide to Understanding, Assessing & Changing Aggressive Behavior in Your Dog* (Ottawa, Canada: DogPsych Publishing, 2007), 17.
    7. Turid Rugaas, *On Talking Terms with Dogs: Calming Signals*, 2nd edition (Wenatchee, WA: Dogwise Publishing, 2006), 7-36.
    8. Emily Willingham, "Dogs Detect the Scent of Seizures," *ScientificAmerican.com*, March 28, 2019, https://www.scientificamerican.com/article/dogs-detect-the-scent-of-seizures/#:~:text=Among%20the%20candidates%3A%20seizure%2Dspecific,a%20human%20having%20an%20episode.
    9. Joana Cavaco Silva, "Can Dogs Detect Cancer?," *MedicalNewsToday.com*, updated January 19, 2024, https://www.medicalnewstoday.com/articles/323620.
    10. Erika Lessa, "8 Surprising Things Your Dog Can Sense," *PetMD.com*, September 29, 2023, https://www.petmd.com/dog/behavior/surprising-things-your-dog-can-sense.
    11. Carrie Arnold, "If You're Chronically Stressed, Your Dog Could Be Too," *NationalGeographic.com*, June 6, 2019, https://www.nationalgeographic.com/animals/article/dogs-stress-anxiety-owners-pets.
    12. Megan Marples, "Dogs Can Smell When Humans Are Stressed, Study Suggests," *CNN.com*, September 28, 2022, https://www.cnn.com/2022/09/28/world/dogs-smell-stress-study-wellness-scn/index.html.
    13. James O'Heare, *The Dog Aggression Workbook: A Positive Reinforcement-Based Guide to Understanding, Assessing & Changing Aggressive Behavior in Your Dog* (Ottawa, Canada: DogPsych Publishing, 2007), 31-32.
    14. Debra Horwitz et al., "Dog Behavior Problems—Aggression—Children," *VCA Animal Hospitals*, accessed August 11, 2024, https://vcahospitals.com/know-your-pet/dog-behavior-problems-aggression-children.
    15. Pat Miller, "Demand Behaviors in Dogs," *WholeDogJournal.com*, updated March 21, 2019, https://www.whole-dog-journal.com/behavior/

demand-behavior/demand-behaviors-in-dogs.

16. Karen Pryor, *Don't Shoot the Dog! The New Art of Teaching and Training*, revised edition (New York, NY: Bantam Books, 1999), 126.

Chapter 9

1. Patricia B. McConnell and Karen B. London, *Love Has No Age Limit: Welcoming an Adopted Dog into Your Home* (Black Earth, WI: McConnell Publishing, Ltd., 2011), 13.

2. Sean Zucker, "5 Surprising Things That Dogs Are Afraid Of," *The Wildest*, July 9, 2024, https://www.thewildest.com/-dog-behavior/things-dogs-are-afraid-of.

3. Ruby Leslie, "The 4F's of Fear- Fear Responses," *Welfare For Animals*, July 11, 2020, https://www.welfare4animals.org/blog/the-4fs-of-fear-fear-responses.

4. James O'Heare, *The Dog Aggression Workbook: A Positive Reinforcement-Based Guide to Understanding, Assessing & Changing Aggressive Behavior in Your Dog* (Ottawa, Canada: DogPsych Publishing, 2007), 32.

5. James O'Heare, *The Dog Aggression Workbook: A Positive Reinforcement-Based Guide to Understanding, Assessing & Changing Aggressive Behavior in Your Dog* (Ottawa, Canada: DogPsych Publishing, 2007), 38–39.

6. Katherine Compitus Zooeyia, "Why We Can Mistake a Pet's Fear as Friendliness," *PsychologyToday.com*, July 15, 2024, https://www.psychologytoday.com/us/blog/zooeyia/202407/fear-disguised-as-friendliness-the-fawn-response-in-pets#:~:text=Fawning%20in%20pets%20is%20a,attentiveness%20to%20owners%20or%20strangers.

7. Adrienne Farricelli, "Flooding Therapy for Dog Behavior Issues: Does It Work?," *PetHelpful.com*, updated March 11, 2023, https://pethelpful.com/dogs/-Flooding-Therapy-for-Dog-Behavior-Issues.

8. Jean Donaldson, *The Culture Clash: A Revolutionary New Way of Understanding the Relationship Between Humans and Domestic Dogs* (Berkeley, CA: James & Kenneth Publishers, 1996), 143.

9. Karen Pryor, *Getting Started: Clicker Training for Dogs* (Waltham, MA: Sunshine Books, Inc., 2005), 14.

10. Patricia B. McConnell and Karen B. London, *Love Has No Age Limit: Welcoming an Adopted Dog into Your Home* (Black Earth, WI: McConnell Publishing, Ltd., 2011), 78.

11. Pat Miller, "Fun Dog Training Techniques Using Shaping!," *WholeDogJournal.com*, updated June 21, 2023, https://www.whole-dog-journal.com/training/fun-dog-training-techniques-using-shaping.

12. Patrica McConnell, "Luring, Prompting and (or) Free Shaping," *PatriciaMcConnell.com*, February 15, 2016, https://www.patriciamcconnell.com/theotherendoftheleash/luring-prompting-and-or-free-shaping.

13. James O'Heare, *The Dog Aggression Workbook: A Positive Reinforcement-Based Guide to Understanding, Assessing & Changing Aggressive Behavior in Your Dog* (Ottawa, Canada: DogPsych Publishing, 2007), 158.

Chapter 10

1. "Behavioral Incompatibilities, Not Behavior Problems," *National Canine Research Council*, February 8, 2022, https://nationalcanineresearchcouncil.com/behavioral-incompatibilities-not-behavior-problems.

2. Peter Singer, *Practical Ethics* (Cambridge, United Kingdom: Cambridge University Press, 1993), 88.

3. Marieta Murg, "Why Do Dogs Play Hide and Seek," *Wag.com*, updated January 30, 2020, https://wagwalking.com/behavior/why-do-dogs-play-hide-and-seek.

4. Charlotte Ruhl, "Cognitive Bias: How We Are Wired to Misjudge," *SimplyPsychology.org*, updated October 24, 2023, https://www.simplypsychology.org/-cognitive-bias.html.

Chapter 11

1. Karen B. London and Patricia B. McConnell, *Feeling Outnumbered? How to Manage and Enjoy Your Multi-Dog Household* (Black Earth, WI: Dog's Best Friend, Ltd, 2001), 9.

2. Karen B. London and Patricia B. McConnell, *Feeling Outnumbered? How to*

Manage and Enjoy Your Multi-Dog Household (Black Earth, WI: Dog's Best Friend, Ltd, 2001), 7.

3. Kahlil Gibran, "On Marriage," *Poetry Foundation*, accessed August 13, 2024, https://www.poetryfoundation.org/poems/148576/on-marriage-5bff1692a81b0.

4. Adrienne Farricelli, "How Can I Stop My Dog From Approaching People?," *PetHelpful.com*, updated April 20, 2024, https://pethelpful.com/dogs/How-Can-I-Stop-My-Dog-From-Running-up-to-People.

5. Pat Miller, "Resource-Guarding and What to Do About It," *Whole-DogJournal.com*, July 15, 2015, https://www.whole-dog-journal.com/behavior/resource-guarding/resource-guarding-and-what-to-do-about-it.

6. James O'Heare, *The Dog Aggression Workbook: A Positive Reinforcement-Based Guide to Understanding, Assessing & Changing Aggressive Behavior in Your Dog* (Ottawa, Canada: DogPsych Publishing, 2007), 102.

7. Saul McLeod, "Attachment Theory in Psychology," *SimplyPsychology.org*, updated January 17, 2024, https://www.simplypsychology.org/attachment.html.

8. Wendy Rose Gould, "How to Spot the Signs of Codependency," *VeryWellMind.com*, updated on May 21, 2024, https://www.verywellmind.com/what-is-codependency-5072124.

9. Loretta G. Breuning, "The Biology of Belonging," *PsychologyToday.com*, December 29, 2020, https://www.psychologytoday.com/us/blog/your-neurochemical-self/202012/the-biology-belonging#:~:text=Each%20small%20act%20of%20trust,alliances%2C%20and%20it%20feels%20good.

10. Karen B. London and Patricia B. McConnell, *Feeling Outnumbered? How to Manage and Enjoy Your Multi-Dog Household* (Black Earth, WI: Dog's Best Friend, Ltd, 2001), 7.

11. Patricia B. McConnell and Karen B. London, *Love Has No Age Limit: Welcoming an Adopted Dog into Your Home* (Black Earth, WI: McConnell Publishing, Ltd., 2011), 61.

Chapter 12

1. Autumn Madden, "Do Dogs Know When They Are Dying?," *PetMd.com*, February 25, 2023, https://www.petmd.com/dog/general-health/do-dogs-know-when-they-are-dying.

2. Charles Trepany, "My Dog Died Two Months Ago. Pet Loss Causes Deep Grief That Our Society Ignores," *USAToday.com*, updated October 31, 2023, https://www.usatoday.com/story/life/health-wellness/2023/10/31/pet-loss-disenfranchised-grief/71375731007.

3. Lorraine Hedtke and John Winslade, *The Crafting of Grief: Constructing Aesthetic Response to Loss* (New York: Routledge, 2017), 144.

4. Lorraine Hedtke and John Winslade, *The Crafting of Grief: Constructing Aesthetic Response to Loss* (New York: Routledge, 2017), xi.

Bibliography

Alexander, Melissa. "'NRMs' No Reward Markers." *Karen Pryor Clicker Training*. July 1, 2003. https://www.clickertraining.com/node/179.

American Psychological Association. "Smarter Than You Think: Renowned Canine Researcher Puts Dogs' Intelligence on Par with 2-Year-Old Human." American Psychological Association press release. 2009. https://www.apa.org/news/press/releases/2009/08/dogs-think#:~:text=According%20to%20several%20behavioral%20measures,of%20these%20differences%2C%20Coren%20says.

Arnold, Carrie. "If You're Chronically Stressed, Your Dog Could Be Too." *NationalGeographic.com*. June 6, 2019. https://www.nationalgeographic.com/animals/article/dogs-stress-anxiety-owners-pets.

Best Friends. "Dog Nose Work: Scent Training Sport for Dogs." *BestFriends.org*. https://resources.bestfriends.org/article/dog-nose-work-scent-training-sport-dogs.

Breuning, Loretta G. "The Biology of Belonging." *PsychologyToday.com*. December 29, 2020. https://www.psychologytoday.com/us/blog/your-neurochemical-self/202012/the-biology-belonging#:~:text=Each%20small%20act%20of%20trust,alliances%2C%20and%20it%20feels%20good.

Brownlee, Christen. "Mapping Aroma: Smells Light Up Distinct Brain Parts." *ScienceNews.com*. May 25, 2005. https://www.sciencenews.org/article/mapping-aroma-smells-light-distinct-brain-parts.

Cherry, Kendra. "How Extinction Is Defined in Psychology." *VeryWellMind.com*. Updated on November 15, 2023. https://www.verywellmind.com/what-is-extinction-2795176.

Cherry, Kendra. "Pavlov's Dogs and the Discovery of Classical Conditioning." *VeryWellMind.com*. Updated on November 20, 2022. https://www.verywellmind.com/pavlovs-dogs-2794989.

Cherry, Kendra. "The Unconditioned Stimulus in Classical Conditioning." *VeryWellMind.com*. Updated on November 20, 2023. https://www.verywellmind.com/what-is-an-unconditioned-stimulus-2796006.

Chopra, Deepak. "The Important Role of Noticing." *Medium.com*. September 14, 2020. https://deepakchopra.medium.com/the-important-role-of-noticing-b755ee8084e7.

Cimons, Marlene. "Your Dog Can Make You Feel Better, and Here's Why." *WashingtonPost.com*. September 19, 2016. https://www.washingtonpost.com/national/health-science/your-dog-can-make-you-feel-better-and-heres-why/2016/09/19/fde4aeec-6a2a-11e6-8225-fbb8a6fc65bc_story.html.

Descouroue, Mary Grace. "What Excessive Screen Time Does to the Adult Brain." *Stanford Lifestyle Medicine*. May 30, 2024. https://longevity.stanford.edu/lifestyle/2024/05/30/what-excessive-screen-time-does-to-the-adult-brain/#:~:text=The%20study%20shows%20that%20in,%2Dmaking%20and%20problem%2Dsolving.

Des Marais, Saya. "The Importance of Play for Adults." *PsychCentral.com*. Updated November 10, 2022. https://psychcentral.com/blog/the-importance-of-play-for-adults#benefits.

Bibliography

Donaldson, Jean. *The Culture Clash: A Revolutionary New Way of Understanding the Relationship Between Humans and Domestic Dogs.* James & Kenneth Publishers, 1996.

Farricelli, Adrienne. "8 Exercises for Training a Dog's Impulse Control and Frustration Tolerance." *PetHelpful.com.* Updated March 6, 2023. https://pethelpful.com/dogs/Understanding-Dog-Frustration-Tolerance.

Farricelli, Adrienne. "Flooding Therapy for Dog Behavior Issues: Does It Work?" *PetHelpful.com.* Updated March 11, 2023. https://pethelpful.com/dogs/--Flooding-Therapy-for-Dog-Behavior-Issues.

Farricelli, Adrienne. "The Four Quadrants of Dog Training (With Examples)." *PetHelpful.com.* Updated May 19, 2024. https://pethelpful.com/dogs/The-Four-Quadrants-of-Dog-Training.

Farricelli, Adrienne. "How Can I Stop My Dog From Approaching People?" *PetHelpful.com.* Updated April 20, 2024. https://pethelpful.com/dogs/How-Can-I-Stop-My-Dog-From-Running-up-to-People.

Farricelli, Adrienne. "How to Use the Premack Principle in Dog Training." *PetHelpful.com.* Updated March 11, 2023. https://pethelpful.com/dogs/-How-to-Use-the-Premack-Principle-to-Train-Your-Dog.

Farricelli, Adrienne. "Understanding Dog Behavior Chains." *PetHelpful.com.* Updated March 26, 2023. https://pethelpful.com/dogs/Understanding-Dog-Behavior-Chains.

Gibran, Kahlil. "On Marriage." *PoetryFoundation.com.* Accessed August 13, 2024. https://www.poetryfoundation.org/poems/148576/on-marriage-5bff1692a81b0.

Gould, Wendy Rose. "How to Spot the Signs of Codependency." *VeryWellMind.com.* Updated on May 21, 2024. https://www.verywellmind.com/what-is-codependency-5072124.

Hedtke, Lorraine, and Winslade, John. *The Crafting of Grief: Constructing Aesthetic Response to Loss.* Routledge, 2017.

Hoshaw, Crystal. "What Is Mindfulness? A Simple Practice for Greater Well-Being." *Healthline.com.* March 29, 2022. https://www.healthline.com/health/mind-body/what-is-mindfulness.

Humane Society International. "About Animal Testing." *Hsi.org.* https://www.hsi.org/news-resources/about/#.

Jowaheer, Roshina. "How Petting a Dog Can Lower Your Blood Pressure by 10%." *CountryLiving.com.* September 28, 2018. https://www.countryliving.com/uk/wellbeing/a23503266/petting-dog-lowers-blood-pressure.

Klein, Paul. "What's Different, and What's Not, About Training Deaf Dogs." *DeafDogsRock.com.* Accessed August 6, 2024. https://deafdogsrock.com/-whats-different-and-whats-not-about-training-deaf-dogs.

Leslie, Ruby. "The 4F's of Fear-Fear Responses." *Welfare For Animals.* July 11, 2020. https://www.welfare4animals.org/blog/the-4fs-of-fear-fear-responses.

Leslie, Ruby. "Intentions + Negative Emotions and Associations = A Poisoned Cue." *Welfare for Animals.* July 5, 2021. https://www.welfare4animals.org/blog/-intentions-negative-emotions-and-associations-a-poisoned-cue.

Lessa, Erika. "8 Surprising Things Your Dog Can Sense." *PetMD.com.* September 29, 2023. https://www.petmd.com/dog/behavior/surprising-things-your-dog-can-sense.

Llera, Ryan, and Buzhardt, Lynn. "How Dogs Use Smell to Perceive the World." *VCAHospitals.com.* https://vcahospitals.com/know-your-pet/how-dogs-use-smell-to-perceive-the-world.

London, Karen B. "After a Fight, Do Dogs Forgive?" *The Wildest.* July 23, 2021. https://www.thewildest.com/dog-behavior/after-fight-do-dogs-forgive.

London, Karen B., and McConnell, Patricia B. *Feeling Outnumbered? How to Manage and Enjoy Your Multi-Dog Household.* Dog's Best Friend, 2001.

Madden, Autumn. "Do Dogs Know When They Are Dying?" *PetMd.com.* February 25, 2023. https://www.petmd.com/dog/-general-health/do-dogs-know-when-they-are-dying.

Marples, Megan. "Dogs Can Smell When Humans Are Stressed, Study Suggests." *CNN.com.* September 28, 2022. https://www.cnn.com/2022/09/28/world/dogs-smell-stress-study-wellness-scn/index.html.

Bibliography

McConnell, Patricia. "Luring, Prompting and (or) Free Shaping." *PatriciaMcConnell.com*. February 15, 2016. https://www.patriciamcconnell.com/theotherendoftheleash/luring-prompting-and-or-free-shaping.

McConnell, Patricia. "What's the Key to Polite Dog Play?" *PatriciaMcConnell.com*. May 1, 2023. https://www.patriciamcconnell.com/theotherendoftheleash/whats-the-key-to-polite-dog-play.

McConnell, Patricia B. *The Other End of the Leash: Why We Do What We Do Around Dogs*. Ballantine Books, 2002.

McConnell, Patricia B., and London, Karen B. *Love Has No Age Limit: Welcoming an Adopted Dog into Your Home*. McConnell Publishing, Ltd., 2011.

McDevitt, Leslie. *Control Unleashed: Creating a Focused and Confident Dog*. Clear Run Productions, 2007.

McDonough, Molly. "The Connections Between Smell, Memory, and Health." *Harvard Medicine The Magazine of Harvard Medical School*. Spring 2024. https://magazine.hms.harvard.edu/articles/connections-between-smell-memory-and-health.

McLeod, Saul. "Attachment Theory in Psychology." *SimplyPsychology.org*. Updated January 17, 2024. https://www.simplypsychology.org/attachment.html.

McLeod, Saul. "Operant Conditioning: What It Is, How It Works, and Examples." *SimplyPsychology.org*. Updated February 2, 2024. https://www.simplypsychology.org/operant-conditioning.html.

Millan, Cesar. "Nose, Eyes, Ears… In that Order." But what does he mean exactly? #cesarsway Dogs see the world differently from the way we do. We communicate using our ears first, then our eyes, and lastly our nose. Dogs begin with the nose, then the eyes, and lastly the ears. Allowing a dog to experience our scent before we engage it in eye contact or speak to it is one way to establish trust early on." Facebook post. December 17, 2013, 12:10 p.m. https://www.facebook.com/cesar.millan/photos/youve-probably-heard-cesar-say-nose-eyes-ears-in-that-order-but-what-does-he-mea/10152161012904954/#.

Miller, Pat. "Demand Behaviors in Dogs." *WholeDogJournal.com*. Updated March 21, 2019. https://www.whole-dog-journal.com/behavior/demand-behaviors-in-dogs.

Miller, Pat. "Fun Dog Training Techniques Using Shaping!" *WholeDogJournal.com*. Updated June 21, 2023. https://www.whole-dog-journal.com/training/fun-dog-training-techniques-using-shaping.

Miller, Pat. "How Dogs Interpret Your Body Language." *WholeDogJournal.com*. Updated January 16, 2018. https://www.whole-dog-journal.com/lifestyle/human-focus/how-dogs-interpret-your-body-language.

Miller, Pat. "Resource-Guarding and What to Do About It." *WholeDogJournal.com*. July 15, 2015. https://www.whole-dog-journal.com/behavior/resource-guarding/resource-guarding-and-what-to-do-about-it.

Murg, Marieta. "Why Do Dogs Play Hide And Seek." *Wag.com*. Updated January 30, 2020. https://wagwalking.com/behavior/why-do-dogs-play-hide-and-seek.

National Canine Research Council. "Behavioral Incompatibilities, Not Behavior Problems." *NationalCanineResearchCouncil.com*. February 8, 2022. https://nationalcanineresearchcouncil.com/behavioral-incompatibilities-not-behavior-problems.

O'Heare, James. *The Dog Aggression Workbook: A Positive Reinforcement-Based Guide to Understanding, Assessing & Changing Aggressive Behavior in Your Dog*. DogPsych Publishing, 2007.

Oliver, Mary. *Dog Songs*. Penguin Press, 2013.

Pryor, Karen. *Don't Shoot the Dog! The New Art of Teaching and Training* (revised edition). Bantam Books, 1999.

Pryor, Karen. *Getting Started: Clicker Training for Dogs*. Sunshine Books, 2005.

Pupford Academy. "Classical Conditioning: How Dogs Learn By Association." *PupfordAcademy.com*. January 23, 2023. https://pupford.com/classical-conditioning-dogs.

Racine, Dr. Elizabeth. "13 Fun Facts About Your Dog's Sense of Smell." *CareCredit.com*. March 27, 2023. https://www.carecredit.com/well-u/

pet-care/how-well-can-your-dog-smell/#:~:text=Scientists%20report%20that%20a%20dog's,more%20acute%20than%20a%20human's.&text=One%20of%20the%20reasons%20a,a%20dog%20has%20about%2050.

Richmond, Mardi. "Classical Conditioning—How Your Dog Learns by Association." *WholeDogJournal.com*. May 4, 2001. https://www.whole-dog-journal.com/training/classical-conditioning-how-your-dog-learns-by-association.

Robson, David. "Catastrophising: How Toxic Thinking Leads You Down Dark Paths." *BBC.com*. July 26, 2022. https://www.bbc.com/worklife/article/20220725-catastrophising-how-toxic-thinking-can-lead-down-dark-path.

Rugaas, Turid. *On Talking Terms with Dogs: Calming Signals* (2nd edition). Dogwise Publishing, 2006.

Ruhl, Charlotte. "Cognitive Bias: How We Are Wired to Misjudge." *SimplyPsychology.org*. Updated October 24, 2023. https://www.simplypsychology.org/cognitive-bias.html.

Sidman, Murray. *Coercion and Its Fallout* (revised edition). Authors Cooperative Inc. Publishers, 2001.

Silva, Joana Cavaco. "Can Dogs Detect Cancer?" *MedicalNewsToday.com*. Updated January 19, 2024. https://www.medicalnewstoday.com/articles/323620.

Silva, Lauren. "Breathwork: What Is It And How Does It Work?" *Forbes.com*. March 2023. Updated January 12, 2024. https://www.forbes.com/health/mind/breathwork.

Singer, Singer. *Practical Ethics*. Cambridge University Press. 1993.

Sternberg, Sue. *Assessing Aggression Thresholds in Dogs: Using the Assess-A-Pet Protocol to Better Understand Aggression*. Dogwise Publishing, 2016.

Stromberg, Joseph. "Why Scientists Believe Dogs Are Smarter Than We Give Them Credit For." *Vox.com*. Updated January 22, 2016. https://www.vox.com/2015/4/7/8360143/dogs-intelligence-science.

Trepany, Charles. "My Dog Died Two Months Ago. Pet Loss Causes Deep Grief That Our Society Ignores." *USAToday.com*. Updated October 31, 2023. https://www.usatoday.com/story/life/health-wellness/2023/10/31/pet-loss-disenfranchised-grief/71375731007.

Willingham, Emily. "Dogs Detect the Scent of Seizures." *ScientificAmerican.com*. March 28, 2019. https://www.scientificamerican.com/article/dogs-detect-the-scent-of-seizures/#:~:text=Among%20the%20candidates%3A%20seizure%2Dspecific,a%20human%20having%20an%20episode.

Wong, Kristin. "How to Add More Play to Your Grown-Up Life, Even Now." *NewYorkTimes.com*. August 14, 2020. https://www.nytimes.com/2020/08/14/smarter-living/adults-play-work-life-balance.html.

Wright, Annie. "How Does Someone Become a Family's 'Identified Patient'?" *PsychologyToday.com*. February 8, 2022. https://www.psychologytoday.com/us/blog/making-the-whole-beautiful/202202/how-does-someone-become-familys-identified-patient.

Zooeyia, Katherine Compitus. "Why We Can Mistake a Pet's Fear as Friendliness." *PsychologyToday.com*. July 15, 2024. https://www.psychologytoday.com/us/blog/zooeyia/202407/fear-disguised-as-friendliness-the-fawn-response-in-pets#:~:text=Fawning%20in%20pets%20is%20a,attentiveness%20to%20owners%20or%20strangers.

Zucker, Sean. "5 Surprising Things That Dogs Are Afraid Of." *The Wildest*. July 9, 2024. https://www.thewildest.com/dog-behavior/things-dogs-are-afraid-of.

Index

acceptance 94–97
accountability 12, 97
acknowledging own feelings 40, 43, 161
adoption: as healing 3, 86, 181–183; lifelong commitment 28; preparation 56, 69, 119, 123, 146; a selfless case 1–2
advocacy 133, 137
alpha 79–82, 86–87
animal rights 40, 149
animal shelters: as community spaces 26, 158, 180–181; ways to be involved 101, 138, 145, 149
anticipatory grief 167
anxiety 4, 56–57, 98, 104, 111, 115, 127, 139, 150, 159–161
associations 36–44, 47–48, 84, 86, 110, 120
attention: intentional focus 12, 24, 68, 107, 117, 128, 168, 174, 181; as reinforcement 14, 23, 29–30, 49–53, 56, 60–61, 88, 100
attune 107
awareness 12–14, 19, 24–25, 29, 67, 95, 99, 142, 151–153, 160

behavior 3–6, 11–13, 17, 20, 25, 27–30, 35–38, 41–61, 66, 71, 75, 77, 79, 81–89, 95–101, 105, 110–115, 119, 121–125, 128, 131, 132, 135–136, 150–154, 162, 182
being seen 45, 132, 142, 154, 178–179
belonging 107
body awareness 72, 112–113, 120
body blocks 108–109
body language 34, 106–111
bonding: as authenticity 61, 134, 137; as creativity 112; as emotional growth 23, 41; as energetic 23; as forgiveness 92–94, 96–106; as lifestyle 125; as mirror 25–28, 174; as spiritual journey 6, 14, 157, 175, 181; as structure 87–88, 98; through play 64–69, 71–79; through stillness 35
boundaries 148–153, 161–162

Bowlby, John 154
breathwork: calming anxiety 6, 35; with your dog 6, 12
building trust 4, 11, 23, 44, 60, 69, 73–76, 113, 116, 124, 150, 152, 164

children 6, 114–115, 141–142, 153, 154, 160, 162
classical conditioning, aka respondent conditioning 40–44, 48, 63
clicker 51–52, 131
Clooney 116–117
codependence vs. interdependence 148–149, 151–155, 157, 161–163
cognitive bias 131, 145–146
compassion 23, 47, 68, 114, 137, 163
conditioned response 41, 48
conditioned stimulus 42
consent 114–115
continuity 44
contract 147
co-regulation 152, 162
cortisol 6
counter classical conditioning 41
crate training 38, 71, 78, 88–89, 100, 161
creative 78, 86, 113

dance party 117
Dayenu 167, 175
decision to bond 11, 19, 158
decompression 68–69, 71, 77–78
detachment 157–159
discernment 137, 158
disenfranchised grief 170–171
dog behavior: fight or flight 120–124; trinity of factors 25, 29
dog parent 30, 71, 81, 100, 148, 150, 177
dog park 73, 130
Donaldson, Jean 76, 123
drop it 63, 141
duty to be well 157, 178

197

Index

eating disorder 9, 57, 107, 114
ego 1, 64, 125–126, 132–134, 140
embody 12, 109, 114, 139, 167, 176
emotionally manipulated 1, 4, 155
energy: as communication 22–26, 30, 34, 42; as invisible but real 29, 31, 33, 35, 81, 86, 94, 111, 117, 133, 139–140, 153, 178, 181
exercise 66, 75
extinction bursts 99–101

family 18, 31, 34, 139, 141–142, 147, 150, 158, 170, 177
Feebe 27–34
fight or flight 120–123
fist 35, 54–55, 63, 71
focusing on what we want 49–50, 56, 61, 98, 106, 162
forgiveness 93, 97, 102–103, 105
Frito 143–146
fun 35, 52, 64–68, 72–76, 117, 161

Gilda 88–90
giving and receiving love 81, 83–86
gotcha day 90
grief: after loss 167–168; support 170–171, 176; in transition 167–168, 170
grounding 83
growth, personal 6, 32, 40, 171

handling identity with care 73–76, 146, 155, 162, 178–179
healing through dogs 1–3, 7, 14, 75, 84, 86, 9, 175
Hedtke, Lorraine 171
here and now 12, 21
hide and seek 141
hierarchy 79–81, 146, 161
Higher Power 14–16, 182
honoring animal power 45, 58–59, 108–110

identified patient 34
identity 73–76, 146, 155, 162, 178–179
ignoring undesired behaviors 29–30, 50, 81–82, 88, 105
impulse control 27–28, 71–73, 77, 111
incompatible behavior 115
interdependence 149, 155, 162
intuition 64, 110, 127

JillieBean 159–164
joy 6, 15, 38, 40, 42, 53, 57, 74, 77, 82, 91, 106, 109
journaling: as a bonding tool 130, 75, 117; to process feelings 48, 121

letter writing 19, 175–176
letting go: grief 77, 164, 167, 175–176; of perfection 7, 76, 101, 130, 136, 153
letting your dog love you 19, 25, 85, 156
liberation 133, 137
London, Karen 41, 50, 69, 71, 75, 80, 94, 98, 108–109, 119, 124, 150, 164
loyalty 44–45, 142

magic mat 71–73, 78
making positive associations 5, 37–40, 42, 44, 47, 75
Mandy 122, 124, 126–129
massage 30, 63, 83
McConnell, Patricia 12, 20, 41, 50, 66, 67, 69, 71, 73, 75, 80, 81, 94, 98, 108, 109, 119, 124, 150, 161, 164
McDevitt, Leslie 13, 14, 20, 25, 52, 59, 60, 72, 73, 83, 84, 87, 89, 94
meditation 13, 83, 101, 182
mindfulness 12, 24, 63, 71, 83, 100, 108, 127
mirroring 6, 10, 25, 28, 86, 93, 174
Mother Nature 17, 47, 83
mourning 47, 167–171
mutual 2, 6, 95, 152

nature 68, 82–83, 91, 131, 133
no reward mark 87–88
nose 48, 59–60, 66–68, 73, 78, 109, 110, 119, 124

O'Heare, James 20, 41, 77, 109, 111, 121, 127, 153
operant conditioning 29, 51–54, 57, 60, 63, 71, 124
oxytocin 6

patience 42, 100–101, 122–123, 131, 138, 142, 151
Pavlov, Ivan 40–41
play 20, 30, 35, 50, 52, 60, 63, 64–69, 71–79, 83, 88, 105, 124, 130, 141, 179
poisoned cue 86
positive reinforcement 30–31, 50, 53, 55, 58, 123
predicting it will be hard 119–123
Premack Principle 58–60
presence, being present 10, 12–13, 17, 21, 23, 35, 46, 61, 68, 83, 93, 125, 126, 131, 138, 145, 152, 161, 169, 174, 180, 181
punishment, fallout of 30, 45, 51–53, 55–58, 81, 93, 99, 114, 120, 126–127
pup bucks 147

real dog 15–16
real you 15, 19
recall 35

reciprocal 25, 84, 147, 155
relapse 103, 116, 119, 168
rescue dogs 1, 4, 8, 11, 36, 56, 87, 119, 137, 139, 158, 163, 174, 183
resilience 123, 126, 128, 155
resource guarding 139, 152–153
Ruffalo 96, 102–104
Rugaas, Turid 92, 110

safety 7, 16, 23, 37, 39, 42, 45, 68, 70, 73, 79, 87, 90, 92, 94, 109, 115, 121, 122, 128, 150, 152, 162, 171
Sassy 42–47
scent training, scent work 67, 76
secure attachment 154–157, 159
self-love 3, 8
self-regulation 52, 128, 152
senior dogs 101–104, 145, 168, 175
senses 13, 24, 67, 109
sensitivity 106, 115, 117, 138
shaping 123–125, 131
Sherlock 73–77
Shiloh 59–60
Sidman, Murray 30, 53, 55, 58
Singer, Peter 141
somatic 106, 170
speciesism 141
Sternberg, Sue 25–26, 139
structure and satisfaction 87–88, 90, 98, 138, 161
success, setting up for 87, 94, 99, 119, 127

threshold 25–27, 32, 39, 45, 72, 97, 121, 138, 153, 161
timing, in training 42, 47
training 2–3, 5, 17, 28, 41–42, 50–52, 67, 70, 76, 94, 97, 98, 108, 115, 170
transition 69, 122, 123, 170
trust 4, 10, 11, 23, 29, 44, 53, 60, 69, 72–73, 75, 76, 89, 113, 116, 124, 128, 130, 131, 150, 152, 156, 162, 164

unconditioned response 41
unconditioned stimulus 41

vulnerability 66, 79, 103, 145

waiting until you're ready 172–173, 175
walks 7, 9, 20, 39, 42, 43, 59, 60, 83, 137, 147
watch me 20–21, 54
wellness 1–2, 6–7, 12, 16, 30, 35, 37, 52–53, 57, 64, 66, 97, 101, 111–115, 125, 130, 136, 140, 150, 152, 160, 172, 177–178, 180, 181
Whiskey 56–57, 62
who you are being 25, 86, 93, 106
willingness 7, 156–157, 171, 181
Winslade, John 171
wonder 16, 24, 33, 40, 50, 64, 91, 103, 121, 134, 169, 173

www.ingramcontent.com/pod-product-compliance
Ingram Content Group UK Ltd.
Pitfield, Milton Keynes, MK11 3LW, UK
UKHW042006140426
5217IPUK00015B/1018